P9-CEE-549

THE
COUNTRY DIARY
BOOK OF
CRAFTS

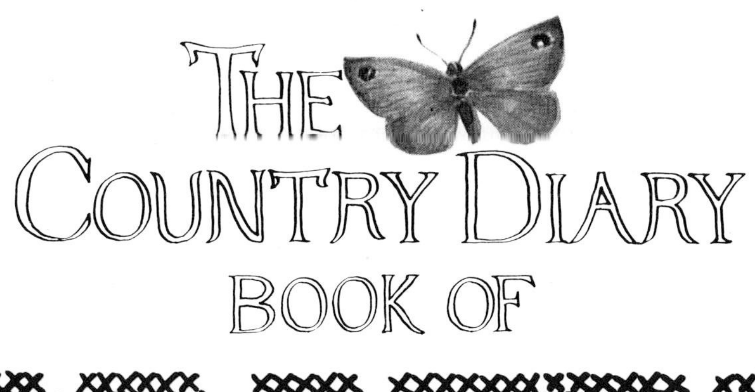

ANNETTE MITCHELL

HENRY HOLT AND COMPANY
NEW YORK

DEDICATION

To Jonathan, my Mother and my late Father
with love and affection.

The publishers would like to thank Rowena Stott,
Edith Holden's great-niece and the owner of the original work,
who has made the publication of this
book possible.

First published in the United States in 1986 by
Henry Holt and Company, Inc., 521 Fifth Avenue,
New York, New York 10175.

Originally published in Great Britain by
Webb & Bower (Publishers) Limited
9 Colleton Crescent, Exeter, Devon EX2 4BY

Library of Congress Cataloging-in-Publication Data

Mitchell, Annette
The country diary book of crafts
1. Handicraft. 2. Textile crafts. I. Title.
TT157.M56 1985 745.5 86-7691

ISBN 0-8050-0079-8

First American Edition

Design Ron Pickless

Production Nick Facer

Typeset in Great Britain by P&M Typesetting Ltd, Exeter, Devon

Printed and bound in Hong Kong by
Mandarin Offset Marketing (HK) Ltd

10 9 8 7 6 5 4 3 2 1

ISBN: 0-8050-0079-8

Contents

MAY

JUNE

JULY

AUGUST

INTRODUCTION

It is difficult to imagine a more appropriate theme than *The Country Diary of an Edwardian Lady* for a book of new craft ideas.
The Country Diary entered our busy lives bringing with it a welcome breath of fresh air. It turned our attention to the beauty of the countryside and to the many pleasures to be gained from the simple things in life. In so doing, it increased our awareness of the need to preserve and encourage the growth of natural beauty, which can all too quickly disappear from view in a fast-moving and highly commercialized world.

Just as there exists a need to preserve the beauty of the countryside, there also exists today a need to preserve the beauty of the crafts and to encourage the survival of creative skills in a world of ever-increasing mass-production. To lose sight of the many pleasures which come from making things by hand would be a great loss to us all. In an effort, therefore, to help safeguard these pleasures, the beautiful illustrations of *The Country Diary* have been used to inspire a new book of craft ideas.
This book is filled with ideas to encourage and rekindle interest in a wide variety of crafts which can be easily carried out in the home. They will provide endless hours of enjoyment, a great sense of personal satisfaction, and encourage all the family to become involved. In order for the crafts to survive, not only must *we* continue to use our creative skills to the full but we must also encourage our children to take an interest from an early age.
The Country Diary of an Edwardian Lady is a reproduction of Edith Holden's 'Nature Notes' for 1906. Edith Holden illustrated her diary by hand, using her skill as an artist to record visually her observations of the countryside. It seems even more fitting, therefore, to use her illustrations as inspiration for new craft designs to be worked by hand using needles and pins, wools and canvas, and cottons and linen.

Each craft item featured in this book carries its own *Country Diary* quotation as a title. 'Silver Tracery'; 'The Carpet Earth'; 'Daffy-down-dilly'; 'Lady's Mantle', and 'A Robe of White' serve as perfect examples of the surprisingly appropriate craft titles which Edith Holden innocently provided so many years ago. It is even more uncanny to find such delightful sayings and snippets of poetry as

> 'Then came old January wrapped well
> In many weeds to keep the cold away.'

and

> 'An Angel mid the woods of May
> Embroidered it with radiance gay.'

The wide range of crafts featured here is used to create almost one hundred different ideas. They include a selection of household items; fashion for men, women and children; dried flower arrangements; soft toys and gift ideas. Knitting, crochet, needlepoint and sewing are featured throughout the year, while rug-making, patchwork, smocking, ribbon-weaving and tatting all have their place.

The Country Diary Book of Crafts is divided into the months of the year, and the designs within each month reflect the changing seasons:

Spring

Spring flowers and butterflies provided inspiration for the early months, while the caterpillar and snake brought about a brief interlude of fun and games to herald April Fools' Day.

Summer

The warm lazy days of May and June, filled with the scent of the rose and honeysuckle, inspired the nostalgic heirloom section. Set in a bedroom reminiscent of romantic Edwardian times is a delightful collection of lace and fine stitchery which shows the true beauty which can be captured by the skills of fine craftsmanship. These wonderful pieces of work would surely be treasured by any son or daughter in the years to come.
The nursery and its playmates found their perfect place in July, inspired by 'For-get-me-nots' and 'Purple Bells'. With August came the opportunity to adorn our tables with poppies from the cornfield.

Autumn

Autumn leaves, fruits and berries inspired much of September and October, giving a chance to show off a fine array of texture and lace. November's fine selection of seed vessels, such as rose-bay willow-herb and beak parsley, opened the doorway for a special tribute to *The Country Diary*. This section is devoted to the art of drying flowers and creating exquisite displays, bringing the beauty of the outdoors into the midst of our living rooms.

Winter

Winter birds, holly and mistletoe set the scene for December and introduce a lively selection of craft ideas for Christmas gifts and decorations. Gifts made by hand are always especially welcome and express the true meaning of the season of goodwill.

Full instructions are given for all the ideas in the book, along with charts and diagrams where necessary. Cut-out pattern guides will need enlarging on squared paper in order to make full-sized pattern pieces for several items. By carefully following the scale indicated on the diagrams concerned, further creative skills can be put to use. Apart from the materials themselves, everything needed to make Edith Holden's enchanting watercolours come to life can be found among the pages of this book.
Many of the designs and work featured are the products of dedicated people who spend much of their time encouraging and promoting the crafts, in order to ensure that they will continue to attract interest and enthusiasm for generations to come. It is hoped that their objective will be furthered with the help of this book.

JANUARY

"Then came old January, wrappèd well
In many weeds to keep the cold away"

FROST CRYSTALS

EMBROIDERERS OF THE CARPET EARTH

AUBURN-TINTED

Frost Crystals *Crochet Sweater*

Measurements

To Fit Bust	86	91	97	cm
	34	36	38	in
Length	60	62	64	cm
	23½	24½	25	in
Sleeve length	44	45	46	cm
	17¼	17¾	18	in

Materials

Knitting worsted				
Main shade [M]	3	3	4	50g balls
Color C1	2	2	2	50g balls
Color C2	2	2	2	50g balls
Color C3	1	1	1	50g ball

size 8/H crochet hook
Pair of No 3 (3¼mm) knitting needles

Gauge

15 dc and 9½ rows to 10cm (4 in) measured over dc patt using 8/H hook

Abbreviations

beg – beginning; **C1(2,3)** – contrast shades; **ch** – chain; **cont** – continue; **dc** – double crochet; **inc** – increase; **k** – knit; **M** – main shade; **p** – purl; **patt** – pattern; **rep** – repeated; **sk** – skip; **st(s)** – stitch(s);
Figures in brackets are for larger sizes

To Make

Back
With 8/H hook and M, make 82 (86, 90) ch loosely. **Foundation Row (wrong side):** 1 dc in 4th ch from hook, 1 dc in each ch to end. 80 (84, 88) sts. Cont in M. **Patt row:** 3 ch, sk 1st dc, 1 dc in each dc, 1 dc in top of turning ch. Rep patt row once. Now cont in patt and stripes of 6 rows C1, 3 rows M, 6 rows C2, 3 rows M, 6 rows C3 and 3 rows M. These 27 rows form stripe sequence and are rep throughout. Cont until back measures 54 (56, 58) cm, 21¼ (22, 23)in, from beg. Fasten off.

Front
Work as back until 8 fewer rows have been worked than on back.

Neck Shaping
1st row: Patt across 33 (34, 35) sts, turn. Patt 1 row. ****3rd row:** patt across 30 (31, 32) sts, turn. Patt 1 row. **5th row:** patt across 28 (29, 30) sts, turn. Patt 1 row. **7th row:** patt across 27 (28, 29) sts, turn. Patt 1 row**. Fasten off. **Next row:** sk center 14 (16, 18) dc and rejoin appropriate color to next dc, 3 ch, patt to end. Work as first side from ** to **. Patt 1 more row. Fasten off.

Sleeves
With 8/H hook and M, make 46 (48, 50) ch loosely. Work foundation row as on back. 44 (46, 48) sts. Patt 2 rows M. Cont in stripe sequence as given for back, inc 1 st at end of every row until there are 72 (76, 80) sts. Patt straight until sleeve measures 40 (41, 42) cm, 15¾ (16, 16½) in, from beg. Fasten off.

Back Welt
With right side facing, using No 3 (3¼mm) needles and M, pick up and k 106 (110, 114) sts evenly along lower edge of back. **1st rib row** (wrong side): p 2, *k 2, p 2; rep from * to end. **2nd rib row:** k 2, *p 2, k 2; rep from * to end. Rep 1st and 2nd rib rows 6 times, then 1st rib row again. Bind off loosely in rib. Work front welt to match.

Sleeve Welts
With right side facing, using No 3 (3¼mm) needles and M, pick up and k 46 (50, 54) sts evenly along lower edge of sleeve. Rib 11 rows as for back. Bind off loosely in rib.

Neckband
Mark center 26 (28, 30) dc on top edge of back for back neck. Join right shoulder seam. With right side facing, using No 3 (3¼mm) needles and M, pick up and k 27 sts down left front neck, 18 (20, 22) sts across sts at center front, 27 sts up right front neck and 38 (40, 42) sts across back neck. 110 (114, 118) sts. Rib 13 rows as for back welt. Bind off loosely in rib.

To Finish
Join left shoulder and neckband seam. Fold neckband in half on to wrong side and catch stitch loosely in place. With center of top edge of sleeves to shoulder seams, sew on sleeves. Join side and sleeve seams.

Silver Tracery
Tatted Collar

Measurement

Depth of collar – 16 cm (6¼in)

Materials

Anchor Mercer Crochet Cotton No 20 (10g) 3 balls of selected color
Tatting shuttle

Gauge

First 3 rings – 3.3 cm (1¼in)

Abbreviations

ds – double stitch; **r** – ring; **ch** – chain; **pct(s)** – picot(s); **smp** – small picot; **sep** – separated; **cl** – close; **prev** – previous; **rw** – reverse work; **rep** – repeat; **sk** – skip

To Make

1st Section
1st Row Tie ball and shuttle threads together. (R of 9 ds, smp, 9 ds, cl, rw. Ch of 9 ds, 3 pcts sep by 1 ds, 9 ds, join by shuttle thread to smp on prev r, rw)
3 times. (R of 12 ds, smp, 12 ds, cl, rw. Ch of 11 ds, 3 pcts sep by 1 ds, 11ds, join by shuttle thread to smp on prev r, rw)
3 times. *R of 9 ds, p, 9 ds, smp, 18 ds, cl, rw. Ch of 13 ds, 3 pcts sep by 1 ds, 13 ds, join by shuttle thread to smp on prev r, rw; rep from * twice more omitting rw at end of last rep.
Ch of 9 ds, 3 pcts sep by 1 ds, 9 ds, join by shuttle thread to smp on prev r, 7 ds, rw. R of 9 ds, join to pct on prev r, 9 ds, smp, 18 ds, cl, rw. Ch of 9 ds, 3 pcts sep by 1 ds, 9 ds, join by shuttle thread to base of prev r. (Ch of 13 ds, 3 pcts sep by 1 ds, 13 ds, join by shuttle thread to smp on prev r, rw. R of 9 ds, join to pct on next r, 9 ds, smp, 18 ds, cl, rw) twice. Ch of 13 ds, 3 ps sep by 1 ds, 13 ds, join by shuttle thread to smp on prev r, join by shuttle thread to smp on next r.
(Ch of 11 ds, 3 pcts sep by 1 ds, 11 ds, join by shuttle thread to smp on next r) 3 times. (Ch of 9 ds, 3 pcts sep by 1 ds, 9 ds, join by shuttle thread to smp on next r) twice. Ch of 9 ds, 3 pcts sep by 1 ds, 9 ds, join by shuttle thread to base of first r.
2nd Row ch of 5 ds, 3 pcts sep by 1 ds, 8 ds, pct, 6 ds, join by shuttle thread to

center pct of 1st ch on prev row, 3 ds, 3 pcts sep by 1 ds, 3 ds, join to center pct of next ch on prev row, 10 ds, pct, 10 ds, join to center pct of next ch on prev row, 4 ds, 3 pcts sep by 1 ds, 4 ds, join to center pct of next ch on prev row, 11 ds, pct, 13 ds, join to center pct of next ch on prev row.
(Ch of 4 ds, 3 pcts sep by 1 ds, 4 ds, join to center pct of next ch on prev row) twice. Ch of 11 ds, rw. R of 13 ds, join to 1st pct of next ch on prev row, 13 ds, cl, rw. Ch of 7 ds, 2 pcts sep by 5 ds, 7 ds, rw. R of 13 ds, sk next pct on prev row, join to next pct, 13 ds, cl, rw. Ch of 11 ds, join to center pct of next ch on prev row, 11 ds, 3 pcts sep by 1 ds, 11 ds, rw. R of 9 ds, join to 1st pct of next ch on prev row, 9 ds, cl, rw. Ch of 9 ds, 3 pcts sep by 1 ds, 9 ds, rw. R of 12 ds, sk next pct on prev row, join to next pct, 7 ds, join to 1st pct of next ch on prev row, 12 ds, cl, rw.
Ch of 9 ds, 3 pcts sep by 1 ds, 9 ds, rw. R of 9 ds, sk next pct on prev row, join to next pct, 9 ds, cl, rw. Ch of 11 ds, 3 pcts sep by 1 ds, 11 ds, join to center pct of next ch on prev row, 11 ds, rw. R of 13 ds, join to 1st pct of next ch on prev row, 13 ds, cl, rw. Ch of 7 ds, 2 pcts sep by 5 ds, 7 ds, rw. R of 13 ds, sk next pct on prev row, join to next pct, 13 ds, cl, rw. Ch of 11 ds, join to center pct of next ch on prev row.
(Ch of 4 ds, 3 pcts sep by 1 ds, 4 ds, join to center pct of next ch on prev row) twice. Ch of 13 ds, pct, 11 ds, join to center pct of next ch on prev row, 4 ds, 3 pcts sep by 1 ds, 4 ds, join to center pct of next ch on previous row 10 ds, pct, 10 ds, join to center pct of next ch on prev row, 3 ds, 3 pcts sep by 1 ds, 3 ds, join to center pct of next ch on prev row, 6 ds, pct, 8 ds, 3 pcts sep by 1 ds, 5 ds, join to base of 1st ch. Tie ends, cut and oversew neatly on wrong side.

2nd Section
Work as 1st section for 1 row. **2nd row** ch of 5 ds, 3 pcts sep by 1 ds, 8 ds, join by ball thread to corresponding pct on 1st section, 6 ds, join by shuttle thread to center pct of next ch on prev row, 3 ds, 3 pcts sep by 1 ds, 3 ds, join to center pct of next ch on 2nd section, 10 ds, sk 3 pcts on 1st section, join by ball thread to next pct, 10 ds, join to center pct of next ch on 2nd section, 4 ds, 3 pcts sep by 1 ds, 4 ds, join to center pct of next ch on 2nd section, 11 ds, sk 3 pcts on 1st section, join by ball thread to next pct, 13 ds, join to center pct of next ch on 2nd section.

(Ch of 4 ds, 3 pcts sep by 1 ds, 4 ds, join to center pct of next ch on 2nd section) twice. Ch of 11 ds, rw. R of 13 ds, join to 1st pct of next ch on 2nd section, 13 ds, cl, rw. Ch of 7 ds, sk 6 pcts on 1st section, join by ball thread to next pct, 5 ds, join by ball thread to next pct on 1st section, 7 ds, rw. R of 13 ds, sk next pct on 2nd section, join to next pct, 13 ds, cl, rw and complete as 1st section.
Make 11 more sections joining each as 2nd section was joined to 1st.

Heading
Tie ball and shuttle threads together. With right side facing attach by shuttle thread to 2nd last pct made on 1st strip. *Ch of 10 ds, sk 2 pcts, join by shuttle thread to next pct. **Ch of 14 ds, sk 2 pcts, join by shuttle thread to next pct; rep from * 12 times more ending last rep at **. Tie ends, cut and oversew neatly on wrong side.

To Finish
Dampen and, using rustproof pins, pin to a padded surface. Measure to insure correct size. Let dry. Sew to garment as desired or secure with ribbon bow at back or front. (Collar can be made smaller by reducing number of sections worked.)

General Working Instructions For All Needlepoint

Mark center lines of canvas (widthwise and lengthwise) with basting stitches. Overcast raw edges and work needlepoint in a frame if possible. Each set of instructions has a chart for the design. Most charts have arrows indicating the center of the design which should correspond with the center lines of the canvas.

Each small square on a chart represents one stitch. Each symbol represents the shade of the yarn to use, as indicated by the key.

To begin work, hold a short 'tail' of yarn against back on canvas so that it is secured by the first few stitches. To finish off, run needle under a few stitches on wrong side and snip yarn. Work design out from the center and fill in the background to the required size when design is complete. Allow sufficient canvas for background together with any extra needed for framing or seams.

Designs are worked in traméed half cross stitch or tent stitch. Outlines (shown on charts by solid lines) are worked in backstitch, using a split strand of yarn, when needlepoint is finished.

Press work lightly on the wrong side using a damp cloth. If work is distorted, pin out flat and square, with wrong side facing. Dampen and leave to dry. Press lightly.

See the 'Glossary' on page 156 for details of stitches.

Daisies

Needlepoint Picture Frame

Measurements

Finished frame 20cm x 24cm (8in x 9½in)
Picture window 7.5cm x 11.5cm (3in x 4½in)

Materials

50cm (19¾in) of 58cm (23in) wide, No 10 Penelope (double-threaded) needlepoint canvas
Anchor Tapestry Wool in 10m (11yd) skeins: 5 skeins 0736; 2 skeins 0670; 1 skein each 0402 White; 3097; 3150; 0242; 0727; 0369; 0217; 3149; 037; 0397
Tapestry needle No 18
Picture or photograph to insert into 'window'
Two pieces of strong cardboard 20cm x 24cm (8in x 9½in)
Strong cardboard for strut

To Make

Important Note:
Read 'General Working Instructions for all Needlepoint'.

1 To work needlepoint design follow charts and key for Daisy A and Daisy B designs on page 16.

2 Lightly fold canvas in both directions and work a line of basting stitches along each crease to mark center lines.

3 Using a soft pencil, center picture window on canvas and draw outline 7.5cm x 11.5cm (3in x 4½in). Note, this should be over an even number of double

Daisies
Needlepoint Picture Frame

Key	
ꞁ	0402
•	3097
×	3150
/	0242
+	0727
V	0369
O	0217
—	3149
\	037

Chart A Design 26 x 39 stitches
Design size
6.5cm x 10cm (2½in x 4in)
10 stitches to 2.5cm (1in)

Chart B Design 23 x 31 stitches
Design size
5.5cm x 7.5cm (2¼in x 3in)
10 stitches to 2.5cm (1in)

(Background for **A** and **B** *0736*)

Special instructions
Backstitch detail:
Petal lines
0670 (shown in red)
0397 (shown in black)
Center leaves Daisy B
0217

Shade numbers refer to Anchor Tapestry wool.

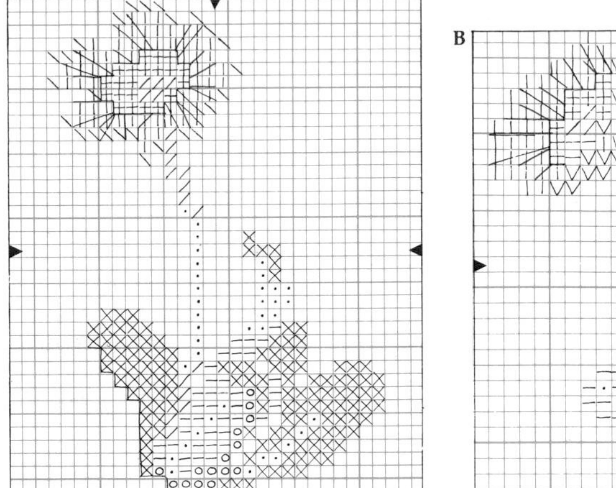

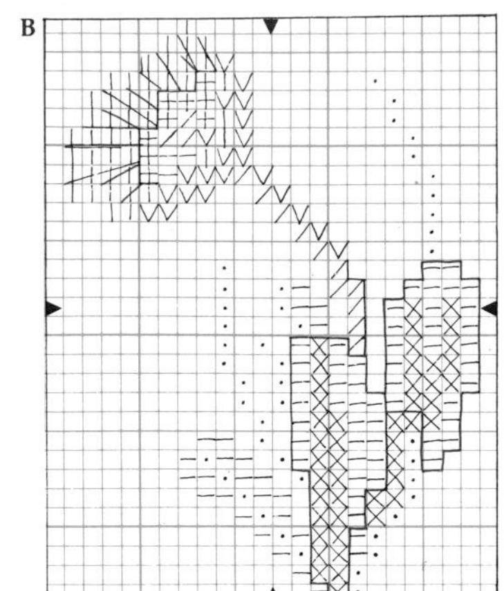

threads in width and depth. Count 25 double threads of canvas out from each side of picture window and draw pencil outline for outer edge of frame.

4 Using 0670 and following the diagrams, work a row of double cross stitches over 2 double threads of canvas, *inside frame outline.* Work another row of double cross stitch *outside picture window outline.*

5 The remaining unworked 21 double threads of canvas (lying between the rows of double cross stitch) are worked in traméed half cross stitch.

6 Following the picture of 'Daisies' on page 15, center Daisy A in lower left corner of frame and work chart A. Work chart in reverse in lower right corner. Center Daisy B in top right corner of frame and work chart B. Repeat chart in reverse in top left corner.

7 Work background in 0736.

8 Work backstitch details using 0397 and 0670 for petal lines. Use 0217 for leaf lines on Daisy B.

9 Remove basting stitches.

10 Trim away surplus canvas inside picture window to within 2.5cm (1in) of needlepoint stitches being worked. Clip into corners. Cut window in 1 piece of cardboard to match size of needlepoint window. Place this piece on wrong side of needlepoint and fold surplus canvas over it. Glue in place. In same way, fold and glue surplus canvas over outer edges of cardboard. Place 2nd piece of cardboard behind frame and glue in place along outer edges of frame only. Cut a piece of cardboard approximately 5cm (2in) wide and glue into position, at center back, to form strut. Insert picture into frame through window edges.

General Working Instructions For All Cross Stitch Embroideries

Most cross stitch embroidery designs found in this book can be used to decorate a variety of household items. Those pictured serve to indicate a suitable selection of ideas including pictures, cushion covers and table linen.

It is important when deciding on a suitable embroidery design to choose one which will be neither too small nor too large for the finished size of the item. Embroidery design sizes are given at the beginning of each set of instructions. These can, however, be increased in size by using a coarser weave fabric or decreased by using a finer one. Quantities of embroidery floss, the number of strands used to work the embroidery, and the size of the needle will vary accordingly.

It is also of great importance when calculating the amount of linen to purchase, to take into consideration the fabric allowance needed for the plain border which surrounds the cross stitch design area, as well as any allowance needed for mounting, framing, seams or hems. If in doubt, do not hesitate to ask for advice at a reputable craft shop or department store before purchasing the fabric.

Start by neatening the edges of the fabric by either hand oversewing or by machine zigzagging. This will help to prevent the fabric from fraying. Work the embroidery using a small embroidery hoop to hold the fabric taut. Move the hoop to different sections as they are worked.

Each set of embroidery instructions has a working chart for the design and a key of embroidery floss shades to use.

Most charts have arrows indicating the center of the design. To find the center of the fabric, lightly fold it in half in both directions and work a fine line of basting stitches along each crease mark. These basting stitches will correspond to center lines marked on the chart by arrows.

The embroidery is worked from the center outwards, to ensure it is correctly placed on the fabric. Begin by holding the loose end of floss behind the fabric until secured with several small stitches. Do not knot the thread. To finish off the thread, run the needle under several stitches at the back of the work and snip the end.

Each small square on the chart represents one cross stitch, which is worked over two threads of linen in each direction. Each symbol on the chart represents the color of cotton to use, as indicated by the key. Each cross stitch is made of two diagonal stitches. Work one row making all left to right diagonal stitches in one color. Return along the same row crossing all stitches with right to left diagonals. All stitches should be crossed in the same direction.

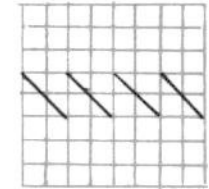

Step 1 working from left to right.
Step 2 working from right to left.
Finished cross stitch.

Details worked in back stitch are indicated on the chart by a solid line. Back stitches form a continuous line, with stitches touching and are used to outline and define certain areas.

When complete, press lightly using a dry cloth on the wrong side.

Ribbon Weaving

Ribbon weaving is one of the easiest needlecrafts to learn and children will enjoy it as much as their mothers. This craft provides a piece of woven fabric made by pinning down ribbons vertically and threading ribbons through horizontally.

Everything needed to make a small cushion will be already available in most homes or workboxes and by following 'The Basic Technique', the cushion can be made immediately.

Tools and Equipment

1 Flat padded surface – an ironing board is perfect for small items. For larger pieces pad a table with a folded blanket and cover with a cotton sheet.

2 Dressmaking pins and sharp scissors. (Large pins with glass heads are best.)

3 Tape measure and a soft pencil.

4 Light weight iron-on interfacing or lining fabric.

5 Large safety pin and kitchen fork.

Ribbons for Weaving

1 Choose ribbons which are colorfast, machine washable, non-iron and virtually non-shrinkable. Offray single face polyester ribbons in satin or grosgrain are best.

2 To create contrasts of texture and color, use different types of ribbon to make the same cushion, eg satins, grosgrains, washable velvet ribbons, Lurex/polyester ribbons or Jacquards.

3 Do not mix polyester satin ribbon with nylon taffeta as nylon taffeta will need ironing after washing.

4 Cushions will complement the color scheme of a room if two or three colors from the curtains, upholstery or carpet are used for the ribbons.

Iron-on Interfacing

Light iron-on interfacing is used to bond the ribbons together into a fabric which can be handled easily or cut into the shape required. This is a great help to beginners. The traditional ribbon-weaving technique of basting the woven ribbons onto a lining can be used and dispenses with the iron-on interfacing.

The Basic Technique

Making a simple 25cm (10in) square woven ribbon cushion cover

Materials

30cm (12in) of light iron-on interfacing
3m (3¼yd) of 25mm (1in) wide Offray polyester satin ribbon in light color
3m (3¼yd) of 25mm (1in) wide Offray polyester satin ribbon in darker color
30cm (12in) of cushion-cover backing fabric
Pillow form to fit
Matching thread

To Make

1 Pencil out a stitching line 25cm (10in) square on light iron-on interfacing. Add 2.5cm (1in) all around for seam allowance to give a final 30cm (12in) square. Pencil large square.

2 With adhesive side of interfacing facing up, pin onto an ironing board or padded table top. Pencil the seam allowance outline again to insure clarity.

3 Cut 10 pieces of 30cm (12in) long ribbons in light shade. These will be pinned vertically (from top to bottom) and are called 'warp ribbons'.

4 Begin 2.5cm (1in) in from left hand corner of large pencilled square and pin ribbons along the top line with edges touching.

5 Cut 10 pieces of ribbon each 30cm (12in) long in darker color to use as weaving ribbons. These are 'weft ribbons' and are woven horizontally.

6 Slip safety pin on end of 1st weft ribbon and lifting *every other* warp ribbon in turn, weave as follows: **Row 1:** over 1, under 1, over 1, under 1. Repeat until row is complete. Pin down at both ends. Diagram A. **Row 2:** using 2nd weft ribbon weave under 1, over 1, under 1, over 1. Repeat until row is complete. Pin down at both ends. Diagram B.

7 Repeat rows 1 and 2 until weaving is complete.

8 Push weft threads close together using a kitchen fork.

9 Pin down warp ends.

10 Set an electric steam iron to wool. Dry press lightly all over weaving, as close to edges as possible, leaving pins in place. Pressing should make ribbons stick to interfacing. Remove pins. Carefully turn over weaving and steam press the back firmly. (Or you can use a damp cloth and a hot iron.) Allow weaving to cool. The woven fabric square is now ready to sew into a cushion cover.

11 Using a 30cm (12in) square of fabric to make cushion cover back, place right sides of front and back pieces together. Stitch 3 sides along stitching line. Turn to right side. Insert pillow form. Stitch remaining side.

Note: The basic technique of making a square woven cushion cover can be used by beginners to make 'Icicles' Cushion Cover in January. The more advanced method actually used for 'Icicles' can be tried out once experience has been gained or by those already experienced in ribbon weaving.

Diagram A

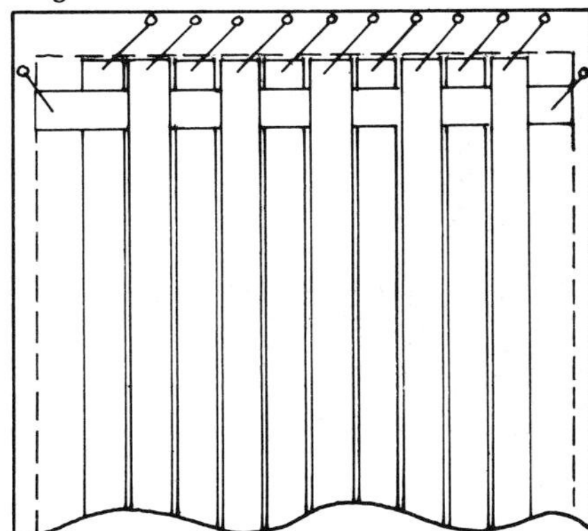

Row 1 of warp ribbon weaving

Diagram B

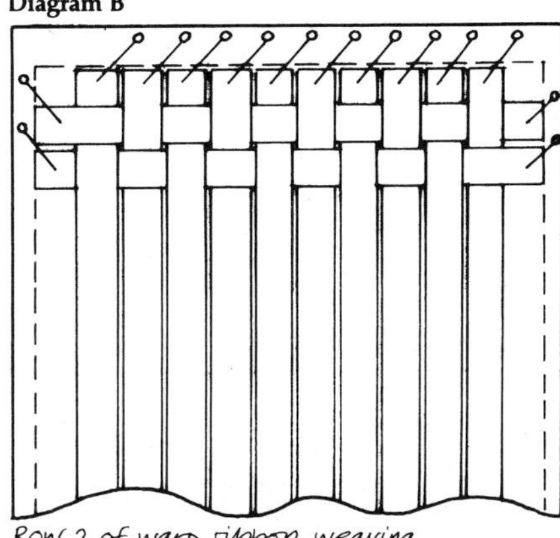

Row 2 of warp ribbon weaving

Snowdrops *Embroidered Cushion Cover* *(Picture on page 12)*

Measurements

Finished cushion cover approx 38cm (15in) square
Snowdrop design approx 30cm (12in) square

Materials

2 pieces of 46cm (18in) square even-weave linen, approximately 26 threads to 2.5cm (1in)
Anchor Embroidery Floss: 2 skeins 01; 1 skein each 0268; 0259; 0261; 0266; 0278; 0297; 0848
Tapestry needle No 24
2 pieces of 46cm (18in) square backing fabric to form cushion lining
Pins
Bias binding for covering piping cord
1.6m (1¾yd) of piping cord
Matching thread
38cm (15in) square pillow form

To Make

Important Note: read 'General Working Instructions for all Cross Stitch Embroideries' on page 16.

1 Fold 1 piece of linen lightly in both directions (widthwise and lengthwise) to mark center lines. Baste along center lines. Arrows on chart mark the center of the design and should coincide with basting stitches.

2 Use 2 strands of floss throughout.

3 To work embroidery follow chart and key for 'Snowdrops' design below. Work chart to form lower half of cushion cover design. Turn fabric, and work design again onto 2nd half of cushion cover front. Each square on chart represents 2 double threads of linen (2 warp and 2 weft) or 1 cross stitch.

4 With embroidery centered, mark out 38cm (15in) square with basting stitches. Pin and baste lining to wrong side of embroidered linen.

5 Open up bias binding to lie flat (press flat if necessary). Enclose piping within a center fold of bias binding. Baste and stitch down binding as close as possible to enclosed cord.

6 Position end of covered cord at center of base edge. Place cord cover on top of embroidered linen matching basting stitches. Pin and baste covered piping in place. Carefully snip into seam edges of piping cover at each corner to enable piping to curve easily around corners. Where piping meets, at center base, trim cord and stitch binding edges to fit neatly together.

7 Mark out 38cm (15in) square on 2nd piece of linen to form back cover. Pin and baste lining to wrong side.

8 With right sides of front and back lined pieces facing, pin, baste and stitch 3 sides. Trim seams and turn onto right side.

9 Insert pillow form and stitch remaining side.

Snowdrops
Embroidered Cushion

Key	
○	0268
I	0259
X	0261
•	01
\	0266
–	0278
+	0297
/	0848

Design 151 x 69 stitches
Design size (approx.)
30cm x 13cm (12in x 5in)
13 stitches to 2.5cm (1in)

(Please note design is worked twice.)

Shade numbers refer to Anchor Embroidery Floss.

Icicles *Woven Ribbon Cushion* *(Picture on page 12)*

(First refer to page 17)

Measurements

Finished cushion: 41cm x 41cm (16in x 16in)
Woven ribbon area: 35cm x 35cm (13¾in x 13¾in)

Materials

Warp ribbons: 18m (19¾yd) of 9mm (⅜in) wide Offray polyester satin ribbon: Light Blue shade no 305
Weft ribbons: (a) 6m (6½yd) of 9mm (⅜in) wide Offray polyester satin ribbon: Aqua shade no 314. (b) 5.6m (6⅛yd) of 12mm (½in) wide Offray polyester satin ribbon: Ice Mint shade no 510.
36cm (14in) square lightweight iron-on interfacing.
75cm (29½in) fabric for backing cushion and for ruche strip and piping cord.
Matching thread.
30cm (12in) zipper to match color of backing fabric.
Pillow form. Glass headed pins.
2m (2¼yd) of piping cord. Soft pencil.

Useful Hints
To make weaving very easy, it helps to have a large safety pin (to attach to the end of a ribbon when weaving) and an ordinary kitchen fork (to push the weft ribbons closely together).

To Make

1 Cut the light blue warp ribbons into 45 ribbons of 40cm (15¾in) length: the aqua weft ribbons into 15 ribbons of 40cm (15¾in) length, and the ice mint weft ribbons into 14 ribbons of 40cm (15¾in) length.

2 Work the ribbon weaving on iron-on interfacing in the standard 'over 1 under 1' weave found in 'The Basic Technique' on page 17. Note that in 'Icicles' the warp ribbons are all light blue and the weft ribbons use aqua and ice mint alternately.

3 Set an electric steam iron to the heat for wool. Dry-press lightly all over the weaving as close to the edges as possible, leaving the pins in place. This light pressing should be sufficient to make the ribbons stick to the interfacing.

4 Carefully turn the weaving over and reset the electric iron. Steam-press the back of the weaving firmly (use a damp cloth and a hot setting if the iron is not a steam iron).

5 Cut backing fabric to 45cm (17¾in) square, which includes 2cm (¾in) seam allowance.

6 Cut strip for ruching 6.5cm (2½in) wide and 193cm (75in) long, along straight grain of fabric (seam allowance included in size of width). Miter 4, evenly spaced, corners and join ends.

7 Using matching thread, neatly gather each edge of ruche strip and pull up gently to fit onto edges of woven ribbon and cushion backing fabric.

8 Machine or hand stitch inner edge of ruche strip to outer edge of ribbon weaving, matching mitered corners with corners of woven fabric.

9 Assemble piping and cushion cover as 'Snowdrops' on page 18.

The Carpet Earth

Crochet Chair or Floor Rug

(Picture on page 12)

Measurements

120cm (48in) square excluding fringes

Materials

5 x 100g balls of Bulky knitting yarn in each of 4 colors
10/J crochet hook

Gauge

10 sts to 10cm (4in) measured over pattern

Abbreviations

ch – chain; **lp(s)** – loop(s); **patt** – pattern; **rep** – repeat; **sc** – single crochet; **st(s)** – stitch(es); **yo** – yarn over

To Make

To make each square make 21ch.
Foundation row: 1 sc in 2nd ch from hook, 1 sc in each ch to end, 1 ch, turn. 20 sts. **1st patt row** (wrong side): *Take yarn round finger to make a long lp, insert hook into next st, draw through 2 strands leaving lp on finger, yo and draw through 3 lps on hook; rep from* to end, 1 ch, turn. **2nd patt row:** 1 sc in each st to end, 1 ch, turn. These 2 rows form the patt. Rep them until square measures 20 cm (8in) measured on the wrong side, not including lps, ending after a 2nd row. Fasten off.
Make 10 in color 1, 10 in color 2, 8 in color 3 and 8 in color 4.

To Finish
Join squares following the diagram, making sure that the lps do not get caught in the seams. Cut remaining yarn into 23cm (9in) lengths and, using two strands together, fringe all round outer edge using colors 3 and 4 as shown. Do not press.

	3	4	3	4	3	4	
3	1	2	1	2	1	2	4
4	2	3	4	3	4	1	3
3	1	4	3	4	3	2	4
4	2	3	4	3	4	1	3
3	1	4	3	4	3	2	4
4	2	1	2	1	2	1	3
	4	3	4	3	4	3	

Auburn-tinted

Knitted Leaf Sweater
With Matching Lacy Scarf

Measurements

Sweater

To fit bust	81	86	91	97cm
	32	34	36	38in
Length at center back, excluding neckband	66	67	69	70cm
	26	26½	27	27½in
Sleeve seam	41	41	41	41cm
	16	16	16	16in

Lacy scarf

width, approximately	97cm 38in
Length, excluding fringe	157cm 62in

Materials

Sweater

Jaeger Gypsy (M)	9	9	10	10	25g balls
Jaeger Mohair Spun — platinum (L)	3	3	3	3	25g balls
cornelian (D)	5	5	5	6	25g balls
Jaeger Cotton Flammé (C)	2	2	3	3	50g balls

Pair of needles each Nos 9 (6mm) and 6 (4½mm)

Lacy Scarf

Jaeger Gypsy (M)	3	25g balls
Jaeger Mohair Spun — platinum (L)	6	25g balls

Pair No 9 (6mm) needles

Gauge

16 sts and 22 rows to 10cm (4in) over main pattern on No 9 (6mm) needles

Abbreviations

k – knit; **p** – purl; **st(s)** – stitch(es); **patt** – pattern; **sl** – slip; **yo** – yarn over needle; **psso** – pass slip st over; **inc** – increase, increasing; **dec** – decrease, decreasing; **beg** – beginning; **rep** – repeat; **cont** – continue; **st st** – stockinette stitch; **tog** – together

To Make

SWEATER

Sleeves

With No 6 (4½mm) needles and M, cast on 32 (32, 36, 36) sts. **1st row** (right side): k 3, (p 2, k 2) to last st, k 1. **2nd row:** k 1, (p 2, k 2) to last 3 sts, p 2, k 1. Rep these 2 rows for 10cm (4in), ending after a 2nd row. **Next row:** k inc once in every st. 64 (64, 72, 72) sts. **Next row:** p inc 9 (13, 9, 13) sts evenly across. 73 (77, 81, 85) sts. Change to No 9 (6mm) needles and main patt thus: (**NB:** C should be used double) **1st row:** in C, k 1, (with yarn back sl 1 purlwise, k 1) to end. **2nd row:** in C, k 1, (bring yarn to front of work, sl 1 purlwise, take yarn to back of work, k 1) to end. **3rd row:** in M, k 2, (sl 1 purlwise, k 1) to last st, k 1. **4th row:** in M, p. **5th row:** in M, p 1, (yo, p 3 tog, yo p 1) to end. **6th row:** in M, k. **7th and 8th rows:** in L, as 5th and 6th. **9th and 10th rows:** in M, as 5th and 6th. **11th to 20th rows:** as rows 1 to 10 but using D in place of M. These 20 rows form main patt. Cont in patt until work measures approximately 41cm (16in) at center, ending after a 6th or 16th row for 1st size, a 4th or 14th row for 2nd size, a 10th or 20th row for 3rd size and an 8th or 18th row for 4th size. **Keeping patt correct, shape as follows: **1st and 2nd rows:** bind off 8 (9, 10, 11) sts, work to end. **3rd row:** k 1, sl 1, k 1, psso, work to last 3 sts, k 2 tog, k 1. **4th row:** p 2, work to last 2 sts, p 2.** Rep 3rd and 4th rows until 51 sts remain, ending after 3rd row. Sl sts on a spare needle.

Front

With No 6 (4½mm) needles and M, cast on 64 (68, 72, 76) sts. Work in rib as on cuffs for 10cm (4in), ending after a 1st row. **Next row:** rib 2 (4, 6, 8), (inc in next st, rib 2, inc in next st, rib 1) 12 times, inc in next st, rib to end. 89 (93, 97, 101) sts. Change to No 9 (6mm) needles and patt as on sleeves until work measures approximately 41cm (16in) at center, ending after same patt row as on sleeves before shaping. Work as sleeves from ** to **. Rep 3rd and 4th rows until 67 sts remain, ending after 3rd row. Slip sts on a spare needle.

Back

Work as front but leave final sts on needle.

Yoke

(**NB:** A 3rd, No 9 (6mm) needle, may be used to hold sts until number is reduced.) Cont in M only. **Next row:** p across sts of back inc 5 sts evenly, p across sts of right sleeve, p across sts of front inc 2 sts evenly, finally p across sts of left sleeve. (243 sts.) Change to st st and beg k row work 2 rows. Cont in st st working from chart thus: First wind off 10 small balls of D, each approximately 345cm (136in) long. Use a separate ball of D for each leaf motif. **1st row:** 5 M, (work 1st row of chart, 7 M) 9 times, work 1st row of chart, 5 M. **2nd to 4th rows:** as 1st but working 2nd to 4th rows of chart. **5th row** (dec row): 1 M, sl 1, k 1, psso all in M, 2 M, (work 5th row of chart, in M, k 2, sl 1, k 2 tog, psso, k 2) 9 times, work 5th row of chart, 2 M, k 2 tog M, 1 M. (223 sts.) **6th row:** 4 M, (work 6th row of chart, 5 M) 9 times, work 6th row of chart, 4 M. **7th to 12th rows:** as 6th but working 7th to 12th rows of chart. **13th row (dec row):** 1 M, sl 1, k 1, psso all in M, 1 M, (work 13th row of chart, in M, k 1, sl 1, k 2 tog, psso, k 1) 9 times, work 13th row of chart, 1 M, k 2 tog M, 1 M. (203 sts.) **14th row:** 3 M, (work 14th row of chart, 3 M) 9 times, work 14th row of chart, 3 M. **15th to 20th rows:** as 14th but working 15th to 20th rows of chart. **21st row (dec row):** 1 M, sl 1, k 1, psso all in M, (work 21st row of chart, sl 1, k 2 tog, psso all in M) 9 times, work 21st row of chart, k 2 tog M, 1 M. (183 sts.). Break D. Cont in M only and work 1 row dec 3 sts evenly across. (180 sts.) Change to rib thus: **1st row:** p 2, (k 2, p 4) 29 times, k 2, p 2. **2nd row:** k 2, (p 2, k 4) 29 times, p 2, k 2. **3rd and 4th rows:** as 1st and 2nd. **5th row:** p 2, (k 2, p 1, p 2 tog, p 1) 29 times, k 2, p 2. (151 sts.) **6th row:** k 2, (p 2, k 3) 29 times, p 2, k 2. **7th to 12th rows:** keeping rib correct, work 6 rows. **13th row:** p 2, (k 2, p 2 tog, p 1) 29 times, k 2, p 2. (122 sts.) **14th row:** k 2, (p 2, k 2) to end. Keeping rib correct, work 3 rows straight. **Next row:** p 3 tog, (p 2 tog, p 1, p 2 tog) 23 times, (p 2 tog) twice. (72 sts.) Change to No 6 (4½mm) needles and beg 1st row work 16 rows in rib as on welt. Bind off loosely.

To Finish

Press upper section of yoke only, following instructions on the yarn band. Join yoke seam and neckband; join shapings. Join side and sleeve seams. Fold neckband in half to wrong side and hem in position. Press seams.

LACY SCARF

With No 9 (6mm) needles and L, cast on 53 sts. Joining in and breaking off M only, work in patt thus: **1st row:** in L, p 1, (yo, p 3 tog, yo, p 1) 13 times. **2nd row:** in L, k. **3rd and 4th rows:** as 1st and 2nd. **5th and 6th rows:** in M, as 1st and 2nd. Rep these 6 rows for 157cm (62in), ending after 4th row. Bind off *loosely* in L. Do not press. Cut remainder of L into 25cm (10in) lengths and taking 3 lengths for each tassel, fringe the 2 short ends.

Chart for working 'Leaf' motif

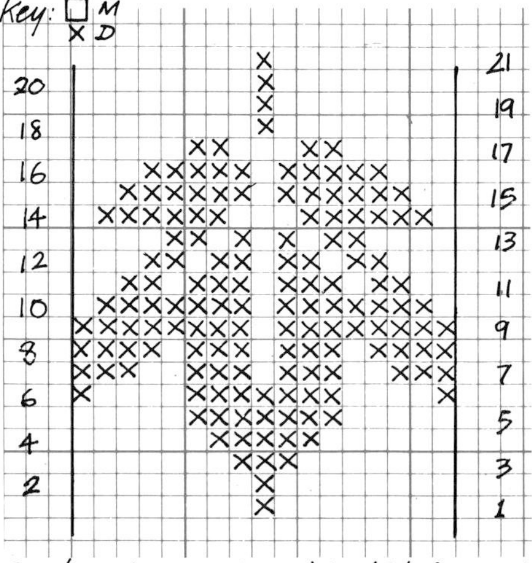

FEBRUARY

Fair Maids of February

WILD ARUM

PRIMROSE/WILLOW CATKINS *(Inset)*

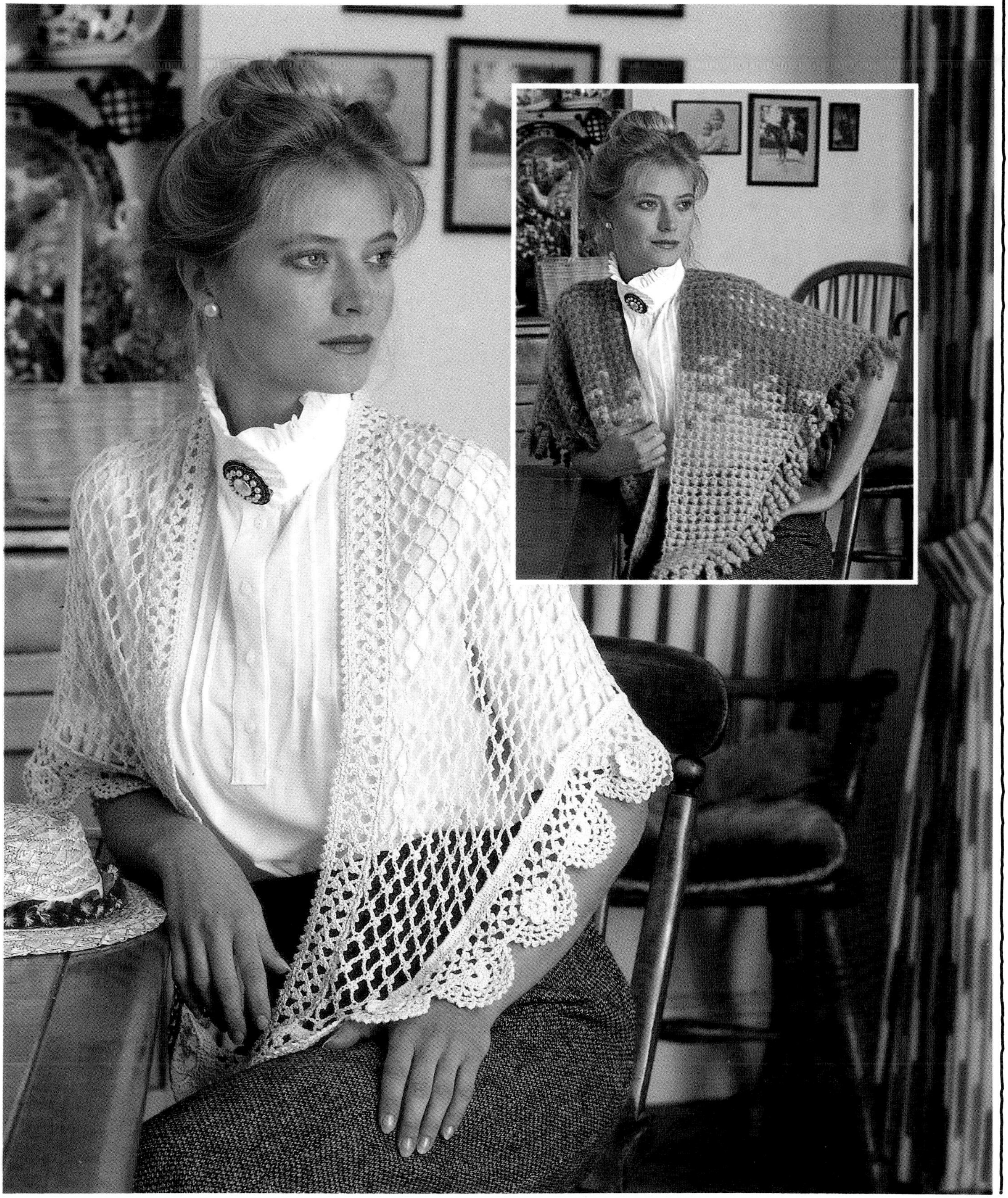

Wild Arum *Knitted Aran Jacket*

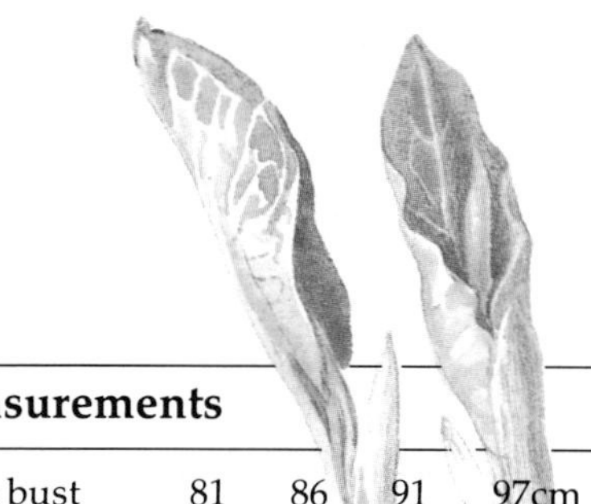

Measurements

To fit bust	81	86	91	97cm
	32	34	36	38in
Length from shoulder	70	71	72	74cm
	27½	28	28½	29in
Sleeve seam	42	42	42	42cm
	16½	16½	16½	16½in

Materials

Fisherman yarn 17 18 18 19 50g balls
Pair of needles each Nos 6 (4½mm) and 4 (3¾mm)
A cable needle
5 buttons

Gauge

18 sts and 28 rows to 10cm (4in) over stockinette stitch on No 6 (4½mm) needles

Abbreviations

k – knit; **p** – purl; **sts** – stitches; **st st** – stockinette st; **patt** – pattern; **inc** – increase, increasing; **dec** – decrease, decreasing; **beg** – beginning; **alt** – alternate; **rep** – repeat; **C8** – slip next 4 sts on cable needle to front of work, k 4 then k 4 from cable needle; **cont** – continue; **g st** – garter st

Cable Panel *(worked over 18 sts)*
1st row: p 5, k 8, p 5. **2nd row:** k 5, p 8, k 5. **3rd to 6th rows:** rep 1st and 2nd rows twice. **7th row:** p 5, C 8, p 5. **8th row:** as 2nd. **9th to 14th rows:** rep. 1st and 2nd rows 3 times. These 14 rows form panel.

To Make

Pocket Linings (2)
With No 6 (4½mm) needles, cast on 28 sts. Work 36 rows in st st, beg k row, and inc 4 sts evenly on last row. Slip 32 sts on a spare needle.

Right Front
With No 4 (3¾mm) needles, cast on 45 (47, 49, 51) sts. **1st row:** k 2, (p 1, k 1) to last st, k 1. **2nd row:** k 1, (p 1, k 1) to end. Work 8 more rows in rib inc 1 st at each end of last row. 47 (49, 51, 53) sts.
Change to No 6 (4½mm) needles and patt thus: **1st row:** k 14 (15, 16, 17), work 1st row of panel, k 15 (16, 17, 18). **2nd row:** p 15 (16, 17, 18), work 2nd row of panel, p to end. **3rd to 14th rows:** rep 1st and 2nd rows 6 times but working 3rd to 14th rows of panel. These 14 rows form patt.
Cont in patt until work measures 19cm (7½in) from beg, ending after a wrong-side row and inc 1st at center of cable on last row.
Place pocket lining thus: **Next row:** k 7 (8, 9, 10), *slip next 33 sts on a spare needle and in place of these patt across a group of lining sts, k to end.
Cont in patt until work measures 34cm (13½in), ending after a wrong-side row.
Shape front slope thus: Keeping panel correct, dec 1 st at front edge on next row, then on every following 8th row until 41 (43, 45, 47) sts remain. Work 2 rows straight. **NB:** on left front, work 1 row only here.
Shape armholes thus: **Next row:** bind off 6 (7, 8, 9) sts, work to end. **NB:** on left front only, now work 1 row straight. Dec 1 st at armhole edge on next 3 rows, then on the 2 following k rows, at the same time dec 1 st at front edge as before on 5th row following. 29 (30, 31, 32) sts.
Cont dec at front edge only on every 8th row from previous front dec until 24 (24, 25, 25) sts remain.
Work straight until front measures 21 (23, 24, 25) cm, 8½ (9, 9½, 10) in from beg of armhole shaping, ending at armhole edge.
Shape shoulder by binding off 8 (8, 9, 9) sts at beg of next and following alt row. Work 1 row. Bind off.

Left Front
Work to match right front reversing patt rows, thus 1st row will be: 'k 15 (16, 17, 18), work 1st row of panel, k 14 (15, 16, 17)' and pocket row will be: 'k 8 (9, 10, 11), work as right pocket row from * to end.'

Back
With No 4 (3¾mm) needles, cast on 95 (99, 103, 107) sts. Work 10 rows in rib inc 1 st at end of last row. 96 (100, 104, 108) sts.
Change to No 6 (4½mm) needles and patt thus: **1st row:** k 15 (16, 17, 18), work 1st row of panel, k 30 (32, 34, 36), work 1st row of panel, k 15 (16, 17, 18). **2nd row:** p 15 (16, 17, 18), work 2nd row of panel, p 30 (32, 34, 36), work 2nd row of panel, p to end. **3rd to 14th rows:** rep 1st and 2nd rows 6 times but working 3rd to 14th rows of panel. These 14 rows form patt.
Cont in patt until work measures same as left front up to armhole shaping, thus ending after a wrong-side row.
Shape armholes by binding off 6 (7, 8, 9) sts at beg of next 2 rows. Dec 1 st at each end of next 3 rows, then on the 2 following alt rows. 74 (76, 78, 80) sts.
Work straight until back measures same as fronts to shoulder shaping, ending after a wrong-side row.
Shape shoulders by binding off 8 (8, 9, 9) sts at beg of next 4 rows, then 8 (8, 7, 7) sts at beg of next 2 rows. Bind off final 26 (28, 28, 30) sts.

Sleeves
With No 4 (3¾mm) needles, bind on 39 (41, 43, 45) sts. Work 10 rows in rib as on right front but inc 7 (9, 11, 13) sts evenly across last row. 46 (50, 54, 58) sts.
Change to No 6 (4½mm) needles and patt thus: **1st row:** k 14 (16, 18, 20), work 1st row of panel, k 14 (16, 18, 20). **2nd row:** p 14 (16, 18, 20), work 2nd row of panel, p to end. **3rd to 14th rows:** rep 1st and 2nd rows 6 times but working 3rd to 14th rows of panel and inc 1 st at each end of 9th row. Cont in patt, shaping sleeve by inc 1 st at each end of next row, then on every following 6th row until there are 62 (66, 70, 74) sts, then on every following 4th row until there are 84 (88, 92, 96) sts.
Work straight until sleeve measures 42cm (16½in), ending after a wrong-side row.
Shape top by binding off 6 (7, 8, 9) sts at beg of next 2 rows. Dec 1 st at each end of every right-side row until 44 sts remain, then on every row until 34 sts remain. Bind off.

Left Border and Collar Section
With No 4 (3¾mm) needles, cast on 11

sts. Work in rib until strip, when slightly stretched, fits up front edge to start of front slope. Change to g st, shaping inner edge of border by inc 1 st at inner edge on next row, then on 3 following alt rows, then on every following 4th row until there are 20 sts, finally on every following 6th row until there are 26 sts. Work 40 rows straight, thus ending at outer edge. Shape thus: **Next row:** k to last 3 sts, turn. **Next row:** slip 1, k to end. K 4 rows on all sts. Rep the last 6 rows 6 times more. Cont without further shaping until shaped edge of collar section (ie g st portion) fits up front slope and round to center back of neck. Bind off.

Right Border and Collar Section
First mark position on left border for 5 buttons, first to be in 5th/6th rows, fifth to be in 3rd/4th rows below top of rib portion of border and remainder spaced evenly between. Work as left section but working shaping at opposite edge and working 41 rows in place of 40, and working buttonholes to match markers thus: **1st row:** rib 4, bind off 3 sts neatly in rib, rib 4 (including st on needle after binding off). **2nd row:** in rib, binding on 3 sts over those bound off.

Pocket Tops
With right side facing, slip a group of pocket sts onto a No 4 (3¾mm) needle. Knit 1 row. Beg 2nd row for wrong side of work, work 6 rows in rib as on welt. Bind off loosely in rib.

To Finish
Omitting ribbing, press following pressing instructions. Sew down pocket linings on wrong side and tops on right side. Join shoulder, side and sleeve seams. Sew in sleeves. Sew on border and collar sections, joining bound-off edges at back of neck. Sew on buttons. Press seams.

Primrose *Crochet Shawl*

Measurements

One size

Materials

7 balls of 3 ply yarn
Nos 4 and 4E steel crochet hooks

Gauge

Worked on No 4 steel hook and 2nd border
10 pattern rows to 7.5cm (3in)

Abbreviations

ch – chain; **alt** – alternate, alternately; **cont** – continue; **dc** – double crochet; **hdc**, – half double crochet; **lp** – loop; **pct(s)** – picot(s); (**Note:** to make picot work 3 ch, 1 dc into 1st of 3 ch); **patt** – pattern; **prev** – previous; **r** – ring; **rep** – repeat; **sk** – skip; **ss** – slip stitch; **sp(s)** – space(s); **st(s)** – stitch(es); **sc** – single crochet.

To Make

Main Part
With No 4 hook make 359 ch. **1st row:** into 2nd ch work 1 sc, *7 ch, sk 6 ch, into next ch work 1 sc/2ch/1 sc, rep from * to within last 7 ch, 7 ch, sk 6 ch, 1 sc into last ch, 51 ch sps made, turn. **2nd row:** 1 ch, ss up 1st 4ch of 7 ch sp, *7 ch, into center ch of next 7 ch sp work 1 sc/2 ch/1 sc, rep from * to within last 7 ch sp, 7 ch, into center ch of last 7 ch sp work 1 dc, turn. Rep prev row until two 7 ch sps remain. Fasten off.

1st Border
With No 4 hook make 19 ch. **1st row:** into 4th ch from hook work 1 dc, 5 ch, sk 6 ch, into next ch work 1 sc/3ch/1 sc, 5 ch, sk 6 ch, 1 dc into each of next 2 ch, turn. **2nd row:** 3 ch, sk 1st dc, 1 dc into next dc, 3 ch, *into center ch of 5 ch sp work 1 sc/3 ch/1 sc,* 5 ch, rep from * to * once, 3 ch, 1 dc into each of next 2 dc, working last dc into top of 3 ch, turn. **3rd row:** 3 ch, sk 1st dc, 1 dc into next dc, 5 ch, rep from * to * of prev row once, 5 ch, 1 dc into each of next 2 dc, turn. Work 178 more rows, rep the prev 2 rows alt. Do not fasten off but continue with pcts along side edge thus: *3 sh, 1 dc into 1st of 3 ch (1 pct made), 1 sc under the bar of the dc on side edge,* rep from * to * all along side edge, working 1 pct to each row. Fasten off. Stitch border to upper edge of main part, fitting into place. Rejoin yarn in 1st pct of upper edge with 3 ch, 1 dc into next dc of 1st border edge, 6 dc into 5 ch sp, 1 dc into 3 ch sp, 6 dc into next 5 ch sp, 1 dc into each of next 2 dc of 1st border, into each of next row work 7 dc all along rounded shawl edge, completing sts along 1st border to match those worked at the beginning.
Fasten off.

2nd Border
With No 4 hook work 1st 5 rows as for 1st border, last row ending with 6 ch, turn. **6th row:** cont with 1st border patt, working 1 dc instead of 3 ch (for 1st dc), turn. **7th row:** cont with 1st border patt ending with 13 dc into 6 ch lp, ss through each of 3 beginning ch of prev row (ie 4th patt row), turn and cont working along 13 dc row. **8th row:** *3 ch, 1 sc into 1st of 3 ch (1 pct made), sk 1 dc, 1 dc into next dc, rep from * 5 times, 1 pct, sk 1 dc, cont in 1st border patt to end of row, turn. **9th row:** cont in 1st border patt to within 1st pct, *3 ch, sk 1st pct, 1 dc into next dc, rep from * 5 times, 3 ch, ss through each of 3 beginning ch of prev row (ie 2nd patt row), turn and cont working along row. **10th row:** *1 pct, 1 dc into 3 ch sp, 1 pct, 1 dc into next dc, rep from * 6 times, last dc to form 1st dc of 1st border patt row, cont in patt to end, turn. **Work 5 1st border patt rows, ending with 6 ch. Rep 6th to 10th row.** Rep from ** to ** 24 times. Fasten off. Attach border to main part, allowing 1 full semi-circle each to 1st border edge, 2 semi-circles to apex, fitting the remaining border evenly on edge of main part.
To make a complete pct edge round shawl, work 6 pcts, evenly spaced, from last pct of upper edge to 1st pct of semi-circle, at each end. Fasten off.

Flower Motifs *(make 14)*
With No 4 hook make 6 ch; ss into 1st ch to form a r. **1st round:** 5 ch, 1 sc into r; *3 ch, 1 sc into r, rep from *3 times; 3 ch, ss through 2nd of 5 ch. **2nd round:** into each of next 3 ch sps work 1 sc/1 hdc/3 dc/1 hdc/1 sc, ss into 1st sc. Fasten off. Attach 1 flower to each of the 2 apex semi-circles; then 1 on every alt semi-circle.

Willow Catkins *Crochet Shawl*

Measurements

One size
Length (excluding fringe) approximately 74cm (29in)

Materials

Pingouin Mohair 70	
Main Shade (M)	5 x 50g balls
1st Contrast (C1)	2 x 50g balls
2nd Contrast (C2)	3 x 50g balls
5/F crochet hook	

Gauge

6 clusters and 6½ rows to 10cm (4in)

Abbreviations

alt – alternately; **beg** – beginning; **C1(2)** – contrast shades; **ch** – chain; **cont** – continue; **dc** – double crochet; **lp(s)** – loop(s); **M** – main shade; **patt** – pattern; **rep** – repeat; **sc** – single crochet; **sk** – skip; **sp** – space; **yo** – yarn over.

To Make

Back

With 5/F hook and C1, make 14 ch loosely. **1st row:** 1 dc in 5th ch from hook, 1 ch, * (yo, insert hook around stem of last dc, yo and pull up yarn to 1cm (⅜in) 4 times, yo and draw through all lps on hook – cluster worked, 1 ch, sk 3 ch, 1 dc in next ch, 1 ch; rep from * once, 1 cluster around stem of last dc, 1 ch, 1 dc in last ch, turn. **2nd row:** 3 ch, *1 dc in the 1 ch sp inside cluster, 1 ch, 1 cluster around stem of last dc, 1 ch; rep from * to end, 1 dc in top of turning ch, turn. **3rd row:** 3 ch, 1 dc in 1st 1 ch sp, 1 ch, *1 cluster around stem of last dc, 1 ch, 1 dc in 1 ch sp inside cluster, 1 ch; rep from * to end, 1 cluster around stem of last dc, 1 ch, 1 dc in sp before turning ch, 1 ch, 1 cluster around stem of last dc, 1 ch, 1 dc in top of turning ch, turn.
The 2nd and 3rd rows form patt for back. Beg with 4th row, cont from chart reading rows alt from left to right and right to left, shaping sides and changing color as shown, until all 48 rows have been completed. Fasten off.

Right Front

With 5/F hook and C1, make 6 ch loosely. **1st row:** 1 dc in 5th ch from hook, 1 ch, 1 cluster around stem of dc, 1 ch, 1 dc in last ch, turn. **2nd row:** 3 ch, 1 dc in the 1 ch sp inside cluster, 1 ch, 1 cluster around stem of dc, 1 ch, 1 dc in top of turning ch, turn. Beg with 3rd row, cont from chart, shaping side and changing color as shown, until all 48 rows have been completed. Fasten off.

Left Front

Work as for right front. Join fronts to back.

Fringe

Work approximately 60 tassels in each of the 3 colors. With 5/F hook make 30 ch very loosely. Working firmly work 1 sc in 3rd ch from hook, 1 sc in each ch to end. Fasten off leaving sufficient yarn to attach tassel to shawl. Attach approximately 15 tassels of each color to each of the 4 shaped edges of shawl arranging colors as desired.

Willow Catkins
Crochet Shawl

Key	
□ Main shade X Contrast 1 • Contrast 2	Each square represents 1 dc, 1 ch, 1 cluster and 1 ch worked in color as indicated by symbol

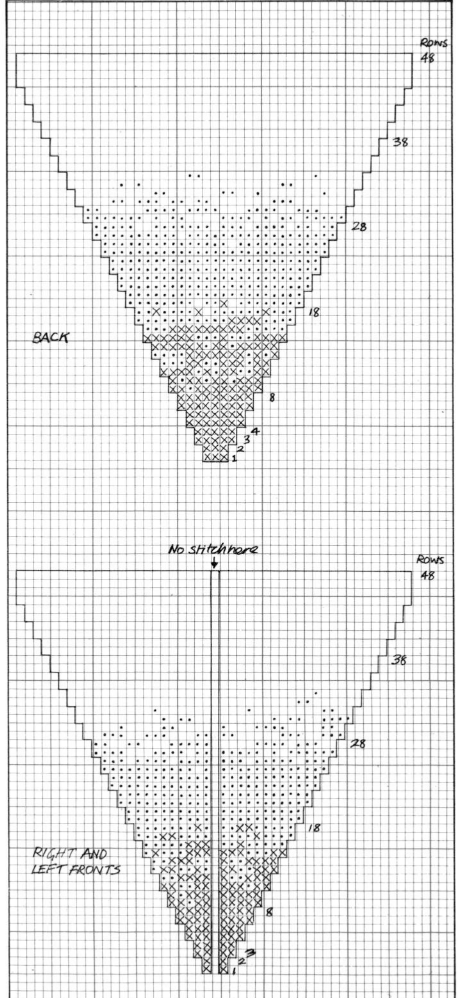

BIRDS

MARCH

"And the Spring arose on the garden fair."

TWO THRUSH'S NESTS

VIOLET WOODS AND DAFFODIL FIELDS

Two Thrush's Nests *Knitted Textured Sweaters*

Measurements

To fit bust/chest					
86	91	97	102	107	112cm
34	36	38	40	42	44in
Length from shoulder					
61	62	65	66	67	69cm
24	24½	25½	26	26½	27in
Sleeve length					
47	48	48	49	49	51cm
18½	19	19	19½	19½	20in

Materials

Mohair yarn, Lady's Sweater,

Dark (D)	12	12	13	13	14	14	50g balls
Light (L)	6	6	7	7	7	7	50g balls
Man's Sweater							
	17	17	18	18	19	20	50g balls

Pair of needles each Nos 8 (5½mm), 6 (4½mm) and 5 (4mm)

Set of four No 7 (4½mm) needles

Gauge

15 sts and 26 rows to 10cm (4in) over ribbed pattern on No 8 (5½mm) needles

Abbreviations

k – knit; **kb** – knit next stitch one row below; **p** – purl; **st(s)** – stitch(es); **patt** – pattern; **inc** – increase, increasing; **dec** – decrease, decreasing; **beg** – beginning; **alt** – alternate; **rep** – repeat; **D** – dark shade; **cont** – continue; **L** – light shade

To Make

LADY'S SWEATER

Front

With No 5 (4mm) needles and D, cast on 77 (81, 85, 89, 93, 97) sts. **1st row:** k 2, (p 1, k 1) to last st, k 1. **2nd row:** k 1, (p 1, k 1) to end. Rep these 2 rows for 10cm (4in), ending after a 2nd row.

Change to No 8 (5½mm) needles and ribbed patt thus: **1st row** (right side): in D, k 1, (kb, p 1) to last 2 sts, kb, k 1. **2nd row:** in D, k 1, (p 1, k 1) to end.** **3rd to 7th rows:** rep 1st and 2nd rows twice, then 1st row again. Using a separate ball of L for each color area, and twisting yarns on wrong side when changing colors, cont in patt thus: **8th row:** (k 1, p 1) 2 (3, 4, 5, 6, 7) times in D, *p 13L, then in D (p 1, k 1) 7 times, p 1; rep from * once, p 13L, rib to end in D. **9th row:** k 1, (kb, p 1) 1 (2, 3, 4, 5, 6) times, kb in D, *p 13L, then in D, (kb, p 1) 7 times, kb; rep from * once, p 13L, rib to end in D. **10th row:** (k 1, p 1) 2 (3, 4, 5, 6, 7) times in D, *k 13L, then in D (p 1, k 1) 7 times p 1; rep from * once, k 13L, rib to end in D. **11th row:** all in D, k 1, (kb, p 1) 1 (2, 3, 4, 5, 6) times , kb, *k 13, (kb, p 1) 7 times, kb; rep from * once, k 13, rib to end. **12th row:** as 2nd row. **13th to 19th rows:** rep 1st and 2nd rows 3 times, then 1st row again. **20th row:** p 3 (5, 7, 9, 11, 13) L, *in D, (p 1, k 1) 7 times, p 1, p 13L; rep from * once, in D (p 1, k 1) 7 times, p 1, p to end in L. **21st row:** p 3 (5, 7, 9, 11, 13)L, *in D (kb, p 1) 7 times, kb, p 13L; rep from * once, in D (kb, p 1) 7 times, kb, p to end in L. **22nd row:** k 3 (5, 7, 9, 11, 13) L, *in D (p 1, k 1) 7 times, p 1, k 13L; rep from * once, in D (p 1, k 1) 7 times, p 1, p to end in L. **23rd row:** all in D, k 3 (5, 7, 9, 11, 13), *(kb, p 1) 7 times, kb, k 13; rep from * once, (kb, p 1) 7 times, kb, k to end in D. **24th row:** as 2nd. These 24 rows form patt.

Cont in patt until work measures 53 (53, 54, 54, 56, 57) cm, 21 (21, 21½, 21½, 22, 22½) in from beg, ending after a wrong-side row (but avoid ending after an 8th or 20th row).

Keeping patt correct, shape neck thus: **NB:** do not work kb on edge sts but work a k 1 in the usual way. **Next row:** patt 33 (34, 36, 37, 38, 40), turn. Cont on this group. Dec 1 st at neck edge on next 5 rows. 28 (29, 31, 32, 33, 35) sts. Work straight until front measures 61 (62, 65, 66, 67, 69) cm, 24 (24½, 25½, 26, 26½, 27) in from beg, ending at side edge.

Shape shoulder by binding off 9 (10, 10, 11, 11, 12) sts at beg of next and following alt row. Work 1 row. Bind off.

With right side facing, slip center 11 (13, 13, 15, 17, 17) sts on a spare needle. Rejoin yarn to remaining sts and work 1 row. Complete as first half.

Back

Omitting neck shaping, work as given for front up to shoulder shaping, ending after a wrong-side row.

Shape shoulders by binding off 9 (10, 10, 11, 11, 12) sts at beg of next 4 rows, then 10 (9, 11, 10, 11, 11) sts at beg of next 2 rows. Slip final 21 (23, 23, 25, 27, 27) sts on a spare needle.

Sleeves

With No 6 (4½mm) needles and L, cast on 31 (31, 33, 35, 35, 37) sts. Work in rib as on welt for 10cm (4in), ending after a 2nd row. **Next row:** rib 3 (3, 4, 1, 2, 3), *inc in next st, rib 3 (2, 2, 3, 2, 2); rep from * to last 4 (4, 5, 2, 3, 4) sts, inc in next st, rib to end. 38 (40, 42, 44, 46, 48) sts. Knit 1 row.

Change to No 8 (5½mm) needles and patt thus: **1st row:** in D, p. **2nd row:** in D, k.** **3rd to 18th rows:** using L, rep 1st and 2nd rows 8 times but inc 1 st at each end of 3rd row following, then on every following 4th row. 46 (48, 50, 52, 54, 56) sts.

Cont in patt as on these 18 rows, shaping sleeve by inc 1 st at each end of 3rd row following, then on every following 4th row until there are 58 (64, 70, 72, 74, 76) sts, then on every following 6th (6th, 6th, 6th, 4th, 4th) row until there are 66 (70, 74, 78, 82, 86) sts. *** Work straight until sleeve measures 47 (48, 48, 49, 49, 51) cm, 18½ (19, 19, 19½, 19½, 20) in at center. Bind off loosely.

Neckband

First join shoulders. With set of No 6 (4½mm) needles and D, right side facing, k across sts of back, k up 14 (16, 18, 20, 20, 20) sts down left front neck, k across center sts, finally k up 14 (16, 18, 20, 20, 20) sts up right front neck. 60 (68, 72, 80, 84, 84) sts. On 1st and 4th sizes only slip first st on 1st needle on to end of 3rd needle. Work 6 rounds in k 1, p 1 rib. Bind off in rib.

Armhole Trimmings

Place a marker approximately 24 (25, 27, 28, 29, 30) cm, 9½ (10, 10½, 11, 11½, 12) in down from each shoulder seam on side edges of back and front. With No 6 (4½mm) needles and D, right side facing, k up 91 (95, 99, 103, 107, 111) sts evenly between 1 set of markers. Beg 2nd row, work 6 rows in rib as on front welt. Bind off evenly in rib.

Finishing

Press patt portions of sleeves only following instructions on the yarn band. Stitch bound-off edges of sleeves to wrong side of base of armhole trimmings. Join side and sleeve seams. Join ends of armhole trimmings. Press seams.

MAN'S SWEATER

Front

Work as for lady's sweater to ** ignoring reference to 'D'. These 2 rows form patt. Cont in patt until work measures 53 (53, 54, 54, 56, 57) cm, 21 (21, 21½, 21½, 22, 22½) in from beg, ending after a 2nd row. Shape neck and complete as for lady's sweater.

Back

Work as for lady's sweater but working patt as on front of man's sweater.

Sleeves

Work as for lady's sweater to ** ignoring reference to 'L' and 'D'. Continue as on these 2 rows, shaping sleeve by inc 1st at each end of 3rd row following, then on every following 4th row until there are 58 (64, 70, 72, 74, 76) sts, then on every following 6th (6th, 6th, 6th, 4th, 4th) row until there are 66 (70, 74, 78, 82, 86) sts. Complete as for lady's sweater working from *** to end.

Neckband, Armhole Trimmings and Finishing

Work as for lady's sweater ignoring reference to 'D'.

Rag Rugs

Rag rugs are fun and easy to do. They are cheap to produce, making good use of old clothes and furnishings. A trip to a local rummage sale will always help to provide extra fabrics if needed.

Rag rugs have a long tradition in England. At the beginning of the century they were mainly worked by country folk who used them to cover the cold floors of their cottages. In town houses rag rugs were only found in servants' rooms or in play rooms, where better quality carpets may have got damaged. Traditionally, rag rugs were made on a backing of sack cloth or hessian. The rag was prodded through the loose weave and usually left without forming a knot. This method was fairly heavy work and was carried out by both men and women in the evenings. The introduction of a latchet hook made the work easier and so knotting became more commonplace. Sewing machines made rag rugs even easier to make. The rags were machined onto a backing and then clipped with scissors to form an even pile.

'The Garden Fair' rag rug has been made in a traditional way but with the help of modern materials and techniques. It serves to immortalize favourite but often threadbare clothes! It is a pleasure to make and will co-ordinate with almost any color scheme in the home. The colors chosen represent spring flowers such as daffodils, primroses and violets.

The abstract design of the rug is simple to create. Colors can be grouped or scattered to represent flowers growing among grass. Autumn, winter and summer designs can be worked in exactly the same way, using colors which represent the season chosen, eg berry and leaf shades for autumn; frost, ice and holly shades for winter, and wild rose and honeysuckle pastels for summer.

The Garden Fair

Rag Rug

Measurements

Approximately 97cm x 130cm (38in x 51in)

Materials

Approximately 138cm (54in) of 102cm (40in) width rug-making canvas
Scraps of fabric (closely woven or knitted natural fibers minimize fraying)
Sharp scissors
Rug-making latchet hook
Bodkin needle

To Make

(**Note:** Rag-rug making is worked on much the same principle as August's 'Poppy' Tufted Hearth Rug on page 104.) With wrong side of canvas facing, following diagrams A, B, C and D, work as follows: begin at top left hand side, completing one row at a time.

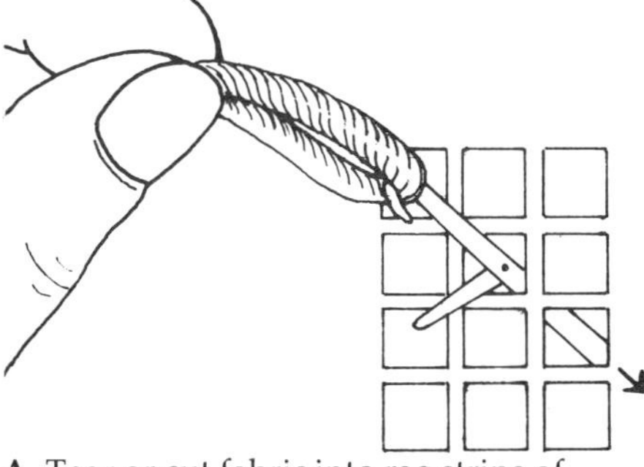

A Tear or cut fabric into rag strips of required length and width. Fold rag in half to form loop. Holding the 2 ends together in left hand, push hook through hole in canvas from right side to underside and pick up loop of rag with hook. Pull back tool through the same hole in the canvas bringing loop to surface of right side (This action will result in the latch on the hook closing and securing loop within hook.)

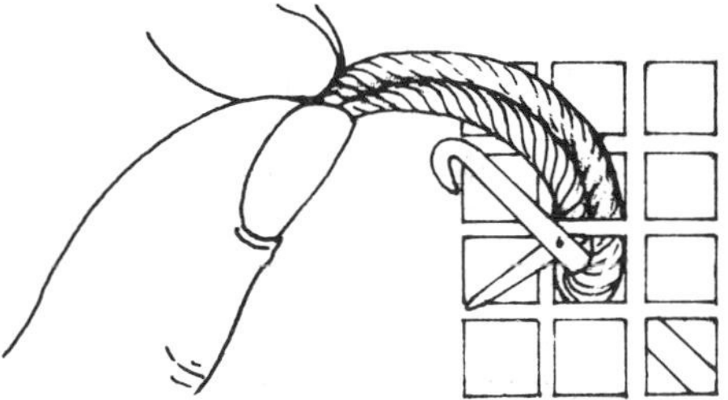

B Holding ends of loop firmly in left hand, to prevent them from coming through onto the wrong side, push hook through hole directly below. This action will release the latch, leaving the loop of the rag lying around the tool on the right side of the canvas above the hole.

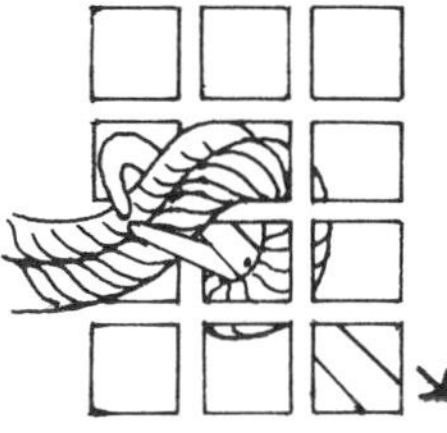

C Place both ends of rag around hook while still holding ends firmly. Push hook forward to enable latch to close around ends. Pull tool back through hole, making sure both ends of rag are pulled up through the rag loop to form knot.

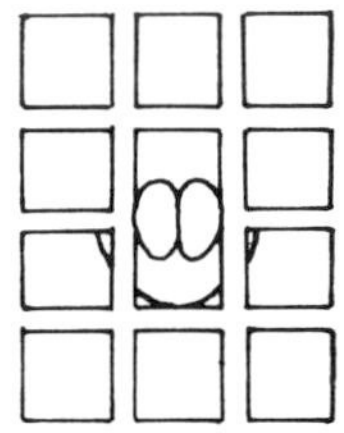

D This action will result in forming a knot which secures the rag firmly around the horizontal line of the canvas. The underside of the knot forms the back of the rug, while the top of the knot and the 2 ends form the surface and the pile. Secure knot by pulling ends of rag gently into place with fingers.

Daffodils and Violets

Crochet Cushion Cover

Measurements

To fit a 41cm (16in) square pillow form.

Measurements

To fit a 41cm (16in) square cushion pad.

Materials

4 balls of 4 ply yarn (M)
1 ball of 4 ply yarn (C1)
1 ball of 4 ply yarn (C2)
1 ball of 4 ply yarn (C3)
pillow form 41cm (16in) square.
4/E and No 1 steel crochet hooks

Key
o chain
I treble
x p'corn stitch

Gauge

Worked on 4/E hook 12 dc and 6 rows of dc to 5cm (2in)

Abbreviations

C(1,2,3) – contrast shade; **ch** – chain; **cont** – continue; **dc** – double crochet; **hdc** – half double crochet; **lp** – loop; **M** – main shade; **pc st** – popcorn stitch; **prev** – previous; **rep** – repeat; **sc** – single crochet; **sk**– skip; **sp(s)** – space(s); **ss** – slip stitch; **st(s)** – stitch(es); **tc** – treble crochet.

Cover
With 4/E hook and M make 98 ch. **1st row:** 1 dc into 6th ch from hook, *1 ch, sk 1 ch, 1 dc into next ch, rep from * to end, turn. 47 ch sps made. **2nd row:** 4 ch, sk 1st dc and ch, 1 dc into next dc, *1 ch, sk 1 ch, 1 dc into next dc*, rep from * to * to end, working last dc into 5th of 6 ch, turn. **3rd row:** 4 ch, sk 1st dc and ch, 1 dc into next dc, rep from * to * to end, working last dc into 3rd of 4ch, turn. Rep prev row 40 times more.
Now cont from chart for front. 1st row of chart is a right-side row. To work a pc st work 5 dc into st, remove lp from hook, insert hook into top of 1st dc from front to back, replace lp on hook and pull through dc. (On wrong-side rows insert hook from back to front so that the pc st is on right side of work.) When chart has been completed fasten off.

Violet (make 7)
With C1 and No 1 hook make 5 ch. **1st round:** 5 tc into 5th ch from hook, ss into top of 4 ch to form a funnel, do not turn. **2nd row:** *into next tc work 1 sc/1 dc/1 tc/1 dc/1 sc*, 1 sc into next tc, rep from * to * once, ss through next tc. Fasten off.

Daffodil (make 4)
With C2 and No 1 hook make 4 ch. **1st round:** 9 dc into 4th ch from hook, ss into top of 3ch to form a funnel, do not turn. **2nd round:** 3 ch, 1 dc into each of next 9 dc, ss into top of 3 ch, do not turn. **3rd round:** *into next dc work 1 sc/2 dc, 1 hdc into next dc, 2 dc/1 sc into next dc, rep from * twice, ss into 1st sc. Fasten off. **4th round:** rejoin yarn in top of 3 ch of 1st round, 5 ch, sk next 3 dc of 1st round, ss through next dc, 5 ch sk 2 dc, ss through next dc, 5 ch, sk 2 dc, ss through top of 3 ch of 1st round, do not turn. **5th round:** *into 5 ch sp work 1 sc/4 dc/1 hdc/4 dc/1 sc, rep from * twice, ss through 1st sc. Fasten off.

Large Leaf (make 4)
With C3 and No 1 hook make 10 ch. **1st round:** 1 tc into 5th ch from hook, 1 dc into each of next 2 ch, 1 hdc into next ch, 1 sc into next ch, 3 sc into next ch, do not turn but cont working along other side of foundation ch, 1 sc into next ch, 1 dc into next ch, 1 tc into each of next 3 ch, 9 tc into last ch, ss through top of 4 ch. Fasten off.

Small Leaf (make 4)
With C3 and No 1 hook make 11 ch. **1st row:** 2 dc into 4th ch from hook, 1 dc into each of next 3 ch, 1 hdc into each of next 2 ch, 1 sc into each of next 2 ch. Fasten off.
Stitch violets, daffodils, large and small leaves into 'window' of cushion cover.

Finishing
Fold work in half and join seams by working through both layers and work

Daffodils and Violets
Crochet Cushion Cover (front)

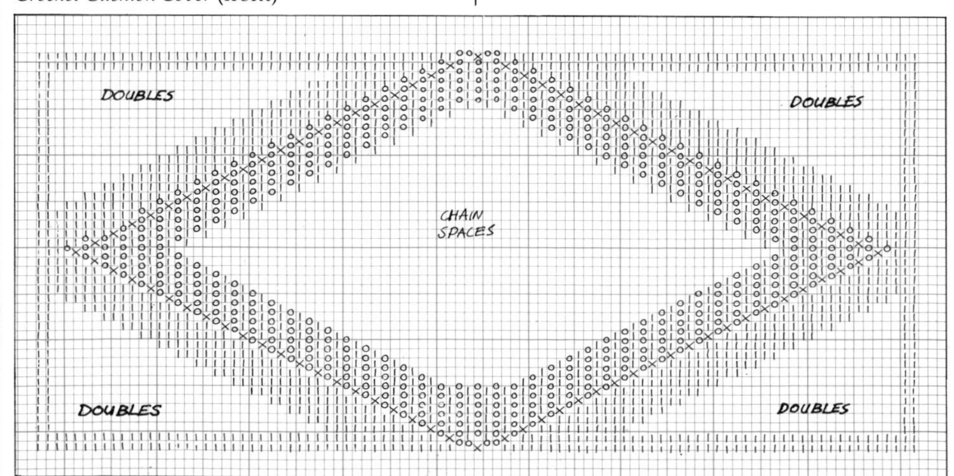

thus: with front of work facing make 1 ss through 1st dc of right hand lower corner; 4 ch, 1 pc st under the bar of dc of 1st row (edge). *1 ch, 1 dc under the bar of dc of next row, 1 ch, 1 pc st under the bar of dc of next row; rep from * to end, working 1 pc st/1 ch/1 dc/1 ch/1 pc st into each of next 3 corners and ending with 1 pc st/1 ch, ss through 3rd of 4 ch and *having inserted pillow form after having joined three sides.*

Daffy-down-dilly

Needlepoint Cushion Cover

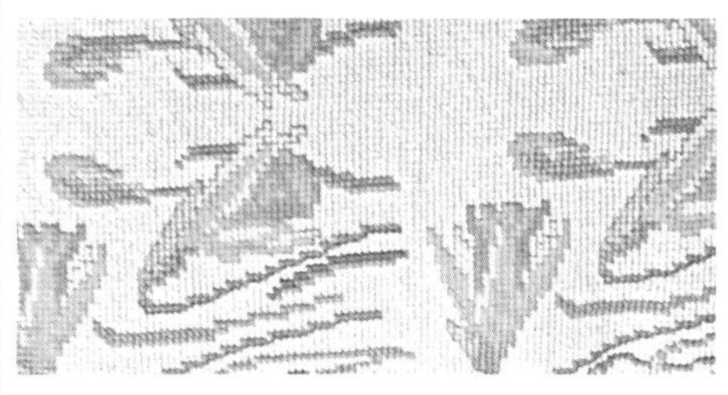

Measurements

38cm (15in) square

Materials

50cm (19½in) of 58cm (23in) wide number 10 Penelope (double-threaded) canvas
Anchor Tapestry Wool in 10m (11yd) skeins: 17 skeins 0386; 2 skeins each of 0717; 0297; 0295; 0305; 3149; 0242; 1 skein each of 3150; 0240
Tapestry needle
45cm (17¾in) square backing fabric
38cm (15in) square pillow form

To Make

Important Note: Read 'General Working Instructions for all Needlepoint,' on page 15.

1 Lightly fold canvas in both directions (widthwise and lengthwise) to form **main** center lines. Mark center lines with running stitches.

2 Cushion cover front is now divided into 4 equal sections.

3 Lightly fold canvas to form crease lines to act as **secondary** center lines in each of 4 sections. Mark these 4 sets of center lines with running stitches using different colored thread.

4 Work design in top right section of canvas matching large solid arrows on chart to **main** center lines, and small solid arrows to **secondary** center lines.

5 Chart and key for 'Daffy-down-dilly' design is below.

Daffy-down-dilly
Needlepoint Cushion Cover

Key	
+	0717
\	0297
I	0295
•	0305
Λ	3150
/	3149
X	0242
–	0240

Shade numbers refer to Anchor Tapestry wool.

Design 61 x 67 stitches

Design size (approx.)
10 stitches to 2.5cm (1in):
15cm (6in) x 17.5cm (7in)

Special instructions
Outline: flower centers with *0717*; light yellow petals and buds *0297*; dark yellow petals *0717*; stems *3150*; bud leaves *0242*

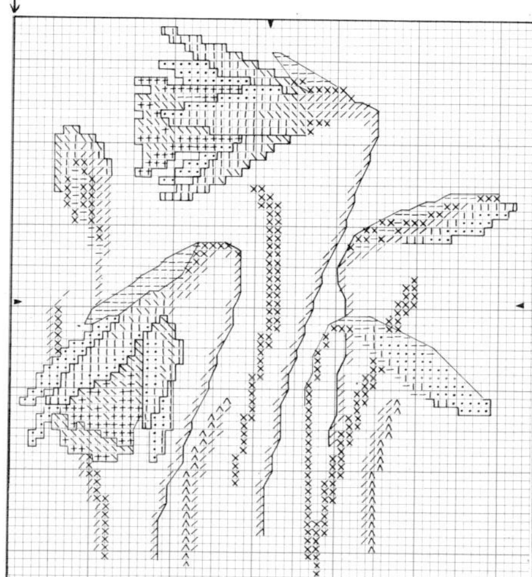

6 Repeat point 5, using same design, in lower right section.

7 Work design in reverse in top and lower left sections, making sure to center design within each section before beginning to work embroidery.

8 Complete background in 0386.

9 Work backstitch details in colors as shown in key to chart.

10 Remove running stitches.

11 Trim away surplus canvas to within 2cm (¾in) of needlepoint and cut backing fabric to match. Stitch pieces together along 3 edges, as close as possible to edge of needlepoint. Turn right side out. Insert pillow form. Stitch remaining side.

12 Model worked in traméed half cross stitch.

Sweet Violets

Crochet Coat-hanger Cover

Materials

1 padded coat hanger
75cm (30in) x No 1 (⅛in) wide ribbon to match C
1 ball of 4 ply yarn (M)
1 ball of 4 ply yarn (C)
4/E crochet hook

Gauge

12 dc and 6 rows of dc to 5cm (2in)

Abbreviations

C – contrast shade; **ch** – chain; **cont** – continue; **dc** – double crochet; **hdc** – half double crochet; **lp** – loop; **M** – main shade; **pc st** – popcorn stitch **Note:** to make pc st work 4 dc into ch sp, remove lp from hook, insert hook from back to front of work through 1st of 4 dc and pull lp from 4th dc through tightly, the pc st being at the back of the work; **prev** – previous; **rep** – repeat; **sc** – single crochet; **sk** – skip; **sp(s)** – space(s); **ss** – slip stitch; **st(s)** – stitch(es); **tc** – treble crochet.

Cover
With M make 32 ch. **Foundation row:** 1 dc into 6th ch from hook, *1 ch, sk 1 ch, 1 dc into next ch, rep from * to end, turn. 14 ch sps made. **2nd row:** *4 ch, sk 1st dc and ch, 1 dc into next dc, *1 ch/1 dc into each of next 2 dc (sk sp in between), **1 pc st into next sp, 1 dc into next dc, 1 ch/1 dc into each of next 2 dc (sk sp in between)**, 1 ch; sk next ch sp, 1 pc st into next dc, 1 ch/1 dc into each of next 3 dc (sk ch sp in between), rep from ** to **, 1 ch, 1 dc into 4th of 5 ch (in all following rows into 3rd of 4 ch), turn. **3rd row:** rep from * to * of 2nd row, 1 ch/1 dc into next dc, *1 pc st into next sp (work pc st as on prev row, but insert hook from front to back of work, the pc st being at the front of the work), 1 dc into next dc*, **sk pc st, 1 ch, 1 dc into next dc, rep from * to * once**, 1 ch/1 dc into next dc, 1 ch/1 dc into pc st, 1 ch/1 dc into each of next 2 dc, rep from * to * and ** to **, 1 ch/1 dc into each of next 2 dc (working last dc into 3rd of 4 ch), turn.
4th row: rep from * to * of 2nd row, 1 ch/1 dc into each of next 2 dc (sk pc st in between), 1 pc st into next sp (as in 2nd row), 1 dc into next dc, sk next pc st, 1 ch/1 dc into each of next 2 dc, 1 ch, 1 pc st into next dc, 1 ch/1 dc into each of next 3 dc, 1 pc st into next sp, 1 dc into next dc, sk pc st, 1 ch/1 dc into each of next dc to end (ie 3 ch sps, turn. **5th row:** rep from * to * of 2nd row, 1 ch/1 dc into each of next dc to within center pc st, 1 ch/1 dc into pc st, 1 ch/1 dc into each of next dc to end, turn. 14 sps made. Rep 2nd to 5th row 9 times more. Fasten off.

Violets (make 7)
With C make 5 ch. **1st round:** 5 tc into 5th ch from hook, ss into top of 4 ch to form a funnel, do not turn. **2nd row:** *into next tc work 1 sc/1 dc/1 tc/1 dc/1 dc*, 1 sc into next tc, rep from * to * once, ss through next tc. Fasten off.

Large Leaf (make 3)
With M make 10 ch. **1st round:** 1 tc into 5th ch from hook, 1 dc into each of next 2 ch, 1 hdc into next ch, 1 sc into next ch, 3 sc into next ch, do not turn but cont working along other side of foundation ch, 1 sc into next ch, 1 dc into next ch, 1 tc into each of next 3 ch, 9 tc into last ch, ss through top of 4 ch. Fasten off.

Small Leaf (make 2)
With M make 11 ch. **1st round:** 2 dc into 4th ch from hook, 1 dc into each of next 3 ch, 1 hdc into each of next 2 ch, 1 sc into next ch, 3 sc into last ch, do not turn but cont with work along other side of foundation ch, 1 sc into next ch, 1 hdc into each of next 2 ch, 1 dc into each of next 3 ch, 4 dc into last ch, ss through top of 3 ch. Fasten off.

To Finish
Place work over hanger, inserting hook through center ch sp and stitch up open seams to form closed sleeve. Sew leaves and violets into place to form a posy. Tie ribbon round posy.

Celandine

Crochet Coat-hanger Cover

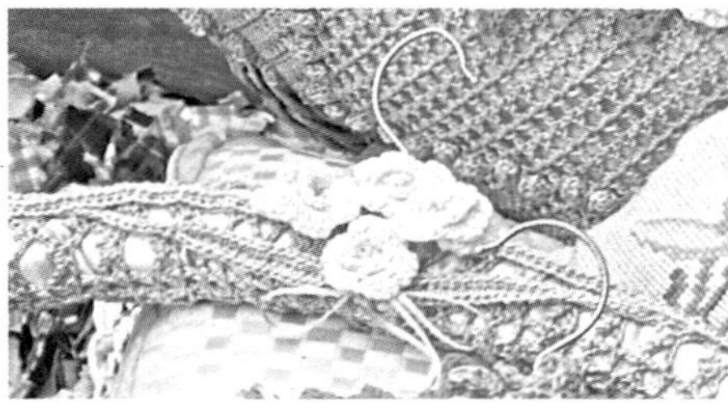

Materials

1 padded coat hanger
75cm (30in) x No 1 (⅛in) wide ribbon to match C
1 ball of 4 ply yarn (M)
1 ball of 4 ply yarn (C)
4/E and No 1 steel crochet hooks

Gauge

Worked with 4/E hook 12 sc and 6 rows of dc to 5cm (2in)

Abbreviations

alt – alternately; **C** – contrast shade; **ch** – chain; **cont** – continue; **dc** – double crochet; **M** – main shade; **prev** – previous; **rep** – repeat; **sc** – single crochet; **sk** – skip; **ss** – slip stitch; **st(s)** – stitch(es).

Cover
With M and 4/E hook make 32 ch. **1st row:** 1 dc into 6th ch from hook, *5 ch, sk 5 ch, into next ch work 1 sc/2 ch/1 sc; rep from * twice, 5 ch, sk 5 ch, 1 dc into next ch, 1 ch, sk 1 ch, 1 dc into last ch, turn. **2nd row:** **4 ch, sk 1st dc and ch, 1 dc into next dc**, 3 ch, *into 3rd of next 5 ch work 1 sc/2 ch/1 sc, 5 ch; rep from * 3 times, ending last rep 3 ch not 5 ch, 1 dc into next dc, 1 ch, 1 dc into 5th of 6 ch (3rd of 4 ch in all following rows), turn. **3rd row:** rep from ** to ** of prev row, *5 ch into center ch of next 5 ch work 1 sc/2 ch/1 sc; rep from * twice, 5 ch, 1 dc into next dc, 1 ch; sk 1 ch, 1 dc into 3rd of 4 ch, turn. Work 38 more rows, rep the prev 2 rows alt. Fasten off.

Celandine (make 2)
With C and No 1 hook make 4 ch. **1st round:** into 4th ch from hook work 9 dc, ss through top of 3 ch to form a funnel. Do not turn. **2nd round:** 3 ch (for 1st dc), 1 dc into each of next dc, ss through top of 3 ch. Do not turn. **3rd round:** as 2nd. **Next round:*** into next dc work 1 sc and 2 dc, 1 hdc into next dc, 2 dc and 1 sc into next dc, rep from * twice, ss through 1st sc. Do not turn. **Next round:** *5 ch, sk 2 petals, ss through 1st sc of next petal, the 5 ch sp being in front of the first two petals, rep from * twice, working last ss through last sc of last petal. Do not turn. **Next round:** into each of next three 5 ch sps work 1 sc/4 dc/1 hdc/4 dc/1 sc, ending with a ss through 1st sc. Fasten off. Work two more celandines but omit 2nd and 3rd round, shortening center of celandine by two rounds.

Stem (make 2)
With M and No 1 hook make 30 ch. **1st row:** 1 sc into 2nd ch from hook, 1 sc into each of next ch to end. Fasten off.

Leaf (make 2)
With M and No 1 hook make 30 ch. **1st row:** ss into 2nd ch from hook, ss into each of next 14 ch, 1 sc into each of next 13 ch, 4 sc into last ch, do not turn but cont work along other side of foundation ch, 1 sc into each of next 13 ch, ss in each ch to end. Fasten off.

To Finish
Place work over hanger, insert hook through center and stitch up open ends to form closed sleeve. Sew stems, leaves and celandines into place. Tie ribbon into bow round flowers.

APRIL

"April weather, rain and sunshine both together."

APRIL FOOL

LADY BUTTERFLY

PEACOCK BUTTERFLY

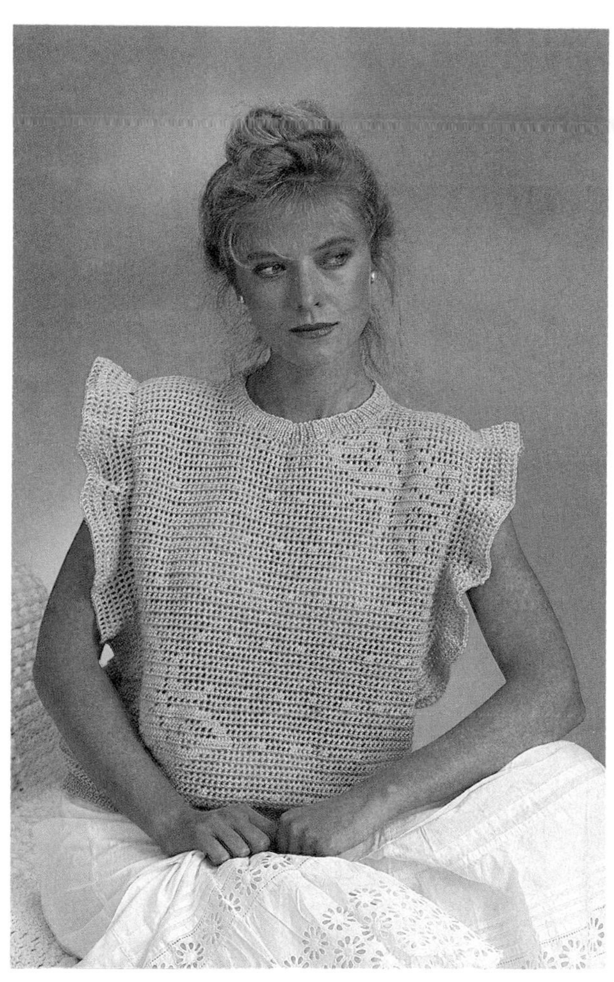

WINGS OF GOLD

Viper *Child's Knitted Sweater and Snake Toy*

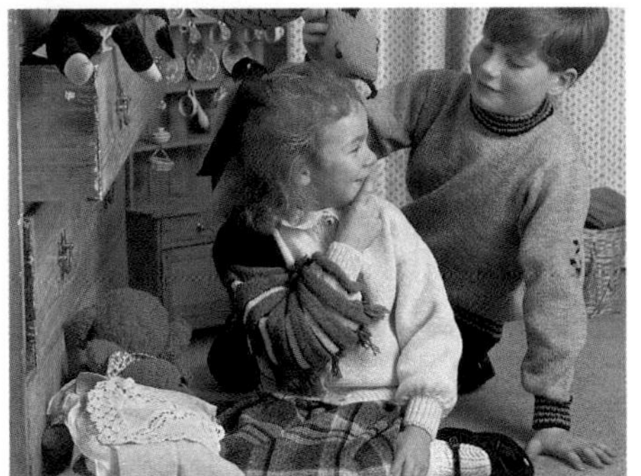

Measurements

To fit chest	61	66	71	76cm
	24	26	28	30in
Length from	42	46	49	53cm
shoulder	16½	18	19½	21in
Sleeve seam	31	34	39	43cm
	12¼	13¾	15½	17in

Materials

Knitting worsted

M (main – grey)	7	7	7	8	50g balls
G (gold)	2	2	2	2	50g balls
B (black)	2	2	2	2	50g balls

Pair of needles each Nos 5 (4mm) and 3 (3¼mm)
Set of four No 3 (3¼mm) needles
Also a pair of needles each Nos 6 (4½mm), 4 (3¾mm) and 2 (3mm) for snake
Polyester fiberfill for stuffing snake

Gauge

22 sts and 30 rows to 10cm (4in) over plain stockinette stitch on No 5 (4mm) needles

Abbreviations

k – knit; **p** – purl; **st(s)** – stitch(es); **patt** – pattern; **sl** – slip; **inc** – increase, increasing; **dec** – decrease, decreasing; **beg** – beginning; **alt** – alternate; **rep** – repeat; **cont** – continue; **B** – black shade; **G** – gold shade; **M** – main shade; **st st** – stockinette stitch; **tog** – together; **cont** – continue; **m1** – make 1

To Make

SWEATER

Front

With No 3 (3¼mm) needles and B, cast on 71 (77, 83, 89) sts. **1st row:** in B, k 2, (p 1, k 1) to last st, k 1. **2nd row:** in B, k 1, (p 1, k 1) to end. **3rd and 4th rows:** in G, as 1st and 2nd. Rep the last 4 rows 3 (4, 4, 5) times more, then 1st and 2nd rows again inc 7 sts evenly on last row. 78 (84, 90, 96) sts. Break B and G.
Change to No 5 (4mm) needles and M and beg k row work in st st until work measures 25 (28, 30, 33) cm, 10 (11, 12, 13) in from beg, ending after a p row.
Shape square armholes by binding off 10 (11, 12, 13) sts at beg of next 2 rows. 58 (62, 66, 70) sts.
Work straight until front measures 38 (41, 44, 47) cm, 15 (16, 17½, 18½) in at center from beg, ending after a p row.
Shape neck thus: **Next row:** k 22 (23, 24, 25), turn. Cont on this group. Dec 1 st at neck edge on next 4 rows. 18 (19, 20, 21) sts. Work straight until front measures 42 (46, 49, 53) cm, 16½ (18, 19½, 21) in from beg, ending at armhole edge.
Shape shoulder by binding off 6 (6, 7, 7) sts at beg of next and following alt row. Work 1 row. Bind off.
With right side facing sl next 14 (16, 18, 20) sts on a spare needle. Rejoin M to remaining sts and k 1 row. Complete as 1st half.

Back

Omitting neck shaping, work as front to shoulder shaping, ending after a p row. Shape shoulders by binding off 6 (6, 7, 7) sts at beg of next 4 rows, then 6 (7, 6, 7) sts at beg of next 2 rows. Slip final 22 (24, 26, 28) sts on a spare needle.

Sleeves

With No 3 (3¼mm) needles and B, cast on 35 (37, 39, 41) sts. Rep 1st to 4th rows of striped rib as on welt 4 (5, 5, 6) times, then 1st row again. **Next row:** in B, rib 1 (3, 1, 6), *inc in next st, rib 3 (2, 2, 1); rep from * to last 2 (4, 2, 7) sts, inc in next st, rib to end. 44 (48, 52, 56) sts. Break B and G.
Change to No 5 (4mm) needles and M, and beg k row work in st st shaping sleeve by inc 1 st at each end of 7th row, then on every following 6th row until there are 54 (62, 76, 82) sts, then on every following 4th row until there are 72 (78, 84, 90) sts.
Work straight until sleeve measures 31 (34, 39, 43) cm, 12¼ (13¾, 15½, 17) in at center. Mark each end of last row. Now work a further 14 (15, 17, 18) rows.
Bind off.

Neckband

First join shoulders. With set of No 3 (3¼mm) needles and B, k across sts of back inc 10 sts evenly, k up 12 (15, 15, 18) sts evenly down left front neck, k across center sts inc 6 sts evenly, finally k up 12 (15, 15, 18) sts evenly up right front neck. 76 (86, 90, 100) sts. Work in rounds of k 1, p 1 rib working 2 rounds B, 2 rounds G repeated throughout for 18 (20, 22, 24) rounds. Bind off *very loosely*.

Emblem

With No 5 (4mm) needles and M, cast on 10 sts. Work in st st thus: **1st row:** p in M. **2nd row:** k, 2 M, 3 B, 5 M. **3rd row:** 4 M, 4 B, 2 M. **4th row:** 1 M, 2 G, 1 M, 3 G, 3 M. **5th row:** 2 M, 3 G, 1 G, 1 M. **6th row:** 2 M, 1 B, 3 M, 3 B, 1 M. **7th row:** 1 M, 2 B, 7 M. **8th row:** 7 M, 2 G, 1 M. **9th row:** 2 M, 2 G, 6 M. **10th row:** 5 M, 2 B, 3 M. **11th row:** 4 M, 2 B, 4 M. **12th row:** 3 M, 2 G, 5 M. **13th row:** 5 M, 2 G, 3 M. **14th row:** 4 M, 3 B, 3 M. **15th row:** 2 M, 3 B, 5 M. **16th row:** in M. Bind off in M.

To Finish

Omitting ribbing, press following pressing instructions. Sew emblem to one sleeve. Join side and sleeve seams as far as markers. Sew in sleeves stitching bind-off sts of armholes to marked rows on sleeves. Fold neckband in half to wrong side and hem in position *loosely* all round. Press seams.

SNAKE TOY

Begin at head. With No 5 (4mm) needles and G, cast on 9 sts. Purl 1 row. Cont in st st, shaping head thus: **1st row:** k 2, m 1 (by picking up and knitting into back of horizontal strand lying before next st), k 1, m 1, k 3, m 1, k 1, m 1, k 2. (13 sts). **2nd and every alt row:** p. **3rd row:** k 3, m 1, k 1, m 1, k 5, m 1, k 1, m 1, k 3. (17 sts). **5th row:** k 4, m 1, k 1, m 1, k 7, m 1, k 1, m 1, k 4. (21 sts). Cont in this way increasing 4 sts on every k row until there are 65 sts. **Next row:** p 5, (p 2 tog, p 4) 10 times. (55 sts). Mark center of last row.
Change to No 6 (4½mm) needles and cont in st st with diamond pattern thus: (**NB:** Carry color not in use loosely over wrong side of work over not more than 5 sts at a time.) **1st row:** (13G, 1B) 3 times, 13G. **2nd row:** 1B, 11G, 1B, 1G, 1B, 11G, 3B, 11G, 1B, 1G, 1B, 11G, 1B. **3rd row:** 1G, 1B, 9G, 1B, 3G, 1B, 9G, 5B, 9G, 1B, 3G, 1B, 9G, 1B, 1G. **4th row:** 2G, 1B, 7G, 1B, 5G, 1B, 7G, 7B, 7G, 1B, 5G, 1B, 7G, 1B, 2G. **5th row:** 3G, 1B, 5G, 1B, 7G, 1B, 5G, 9B, 5G, 1B, 7G, 1B, 5G, 1B, 3G. **6th row:** 4G, 1B, 3G, 1B, 9G, 1B, 3G, 11B, 3G, 1B, 9G, 1B, 3G, 1B, 4G. **7th row:** 5G, 1B, 1G, 1B, 5G, 1B, 5G, 1B, 1G, 13B, 1G, 1B, 5G, 1B, 5G, 1B, 1G, 1B, 5G. **8th row:** 6G,

1B, 5G, 3B, 5G, 15B, 5G, 3B, 5G, 1B, 6G. **9th row:** as 7th. **10th row:** as 6th. **11th row:** as 5th. **12th row:** as 4th. **13th row:** as 3rd. **14th row:** as 2nd. These 14 rows form patt.
Cont in patt until work measures 48cm (19in) from marker. Change to No 5 (4mm) needles and cont until work measures 63cm (25in) from marker. Change to No 4 (3¾mm) needles and cont until work measures 74cm (29in) from marker. Change to No 3 (3¼mm) needles and keeping patt correct dec 1 st at each end of next and every following 4th row until 39 sts remain. Work 3 rows straight. Change to No 2 (3mm) needles and cont dec 1 st at each end of next row, then on every following 4th row until 15 sts remain, then on every k row until 3 sts remain. Work 1 row. Bind off.

To Finish
Press following pressing instructions. Using B embroider eyes on head. Beginning at tail, join seam inserting polyester fiberfill as you go; finally join bound-on edges to form mouth. If desired, a row of stitching in B may be worked to outline mouth. Using 3 lengths of B approximately 15cm (6in) long for each cord, make 2 very tightly twisted cords for tongue. Insert into mouth to length desired, and secure.

April Fool

Child's Knitted Fun Jacket with Caterpillar Sleeve

Measurements

To fit chest

56	61	66	71cm
22	24	26	28in

Length from shoulder

38	42	46	49cm
15	16½	18	19½in

Sleeve length of plain sleeve

28	32	36	39cm
11	12½	14	15½in

Materials

Knitting worsted

Light (L)	6	6	7	7	50g balls
Medium (M)	1	1	2	2	50g balls
Dark (D)	1	1	1	1	50 g ball

Pair of needles each Nos 5 (4mm), and 3 (3¼mm).
7 buttons.
Polyester fiberfill for stuffing head
Two buttons for eyes

Gauge

22 sts and 30 rows to 10cm (4in) over stockinette stitch on No 5 (4mm) needles

Abbreviations

k – knit; **p** – purl; **st(s)** – stitch(es); **patt** – pattern; **inc** – increase, increasing; **dec** – decrease; **beg** – beginning; **alt** – alternate; **rep** – repeat; **cont** – continue; **st st** – stockinette stitch.

To Make

Back
With No 3 (3¼mm) needles and L, cast on 65 (71, 77, 83) sts. **1st row:** k 2, (p 1, k 1) to last st, k 1. **2nd row:** k 1, (p 1, k 1) to end. Work 18 (20, 24, 26) more rows in rib inc 8 sts evenly on last row. 73 (79, 85, 91) sts.
Change to No 5 (4mm) needles and beg k row work in st st until back measures 38 (42, 46, 49) cm, 15 (16½, 18, 19½) in, ending after a p row.
Shape shoulders by binding off 8 (9, 10, 10) sts at beg of next 4 rows, then 9 (9, 9, 11) sts at beg of next 2 rows. Slip final 23 (25, 27, 29) sts on a spare needle.

Right Front
With No 3 (3¼mm) needles and L, cast on 31 (33, 37, 39) sts. Work in rib as on back but inc 4 (5, 4, 5) sts evenly on last row. 35 (38, 41, 44) sts.
Change to No 5 (4mm) needles and beg k row work in st st until front measures 34 (37, 41, 43) cm, 13½ (14¾, 16, 17¼) in from beg, ending at front edge.
Shape neck thus: **Next row:** bind off 6 (7, 8, 9) sts, work to end. Dec 1 st at neck edge on next 4 rows. 25 (27, 29, 31) sts. Work straight until front measures same as back to shoulder shaping, ending at side edge.
Shape shoulder by binding off 8 (9, 10, 10) sts at beg of next and following alt row. Work 1 row. Bind off.

Left Front
Work as right front, working 1 row less before shaping neck.

Left Sleeve
With No 3 (3¼mm) needles and L, cast on 33 (35, 37, 39) sts. Work 20 rows in rib as on back. **Next row:** k 1, (inc in next st) 30 (32, 34, 36) times, k 2. **Next row:** p inc 1 (3, 5, 7) sts evenly across. 64 (70, 76, 82) sts.**
Change to No 5 (4mm) needles and st st until sleeve measures 28 (32, 36, 39) cm, 11 (12½, 14, 15½) in from beg.
Bind off loosely.

Right Sleeve
Work as left sleeve to **.
Change to No 5 (4mm) needles and patt thus: **1st row:** in M, k. **2nd to 10th rows:** in M, beg k row work 9 rows in reversed st st. **11th to 18th rows:** beg k row work in st st working 2 rows D, 4 rows L, 2 rows D. Rep these 18 rows 5 (6, 7, 8) times more, then rows 1 to 10 again. Bind off loosely in M.

Head of Caterpillar
With No 5 (4mm) needles and D, cast on 45 (49, 49, 53) sts. Beg k row work 6 (8, 10, 12) rows straight.
Shape thus: Dec row: k 2, (k 2 tog through back of loops, k 3) twice, k to last 12 sts, (k 2 tog, k 3) twice, k 2. Work 3 rows straight. Rep the last 4 rows until 25 (25, 29, 29) sts remain. Purl 1 row. **Next row:** (k 2 tog) to last st, k 1. Bind off.

Neckband
First join shoulders. With No 3 (3¼mm) needles and L, right side facing, k up 57 (65, 73, 81) sts evenly round neck, including sts on spare needle. Beg 2nd row work 8 rows in rib as on back. Bind off in rib.

Borders
With No 3 (3¼mm) needles and L, cast on 9 sts. Work a strip in rib as on back to fit up front edge to top of neckband allowing for strip to be slightly stretched. Bind off in rib. Mark position on border for 7 buttons, 1st to be in 3rd/4th rows, last to be in 3rd/4th rows from top and remaining 5 spaced evenly between. Work buttonhole border as 1st border but working holes to match markers thus: **1st row:** rib 3, bind off 3 sts, rib to end. **2nd row:** in rib casting on 3 sts over those bound off.

Emblem
With No 5 (4mm) needles and L, cast on 7 sts. Purl 1 row. Cont in st st thus: **1st row:** 3 L, 1 M, 3 L. **2nd row:** 2 L, 3 M, 2 L. **3rd row:** 2 L, 3 D, 2 L. **4th row:** in L. Rep 1st to 4th rows twice more, then 1st and 2nd rows again. **Next 3 rows:** as 3rd row. **Next row:** in L. Bind off in L.

To Finish
Omitting ribbing and right sleeve, press following pressing instructions. Stitch bound-off edges of sleeves to yoke allowing approximately 14 (15, 17, 18)

cm, 5¾ (6¼, 6¾, 7¼) in for armhole. Join side and sleeve seams. Sew on borders and buttons. Cut M into approximately 13cm (5in) lengths and taking 3 strands for every tassel, using a medium crochet hook, work a tassel on the 16th (18th, 20th, 22nd) st from each end of row on each D stripe on right sleeve. Stitch cast-on edge of caterpillar head to armhole seam as in photograph, then stitch outer edges to yoke inserting a little polyester fiberfill as you go. Sew emblem to left sleeve. Sew on buttons for eyes. Press seams.

Lady Butterfly

Knitted Mohair Jacket

Measurements

To fit bust	81	86	91	97cm
	32	34	36	38in
Length at center back	53	54	56	57cm
	21	21½	22	22½in
Sleeve seam	39	39	39	39cm
	15½	15½	15½	15½in

Materials

Mohair yarn 17 17 18 18 25g balls
Pair of needles each Nos 9 (6mm), 8 (5½mm) and 6 (4½mm)
9 small buttons

Gauge

16 sts and 20 rows to 10cm (4in) over stockinette stitch on No 8 (5½mm) needles

Abbreviations

k – knit; **p** – purl; **st(s)** – stitch(es); **st st** – stockinette stitch; **patt** – pattern; **sl** – slip; **yfwd** – yarn forward; **psso** – pass slipped st over; **inc** – increase; **dec** – decrease; **beg** – beginning; **rep** – repeat; **cont** – continue; **m 1** – make 1 by picking up and purling into back of horizontal strand lying before next st; **tbl** – through back of loops; **tog** – together

To Make

Back
With No 6 (4½mm) needles, bind on 67 (71, 75, 79) sts. **1st row** (right side): k 2, (p 1, k 1) to last st, k 1. **2nd row:** k 1, (p 1, k 1) to end. Rep these 2 rows for 10cm (4in), ending after a 1st row. **Next row:** rib 3 (5, 7, 9), (inc in next st, rib 4) 12 times, inc in next st, rib to end. 80 (84, 88, 92) sts.
Change to No 8 (5½mm) needles and beg k row work in st st until back measures 25cm (10in) at center, ending after a p row.
Shape raglan thus: **1st and 2nd rows:** bind off 2 sts, work to end.
1st and 2nd sizes only: **Next row:** k. **Next row:** k 1, p to last st, k 1.
All sizes:
Next row: k 1, k 2 tog tbl, k to last 3 sts, k 2 tog k 1. **Next row:** k 1, p to last st, k 1. Rep the last 2 rows until 24 (26, 26, 28) sts remain. Work 1 row. Sl sts on a spare needle.

Right Front
With No 6 (4½mm) needles, cast on 33 (35, 37, 39) sts. Work in rib as on back for 10cm (4in), ending after a 2nd row and inc 6 sts evenly on last row. 39 (41, 43, 45) sts.
Change to No 8 (5½mm) needles and st st until front measures 6 rows less than back up to raglan shaping, ending after a p row.**
Commence front slope shaping thus: Dec 1 st at front edge on next row, then on the following 6th row. 37 (39, 41, 43) sts.
Shape raglan thus: **Next row:** bind off 2 sts, p to end.
1st and 2nd sizes only:
Work 2 straight, p row having a 'k 1' at raglan edge.

All sizes:
Next row: k to last 3 sts, k 2 tog, k 1. **Next row:** k 1, p to end. *** Cont dec at raglan edge as on last 2 rows at the same time cont shaping front slope by dec 1 st at neck edge on next (next, 3rd, 3rd) row following, then on every following 6th row until 8 (6, 7, 5) sts remain. Cont dec at raglan edge only as before until 2 sts remain. Work 1 row. Bind off.

Left Front
Work as right front to **.
Commence front slope shaping thus: Dec 1 st at front edge on next row. 38 (40, 42, 44) sts. Work 5 rows straight.
Shape raglan thus: **Next row:** bind off 2 sts, k to last 2 sts, k 2 tog. **Next row:** p.
1st and 2nd sizes only:
Work 2 rows straight, p row having a 'k 1' at raglan edge.
All sizes:
Next row: k 1, k 2 tog tbl, k to end. **Next row:** p to last st, k 1. Complete as right front working from *** to end.

Sleeves
With No 6 (4½mm) needles, bind on 31 (33, 33, 35) sts. Work in rib as on back for 10cm (4in), ending after a 2nd row. **Next row:** k inc once in every st. 62 (66, 66, 70) sts. **Next row:** p inc 8 (8, 12, 12) sts evenly across. 70 (74, 78, 82) sts.
Change to No 8 (5½mm) needles and st st until sleeve measures 39cm (15½in), ending after a p row.
Shape raglan thus:
1st and 2nd rows: bind off 2 sts, work to end. **3rd row:** k 1, k 2 tog tbl, k to last 3 sts, k 2 tog, k 1. **4th row:** k 1, p 2 tog, p to last 3 sts, p 2 tog tbl k 1. Rep 3rd and 4th rows 0 (1, 2, 3) times. (62 sts.) **Next row:** as 3rd. **Next row:** k 1, p to last st, k 1. Rep the last 2 rows until 10 sts remain. Work 1 row. Sl sts on a spare needle.

Border (worked in 2 sections with a join at center back neck).
First join raglan shapings. With No 6 (4½mm) needles and right side facing, k up 20 sts from front edge of right welt, 25 sts up to start of front slope, 60 (61, 63, 64) sts up front slope to first raglan seam, finally k across sleeve sts, then k across first 12 (13, 13, 14) sts of back neck. 127 (129, 131, 133) sts. Beg 2nd row work 2 rows in rib as on back. Bind off firmly and evenly in rib. Work 2nd half to match commencing with remaining back neck sts.

Collar (2 pieces alike)
With No 9 (6mm) needles, cast on 105 (105, 117, 117) sts. **1st row** (right side): *(k 1, y fwd, sl 1, k 2 tog, psso, y fwd) twice (k 1, p 1) twice; rep from * to last 9 sts, (k 1, y fwd, sl 1, k 2 tog, psso, y fwd) twice, k 1. **2nd row:** p 9, *(k 1, p 1) twice, p 8; rep from * to end. These 2 rows form basic patt. **3rd and 4th rows:** as 1st and 2nd. **5th row** (inc row): *(k 1, y fwd, sl 1, k 2 tog, psso, y fwd) twice, (k 1, inc 1 purlwise) twice; rep from * to last 9 sts, (k 1, y fwd, sl 1, k 2 tog, psso, y fwd) twice, k 1. 121 (121, 135, 135) sts. **6th row:** p 9,

*(k 2, p 1) twice, p 8; rep from * to end. **7th and 8th rows:** keeping patt correct, work 2 rows straight. **9th row** (inc row): *(k 1, y fwd, sl 1, k 2 tog, psso, y fwd) twice, (k 1, p 1, m 1 twice; rep from * to last 9 sts, (k 1, y fwd, sl 1, k 2 tog, psso, y fwd) twice, k 1. 137 (137, 153, 153) sts. **10th row:** p 9, *(k 3, p 1) twice, p 8; rep from * to end. **11th and 12th rows:** as 7th and 8th. **13th row** (inc. row): *(k 1, y fwd, sl 1, k 2 tog, psso, y fwd) twice, (k 1, p 1, m 1, p 2) twice; rep from * to last 9 sts (k 1, y fwd, sl 1, k 2 tog, psso, y fwd) twice, k 1. 153 (153, 171, 171) sts. Work a few rows straight until collar measures 9cm (3½in), ending after a right-side row. Bind off to form picot thus: (**NB** work loosely): Bind off 2 sts, *sl st on right needle onto left needle and cast on 2 sts, now bind off 6 sts; rep from * until all sts are bound off. Work 2nd piece the same.

To Finish
Do not press. Join side and sleeve seams. Join borders at back of neck. Join one side edge of each collar piece to form one long strip, now stitch cast-on edge of collar to base of border, leaving welt sections free and slightly easing on collar all round. Catch side edges of collar to top of welt. Sew buttons to left front edge up to front slope, evenly spaced. Now work a loop to correspond with each on edge of right-front border.

Lady's Smock

Floral Skirt with Frill (*Picture on page 39*)

Measurements

To fit all sizes: length 90.5cm (35½in)

Materials

3m (3¼yd) of 145cm (57in) wide floral fabric
Matching thread
1.3cm (½in) wide elastic, 3 times waist measurement plus 7.5cm (3in)

To Make

1 Cut out from fabric 2 pieces each 99cm (39in) by desired length, less frill depth and plus 6cm (2⅜in) for top casing and seam allowances.

2 For frill, cut out 3 fabric widths by desired length plus 2.5cm (1in) for hem and seam allowance.

3 Place main fabric pieces with right sides together. Pin, baste and stitch both side seams, taking 1.5cm (⅝in) seam allowance to within 6cm (2⅜in) of top edge at one side. Neaten and press seam open, pressing under allowances on either side of top opening.

4 Place right sides of frill pieces together. Pin, baste and stitch together to make a ring. Neaten and press seams open. Turn a double 6mm (¼in) deep hem along base edge of frill; pin, baste and stitch in place. Work 2 rows of gathering stitches along top edge of frill.

5 Place frill to skirt with right sides together, pulling up gathers evenly to fit. Pin, baste and stitch frill in place.

6 Turn down 6cm (2⅜in) at top edge to wrong side with pressed under edges meeting together. Turn under 1cm (⅜in). Pin, baste and stitch folded edge. Stitch around top casing twice more, spacing stitching about 1.5cm (⅝in) apart.

7 Cut 3 lengths of elastic to the waist measurement plus 2.5cm (1in). Thread length of elastic through opening in each casing in turn, overlapping ends of elastic and stitching them together. Neatly stitch open seam.

Peacock Butterfly

Crochet Summer Top with Butterfly Motifs

Measurements

To fit bust	86	91	97cm
	34	36	38in
Length	57	60	63cm
	22½	23½	24¾in

Materials

3 ply yarn	5	5	6	100g balls

2/C crochet hook
Pair of No 3 (3¼mm) knitting needles

Gauge

16 sps and 15 rows to 10cm (4in)

Abbreviations

alt – alternately; **beg** – beginning; **dc** – double crochet; **ch** – chain; **cont** – continue; **k** – knit; **p** – purl; **patt** – pattern; **rep** – repeat; **sk** – skip; **sp(s)** – space(s); **st(s)** – stitch(es)

To Make

Front
Make 174 (184, 194) ch loosely. **1st row:** 1 dc in 6th ch from hook, *1 ch, sk 1 ch, 1 dc in next ch; rep from * to end. 85 (90, 95) 1 ch sps. **Next row:** 4 ch, sk 1st dc, *1 dc in next dc, 1 ch; rep from * to end, 1 dc in 4th of 5 ch. **Patt row:** 4 ch, sk 1st dc, *1 dc in next dc, 1 ch; rep from * to end, 1 dc in 3rd of 4 ch. Rep patt row 3 (5, 7) times. Now cont from chart, following key and beg at row marked * . Read rows alt from right to left then left to right. Shape armholes and neck as shown. Fasten off at end.

Back
Work as for front but omit butterfly motifs continuing 'dot' patt across. Omit neck shaping working straight after completing armhole shaping.

Frills (make 2)
Make 224 ch loosely. Work 1st row as front. 110 one ch sps. **2nd row:** 4 ch, sk 1st dc, *1 dc/1 ch in each of next 9 dc, 1 dc/1 ch twice in next dc; rep from * 9 times, 1 dc/1 ch in each of next 9 dc, 1 dc in 4th of 5 ch. 120 one ch sps. **3rd row:** as patt row of front. **4th row:** 4 ch, sk 1st dc, *1 dc/1 ch in each of next 9 dc, 1 dc/1 ch twice in each of next 2 dc; rep from * 9 times, 1 dc/1 ch in each of next 9 dc, 1 dc in 3rd of 4 ch. 140 one ch sps. **5th row:** patt to end. **6th row:** 4 ch, sk first dc, *1 dc/1 ch in each of next 9 dc, 1 dc/1 ch twice in each of next 4 dc; rep from * 9 times, 1 dc/1 ch in each of next 9 dc, 1 dc in 3rd of 4 ch. 180 one ch sps. Patt 2 rows. Fasten off.

Neckband
Mark center 31 (34, 37) sps on top edge of back for back neck. Join right shoulder

seam. With right side facing and using No 3 (3¼mm) needles, pick up and k 112 (116, 120) sts evenly around neck. Work 7 rows in k 1, p 1 rib. Bind off loosely in rib.

Armbands
Join left shoulder and neckband seam. With right side facing and using No 3 (3¼mm) needles, pick up and k 90 (94, 98) sts evenly around armhole. Work 5 rows in k 1, p 1 rib. Bind off loosely in rib.

Welts
With right side facing and using No 3 (3¼mm) needles, pick up and k 114 (118, 122) sts evenly along lower edge of front. Work 8cm (3¼in) in k 1, p 1 rib. Bind off loosely in rib. Work back welt to match.

To Finish
Place center of shorter edge of frill to shoulder seam at armhole edge (within armband). Following the same vertical line of dc on back and front, sew frills in place. Sew down ends of frills. Join side seams.

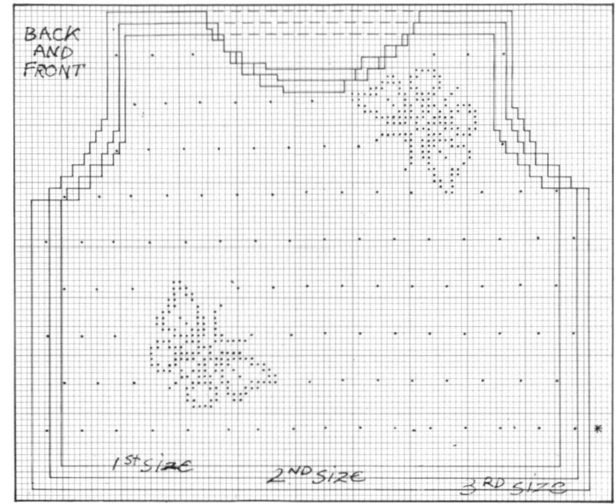

Peacock Butterfly
Crochet Summer Top

Key
□ Space = 1 dc in dc, 2 ch, sk 2 sts
• Block = 1 dc in dc, 2 dc in sp or 1 dc in each of 3 dc

Wings of Gold

Embroidered Butterfly Picture

Measurements

Embroidered area 26cm (10¼in) square

Materials

40cm (15¾in) of 56cm (22in) wide white evenweave embroidery linen with 29 threads to 2.5cm (1in)
Anchor Embroidery floss: 1 skein each of 0264; 0266; 0293; 0297; 0300; 0302; 0306; 0378; 0851; 0884; 0936; 0945
Tapestry needle No 24
Picture frame with backing board large enough to take embroidery

To Make

Important Note: Read 'General Working Instructions for all Cross Stitch Embroideries' on page 16.

1 Cut a piece of linen 40cm (15¾in) square and fold in both directions lightly (widthwise and lengthwise) to form center lines. Work basting stitches along center lines.

2 Center of chart is indicated by arrows which should coincide with basting stitches.

3 Each square on chart represents 2 double threads of linen (2 warp and 2 weft threads), or 1 cross stitch.

4 Following chart and key for 'Wings of Gold' design, work design in cross stitch, working as far as possible out from center. Use 2 strands of cotton throughout.

5 Remove basting stitches.

6 Follow mounting and framing instructions on page 62.

Wings of Gold
Embroidered Butterfly Picture

Design 135 x 135 stitches

Design size 26cm (10¼in) square

Shade numbers refer to Anchor Embroidery Floss.

Key

•	0264
/	0266
—	0293
!	0297
+	0300
1 X	0302
●	0306
<	0378
■	0851
>	0884
V	0936
\	0945

MAY

"An angel mid the woods of May
Embroidered it with radiance gay"

BLUE-BELLS

FAIRE MAY

TINTED PETALS

BUTTERCUP AND SPEEDWELL

Blue-bells *Knitted Sweater*

Measurements

To fit bust	81	86	91	97cm
	32	34	36	38in
Length from shoulder,	57	58	58	60cm
approximately	22½	23	23	23½in
Sleeve seam	33	33	33	33cm
	13	13	13	13in

Materials

Knitting worsted

M (Main Shade)	8	8	9	9	50g balls
A (Dark Green)	1	1	1	1	25g ball
B (Light Green)	1	1	1	1	25 g ball
C (Lilac)	1	1	1	1	25g ball

Pair of needles each Nos 5 (4mm) and 3 (3¼mm)
Set of four No 3 (3¼mm) needles

Gauge

22 sts and 30 rows to 10cm (4in) over stockinette stitch using M and No 5 (4mm) needles

Abbreviations

k – knit; **p** – purl; **st(s)** – stitch(es); **st st** – stockinette stitch; **inc** – increase, increasing; **dec** – decrease; **beg** – beginning; **alt** – alternate; **rep** – repeat; **cont** – continue; **A** – dark green shade; **B** – light green shade; **C** – lilac shade; **M** – main shade

To Make

Front
With No 3 (3¼mm) needles and M, cast on 92 (96, 104, 108) sts. **1st row** (right side): k 3, (p 2, k 2) to last st, k 1. **2nd row:** k 1, (p 2, k 2) to last 3 sts, p 2, k 1. Rep these 2 rows for 11cm (4½in), ending after a 1st row. **Next row:** rib 8 (5, 7, 3), *inc in next st, rib 4 (4, 5, 5); rep from * to last 9 (6, 7, 3) sts, inc in next st, rib to end. 108 (114, 120, 126) sts.**
Change to No 5 (4mm) needles and beg k row work 12 rows in st st. Now using a separate ball of yarn for each color area, twisting yarns on wrong side when changing colors, cont in st st working from charts thus: **1st row:** k, 33 (35, 37, 39) M, work 1st row of chart A reading from right to left, 4 (6, 8, 10) M, work 1st row of chart A reading from left to right, 33 (35, 37, 39) M. **2nd row:** p, 33 (35, 37, 39) M, work 2nd row of chart A reading from right to left, 4 (6, 8, 10) M, work 2nd row of chart A reading from left to right, 33 (35, 37, 39) M. **3rd to 68th rows:** rep 1st and 2nd rows 33 times but working rows 3 to 68 of chart A.
Change to chart B. **1st row:** k 2 (4, 6, 8) M, work 1st row of chart B reading from right to left, 22 (24, 26, 28) M, work 1st row of chart B, reading from left to right, 2 (4, 6, 8) M. **2nd row:** p 2 (4, 6, 8) M, work 2nd row of chart B reading from right to left, 22 (24, 26, 28) M, work 2nd row of chart B reading from left to right, 2 (4, 6, 8) M. **3rd to 24th rows:** rep the last 2 rows 11 times but working rows 3 to 24 of chart B.
Keeping chart correct, shape neck thus: **Next row:** k 43 (45, 47, 49), turn. Cont on this group. Dec 1 st at neck edge on next 4 rows, then on the 3 following alt rows. 36 (38, 40, 42) sts.
Noting that when chart is complete M only for remainder will be used, work straight until front measures 10 (11, 11, 13) cm, 4 (4½, 4½, 5) in from beg of neck shaping, ending at side edge.
Shape shoulder by binding off 9 (9, 10, 10) sts at beg of next and 2 following alt rows. Work 1 row. Bind off. With right side facing, slip center 22 (24, 26, 28) sts on a spare needle. Rejoin yarns to remaining sts and complete as 1st half.

Back
Work as front to **.
Change to No 5 (4mm) needles and beg k row work in st st until back measures same as front to shoulder shaping, ending after a p row.
Shape shoulders by binding off 9 (9, 10, 10) sts at beg of next 6 rows, then 9 (11, 10, 12) sts at beg of next 2 rows. Slip final 36 (38, 40, 42) sts on a spare needle.

Sleeves
With No 3 (3¼mm) needles and M, cast

Blue-bells
Knitted Sweater

Key
□ M
• A
/ B
× C

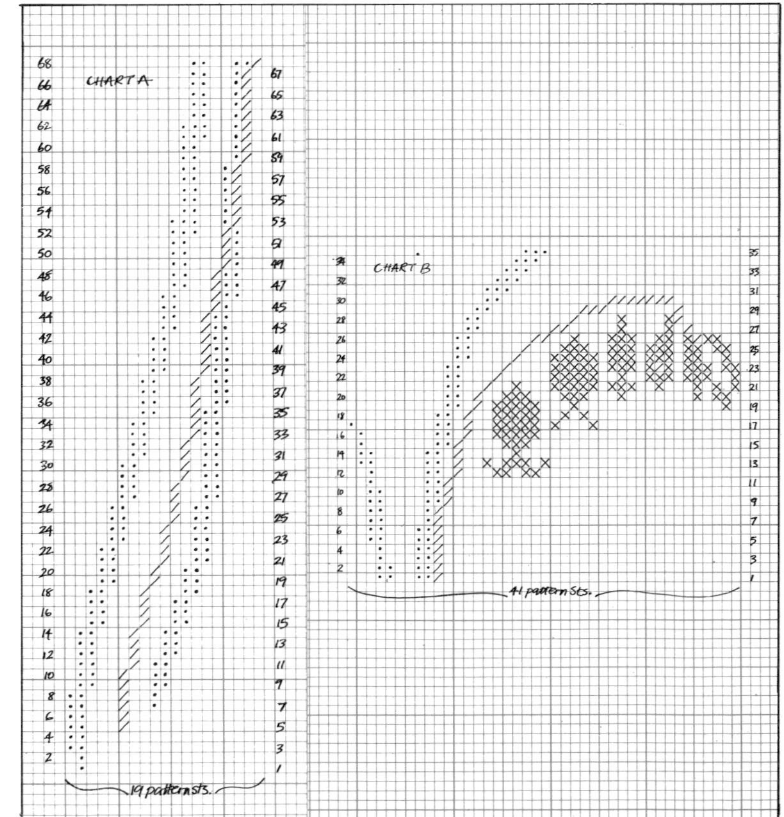

on 51 (53, 55, 57) sts *loosely*. Beg p row work 16 rows in reversed st st. **Next row (hem):** fold work in half and k to end knitting each st on needle together with corresponding loop from cast-on edge. **Next row:** p 3 (3, 2, 2), inc once in next 45 (47, 51, 53) sts, p to end. 96 (100, 106, 110) sts.
Change to No 5 (4mm) needles and beg k row work in st st until sleeve measures 33cm (13in). Bind off loosely.

Neckband
First join shoulders. With set of No 3 (3¼mm) needles and M, right side facing, k up 112 (120, 124, 132) sts evenly round neck, including sts on spare needles. Purl 9 rounds. Now work 6 rounds in k 2, p 2 rib. Bind off loosely.

To Finish
Omitting welt, press following pressing instructions on yarn band. Allowing approximately 22 (23, 24, 24.5) cm, 8¾ (9, 9½, 9¾) in for armholes, stitch bound-off edges of sleeves to yoke. Join side and sleeve seams. Fold neckband in half to wrong side and hem in position.
Press seams.

Faire May

Crochet Rose Camisole

Measurements

To fit bust	81/86	86/91	91/97cm
	32/34	34/36	36/38in
Length	52	53	54cm
	20½	21	21¼in

Materials

4 ply mercerized cotton	5	6	6	50g balls

No 6 steel crochet hook

Gauge

18 sps and 16 rows to 10cm (4in)

Abbreviations

alt – alternately; **ch** – chain; **cont** – continue; **dc** – double crochet; **dec** – decrease; **patt** – pattern; **rep**– repeat; **sc** – single crochet; **sk** – skip; **sp(s)** – space(s); **ss** – slip stitch; **st** – stitch

To Make

Back
Make 158 (170, 182) ch loosely. **1st row:** 1 dc in 6th ch from hook, *1 ch, sk 1 ch, 1 dc in next ch; rep from * to end. 77 (83, 89) 1 ch sps. **Next row:** 4 ch, sk 1st dc, *1 dc in next dc, 1 ch; rep from * to end, 1 dc in 4th of 5 ch. **Patt row:** 4 ch, sk 1st dc, *1 dc in next dc, 1 ch; rep from * to end, 1 dc in 3rd of 4 ch.** Rep patt row 42 times.

Armhole Shaping
1st row: ss in each st to 5th dc of row, patt to within last 4 sps, turn. Patt 1 row. **Dec row:** ss in each st to 2nd dc of row, patt to within last sp, turn. Rep last 2 rows 15 (16, 17) times. 37 (41, 45) sps. Fasten off.

Front
Work as back to **. Rep patt row 5 times. Now cont from chart which shows half the front. Follow key reading each row from right to left, then omit square before dotted line (center st) and work each row from left to right. Cont from chart shaping armholes and neck as shown. **Note:** when neck shaping starts read rows alt from right to left and left to right. Fasten off. Join shoulder and side seams.

Lower Edging
1st round: Join yarn to lower edge at side seam, *1 sc in same ch as dc, 1 ch; rep from * all round, ss to 1st sc. **Patt round:** ss in 1 ch sp, 1 dc in same place as ss, *1 ch, 1 dc in next sp; rep from * to end, 1 ch, ss to 1st dc. Rep patt round 5 times. Fasten off.

Armhole Edging
1st round: Join yarn to top of side seam, 1 sc in same place as join, *1 ch, 1 sc; rep from * evenly around armhole, 1 ch, ss to 1st sc. Rep patt round of lower edging once. Fasten off.

Neck Edging
Join yarn to neck edge at shoulder seam and work 1 round of ss. Fasten off. Press lightly.

Faire May
Crochet Rose Camisole

Key
□ Space = 1 dc in dc, 2 ch, sk 2 sts
• Block = 1 dc in dc, 2 dc in sp or 1 dc in each of 3 dc

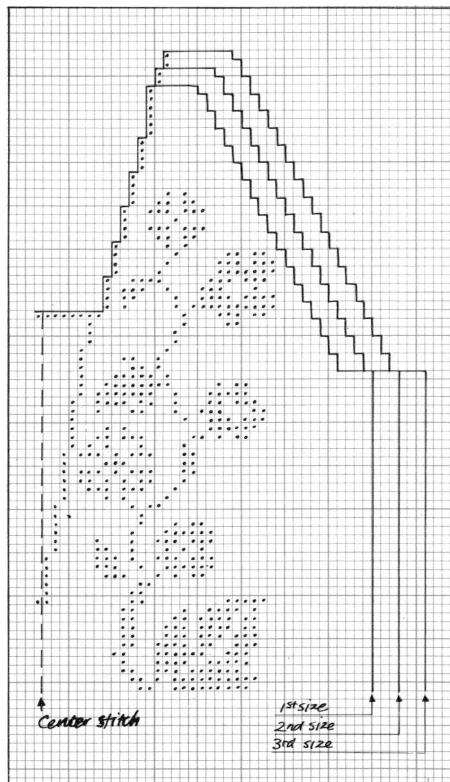

Tinted Petals

Knitted Sweater

Measurements

To fit bust	81/86	86/91	91/97cm
	32/34	34/36	36/38in
Length from	58	58	58cm
shoulder	23	23	23in
Sleeve seam,	46	46	46cm
approximately	18	18	18in

Materials

Knitting worsted,

M (Cream)	7	7	8	50g balls
A (Pink)	2	2	2	50g balls
B (Mauve)	1	1	1	50g ball
C (Yellow)	1	1	1	50g ball

Pair of needles each Nos 5 (4mm) and 3 (3¼mm)
Cable needle
Set of 4 No 3 (3¼mm) needles

Gauge

23¾ sts in width to 10cm (4in) over flower pattern on No 5 (4mm) needles.

Abbreviations

k – knit; **p** – purl; **st(s)** – stitch(es); **patt** – pattern; **inc** – increase, increasing; **dec** – decrease, decreasing; **beg** – beginning; **alt** – alternate; **A** – pink shade; **rep** – repeat; **B** – mauve shade; **C** – yellow shade; **M** – cream shade; **CB** – slip next st on cable needle to back of work, k 1, now p 1 from cable needle; **CF** – slip next st on cable needle to front of work, p 1, now k 1 from cable needle; **cont** – continue; **tw 2** – slip next st on cable needle to front of work, k 1, now k 1 from cable needle; **st st** – stockinette stitch; **tog** – together

To Make

Center Front Panel and Welt
With No 3 (3¼mm) needles and M, cast on 96 (104, 112) sts. **1st row:** k 3, (p 2, k 2) to last st, k 1. **2nd row:** k 1, (p 2, k 2) to last 3 sts, p 2, k 1. Rep these 2 rows for 11cm (4½in) ending after a 2nd row. **Next row:** bind off 27 sts *loosely*, rib to end. **Next row:** bind off 27 sts *loosely*, rib to end inc 8 sts evenly on last row. 50 (58, 66) sts. Change to No 5 (4mm) needles and trellis patt thus: **1st row:** p 4, (tw 2, p 6) to last 6 sts, tw 2, p 4. **2nd row:** k 4, (p 2, k 6) to last 6 sts, p 2, k 4. **3rd row:** p 3, (CB, CF, p 4) to last 7 sts, CB, CF, p 3. **4th and every following alt row:** k all k sts and p all p sts. **5th row:** p 2, (CB, p 2, CF, p 2) to end. **7th row:** p 1, (CB, p 4, CF) to last st, p 1. **9th row:** p 1, k 1, (p 6, tw 2) to last 8 sts, p 6, k 1, p 1. **11th row:** p 1, (CF, p 4, CB) to last st, p 1. **13th row:** p 2, (CF, p 2, CB, p 2) to end. **15th row:** p 3, (CF, CB, p 4) to last 7 sts, CF, CB, p 3. **16th row:** as 2nd. These 16 rows form patt.**
Cont in patt until work measures 48cm (19in) from lower edge, ending after a wrong-side row.
Keeping patt correct, shape neck thus: **Next row:** patt 13 (16, 19), turn. Cont on this group. Dec 1 st at neck edge on next 5 rows, then on the 2 following alt rows. 6 (9, 12) sts. Work straight until front measures 10cm (4in) from beg of neck shaping. Bind off. With right side facing, slip center 24 (26, 28) sts on a spare needle. Rejoin M to remaining sts and patt 1 row. Complete as 1st half.

Center Back Panel and Welt
Work as front section to **. Cont in patt until back measures same as front to shoulder. **Next 2 rows:** bind off 6 (9, 12) sts, work to end. Slip final 38 (40, 42) sts on a spare needle.

Right Front and Left Back Side Sections
(2 pieces alike worked sideways)
Beg at inner edge. With No 5 (4mm) needles and M, cast on 113 sts for all sizes. Beg k row, work in st st from flower chart thus: **1st and 2nd rows:** in M. **3rd row:** k, 3M, (work 1st row of chart reading from right to left, 3M) to end. **4th row:** p, 3M, (work 2nd row of chart reading from left to right, 3M) to end. **5th to 18th rows:** rep 3rd and 4th rows 7 times but working rows 3 to 16 from chart. **19th and 20th rows:** in M. **21st row:** k, 14M (work 1st row of chart but using B in place of A, 3M) to last 11 sts, 11M. **22nd row:** p, 14M, (work 2nd row of chart but using B in place of A, 3M) to last 11 sts, 11M. **23rd to 36th rows:** rep 21st and 22nd rows 7 times but working rows 3 to 16 from chart using B in place of A. These 36 rows form flower patt.
Cont in patt until work measures 17cm (6¾in) from beg, ending after a k row. Shape side seam and sleeve thus: Keeping patt correct, bind off 55 (51, 47) sts in M at beg of next row. (**NB:** fewer sts are bound off on the larger sizes to allow greater depth in the armhole.) Cont on the remaining 58 (62, 66) sts. Dec 1 st at underarm on 5th row following, then on every following 6th row until 44 (48, 52) sts remain. Work straight until sleeve seam measures 34cm (13½in), ending after a 1st row. **Next row:** in M, (p 2 tog) to end. Slip final 22 (24, 26) sts on a spare needle.

Left Front and Right Back Side Sections
(2 pieces alike worked sideways)
Work as right front and left back side sections but ending after a p row before shaping and leaving final 22 (24, 26) sts on needle.

Cuffs
First join shoulder seams on side sections. With No 3 (3¼mm) needles and M, k across 44 (48, 52) sts of lower sleeve edge. Beg 2nd row, work in rib as on center front panel and welt for 11cm (4½in). Bind off loosely in rib.

Neckband
First join the groups of 6 (9, 12) bound-off sts of center panels. Now neatly join the cast-on edges of side sections to the side edges of center panels. With set of No 3 (3¼mm) needles and M, right side facing, k across back sts dec 6 sts evenly, k up 24 sts down left front neck, k across center sts dec 4 sts evenly, finally k up 24 sts up right front neck. 100 (104, 108) sts. Work 14 rounds in k 2, p 2 rib.
Bind off loosely.

To Finish
Omitting ribbing, press following pressing instructions. Stitch side edges of side panels to top of welt, easing in side sections to fit welt. Join side and sleeve seams. Fold neckband in half to wrong side and hem in position. Press seams.

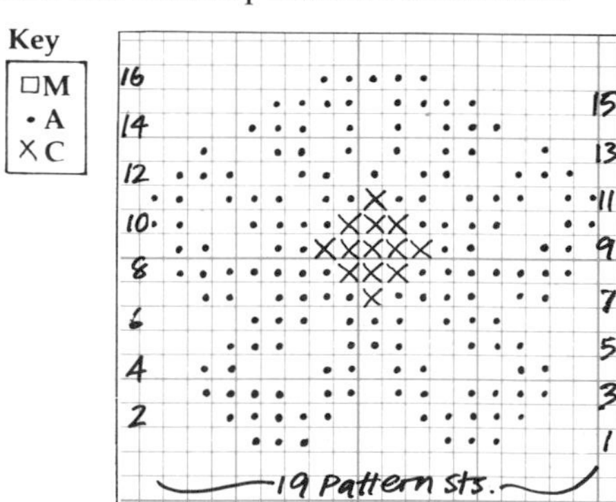

Tinted Petals Knitted Sweater
NB A small ball of C should be used for each rose center; elsewhere color not in use should be carried loosely over back of work, over not more than 5 sts at a time

Flowers in Bloom *Floral Skirt*

(Picture on page 48)

Measurements

To fit all sizes: length 90.5cm (35½in)

Materials

2m (2¼yd) of 150cm (59in) wide floral fabric
Matching thread
1.3cm (½in) wide elastic, three times waist measurement plus 7.5cm (3in)

To Make

1 Cut one piece the fabric length by 100.5cm (39½in). Fold fabric in half with right sides together. Pin, baste and stitch center back seam, taking 1.5cm (⅝in) seam allowance to within 6cm (2⅜in) of top edge. Neaten and press seam open, pressing under allowances on either side of top opening.

2 Turn down 6cm (2⅜in) at top edge to wrong side, aligning pressed seam allowances. Turn under 1cm (⅜in); pin, baste and stitch along folded edge. Stitch round top casing twice more, spacing stitching 1.5cm (⅝in) apart.

3 Cut 3 lengths of elastic to the waist measurement plus 2.5cm (1in). Thread a length of elastic through the opening in each casing in turn, overlapping ends and stitching them together. Neatly stitch open seams.

4 Turn up lower edge for 4cm (1½in). Turn in raw edge to give neat finish to hem. Hem in place.

Buttercups and Speedwell *Knitted Tops*

Measurements

To fit chest/bust	61	66	71	86	91	97cm
	24	26	28	34	36	38in
Length from shoulder	41	44	48	60	61	62cm
	16	17½	19	23½	24	24½in

Materials

Patons Cotton Perle

L (white)	4	4	5	8	8	8	50g balls

Patons Cotton Soft

A (green)	1	1	2	2	2	2	50g balls
B (pink)	1	1	1	2	2	2	50g balls
C (yellow)	1	1	1	2	2	2	50g balls
D (blue)	1	1	1	1	1	1	50g ball

Pair long needles each Nos 5 (4mm) and 2 (3mm)
Set of four No 2 (3mm) needles

Gauge

26 sts and 26 rows to 10cm (4in) over pattern on No 5 (4mm) needles

Abbreviations

k – knit; **p** – purl; **st(s)** – stitch(es); **patt** – pattern; **inc** – increase, increasing; **dec** – decrease, decreasing; **beg** – beginning; **alt** – alternate; **st st** – stockinette stitch

To Make

Front
With No 2 (3mm) needles and L, cast on 67 (73, 79, 95, 101, 107) sts. **1st row:** k 2, (p 1, k 1) to last st, k 1. **2nd row:** k 1, (p 1, k 1) to end. Work 20 (22, 24, 36, 38, 40) more rows in rib. **Next row:** k 4 (7, 10, 6, 9, 12), (inc in next st, k 1, inc in next st, k 2, inc in next st, k 2) 7 (7, 7, 10, 10, 10) times, inc in next 3 (3, 3, 2, 2, 2) sts, k to end. 91 (97, 103, 127, 133, 139) sts. Purl 1 row.
Change to No 5 (4mm) needles and beg k row work in st st with patt thus: **1st row:** 2L, (3A, 3L) to last 5 sts, 3A, 2L. **2nd row:** 2A, (1L, 1A, 1L, 3A) to last 5 sts, 1L, 1A, 1L, 2A. **3rd row:** 3L, (1B, 5L) to last 4 sts, 1B, 3L. **4th row:** 2L, (3B, 3L) to last 5 sts, 3B, 2L. **5th row:** 1L, (2B, 1L) to end. **6th row:** As 4th. **7th row:** As 3rd. **8th row:** In L. **9th and 10th rows:** As 1st and 2nd. **11th row:** 2L, (3C, 3L) to last 5 sts, 3C, 2L. **12th and 13th rows:** 1L, (5C, 1L) to end. **14th row:** 2L, (1C, 1L, 1C, 3L) to last 5 sts, 1C, 1L, 1C, 2L. **15th row:** In L. **16th and 17th rows:** As 1st and 2nd. **18th row:** 3L, (1D, 5L) to last 4 sts, 1D, 3L. **19th and 20th rows:** 2L, (3D, 3L) to last 5 sts, 3D, 2L. **21st row:** 1L, (1D, 1L) to end. **22nd row:** In L. These 22 rows form patt.
Continue in patt until work measures 24 (27, 29, 36, 36, 36) cm, 9½ (10½, 11½, 14, 14, 14) in from beg, ending after a p row.
Working extra sts into patt shape sleeve thus: (**NB:** On the 3 larger sizes a 3rd No 5 (4mm) needle may be used to hold sts.)
Inc 1 st at each end of next 5 rows. Now cast on 22 (22, 22, 82, 82, 82) sts at each end of next row. 145 (151, 157, 301, 307, 313) sts.**
Work straight until front measures 7 (9, 9, 11, 11, 11) cm, 3 (3½, 3½, 4½, 4½, 4½) in from sleeve cast-on sts, ending after a p row.
Shape neck thus: **Next row:** Patt 55 (57, 59, 123, 125, 127), turn. Continue on this group. Dec 1 st at neck edge on next 5 rows. 50 (52, 54, 118, 120, 122) sts. Work straight until front measures 14 (15, 17, 21, 23, 24) cm, 5½ (6, 6½, 8½, 9, 9½) in from sleeve cast-on sts, ending at side edge.
Shape shoulder by binding off 29 (31, 33, 88, 90, 92) sts at beg of next row, then 7 (7, 7, 10, 10, 10) sts at beg of next and following alt row. Work 1 row. Bind off.
With right side facing, slip center 35 (37, 39, 55, 57, 59) sts on a spare needle. Rejoin appropriate color/s and patt 1 row. Complete as first half.

Back
Work as front to **. Work straight until back measures same as front to shoulder shaping, ending after a p row.
Shape shoulders by binding off 29 (31, 33, 88, 90, 92) sts at beg of next 2 rows, then 7 (7, 7, 10, 10, 10) sts at beg of next 6 rows.
Slip final 45 (47, 49, 65, 67, 69) sts on a spare needle.

Neckband
First join shoulders. With set of No 2 (3mm) needles and L, right side facing, k across back sts dec 8 (8, 9, 11, 12, 12) sts evenly across, k up 19 (19, 22, 28, 31, 34) sts evenly down left front neck, k across center sts dec 6 (6, 7, 9, 10, 10) sts evenly across, finally k up 19 (19, 22, 28, 31, 34) sts evenly up right front neck. 104 (108, 116, 156, 164, 174) sts. Work 14 (16, 16, 20, 20, 20) rounds in k 1, p 1 rib. Bind off.

To Finish
Omitting ribbing, press following pressing instructions. Join side and sleeve seams. Fold neckband in half to wrong side and hem in position. Press seams. Fold under the outer 6 (6, 6, 28, 28, 28) sts on sleeves to wrong side and catch lightly in position all round. On Lady's version, fold over approximately 9cm (3½in) of sleeves to right side.

COUNTRY DIARY HEIRLOOMS

WHITE BLOSSOM

THE ROSE

A Robe of White *Crochet Patchwork Bedspread*

Measurements

180cm (72in) square (excluding border, approximately 17cm/6¾in deep)

Materials

43 x 100g hanks knitting worsted
8/H crochet hook

Gauge

13 sts to 10cm (4in) measured over flat pattern

Abbreviations

ch – chain; **cont** – continue; **dc** – double crochet; **hdc** – half double crochet; **lp(s)** – loop(s); **pct** – picot; **prev** – previous; **r** – ring; **rep** – repeat; **sc** – single crochet; **sk** – skip; **ss** – slip stitch; **st(s)** – stitch(es); **tc** – treble crochet; **yo** – yarn over

Note: work instructions in brackets the number of times given.

To Make

Flat Pattern (make a total of 18 squares)
With 8/H hook, make 41 ch. **1st row:** 1 sc in 2nd ch from hook, (1 dc in next ch, 1 sc in next ch) to last ch, 1 dc in last ch, 1 ch, turn. **2nd row:** *1 sc in next dc, 1 dc in next sc; rep from * to end, 1 ch, turn. Rep 2nd row for patt until work measures 30cm (12in). Fasten off.

Pineapple Pattern (make a total of 18 squares)
With 8/H hook, make 40 ch. **1st row:** 1 sc in 2nd ch from hook, 1 sc in each ch to end, 1 ch, turn. 39 sts. **2nd row:** 1 sc in each sc to end, 1 ch, turn. **3rd row:** as 2nd row. **4th row:** 1 sc in each of first 3 sts, *insert hook into next st, yo, draw lp through, (yo, insert hook into the same st 2 rows below, yo, draw lp through, yo, draw through 2 lps) 6 times, yo, draw through all 8 lps on hook – called 1 pineapple – 1 sc into each of next 3 sc; rep from * to end, 1 ch, turn. **5th to 7th rows:** as 2nd row. **8th row:** 1 sc in each of first 2 sts, *1 pineapple in next sc, 1 sc in each of next 3 sc; rep from * to last st, 1 pineapple in last sc, 1 ch, turn. **9th to 11th rows:** as 2nd row. **12th row:** 1 sc in first sc, *1 pineapple in next sc, 1 sc in each of next 3 sc; rep from * to last 2 sts, 1 pineapple in next sc, 1 sc in last sc, 1 ch, turn. **13th to 15th rows:** as 2nd row. **16th row:** 1 pineapple in next sc, *1 sc in each of next 3 sc, 1 pineapple in next sc; rep from * to last 2 sts, 1 sc in each of next 2 sc, 1 ch, turn. These 16 rows form the patt. Rep them until work measures 30cm (12in). Fasten off.

To Finish
Join the squares in rows of 6 squares, alternating the patterns as shown.

The border (work a total of 4 lengths)
1st motif: with 8/H hook, make 8 ch and join into a r with ss. **1st round:** 1 ch, 11 sc into r, join with ss. **2nd round:** *5 ch, sk 1 sc, 1 sc into next sc; rep from * 4 times more, 5 ch, 1 sc into ss at end of round 1. **3rd round:** into each 5 ch lp, work 1 sc, 1 hdc, 5 dc, 1 hdc, 1 sc. Called petals. **4th round:** keeping hook behind petals just worked, work 1 sc into 1st sc on round 2, *4 ch, 1 sc into 3rd ch from hook – pct made – 5 ch, pct, 2 ch, 1 sc into sc on round 2 between next 2 petals; rep from * all round, ending with ss into 1st sc. Fasten off. **2nd motif:** work as given for 1st motif until all 4 rounds have been completed but do not fasten off. To join motifs, work in rows thus: **1st row:** ss along to center of next pct lp, 1 sc in same lp, 4 ch, pct, 5 ch, pct, 2 ch – pct lp made – 1 sc into center of next pct lp, turn. **2nd row:** 1 pct lp, 1 sc into center of next pct lp, 1 pct lp, 1 sc into sc at base of pct lp on prev row, turn. **3rd row:** ss to center of next pct lp, 1 sc into same lp, 1 pct lp, 1 sc into center of next pct lp, turn. **4th row:** 4 ch, pct, 1 ch, 1 sc in center of any lp on 1st motif, 3 ch, pct, 2 ch, 1 sc in next pct lp of 2nd motif, 3 ch, pct, 2 ch, 1 sc in next pct lp of 1st motif, 3 ch, pct, 2 ch, 1 sc in sc at base of prev row. Fasten off. **3rd motif:** work as 2nd motif until 3rd row has been completed. **5th row:** work as 4th row of 2nd motif, joining in 2 lps opposite the prev 2 joins. Cont in this way making and joining motifs until each border fits along side edge of the bedspread. Fasten off.

The heading
With right side facing, join yarn to pct lp at top of first motif, 1 sc into same place as join, *(5 ch, 1 dc in next pct lp) 4 times, 5 ch, 1 sc in next pct lp; rep from * to end. Fasten off.

The lower scallop
With right side of lower edge facing, join yarn to lp before the top lp of 1st motif, 5 ch, pct, 3 ch, *into next lp (at top of motif) work (1 tc, 3 ch, 1 sc into top of tc) 6 times, then 1 sc, 5 ch, 1 tc into pct lp at join of motifs, 1 pct lp, 1 sc into next lp, 5 ch; rep from * along edge, ending with tc groups as before, 5 ch, pct, 2 ch, 1 sc into next lp. Fasten off. Sew heading ch edge along each side edge of bedspread. At each corner join the 1st pct lp below ch heading. Press border lightly and squares' seams if needed. Alternatively the bedspread may be pressed by being laid flat with a damp cloth over it until the cloth has dried out.

Lady's Mantle

Crochet Mantelpiece Cloth or Table Runner

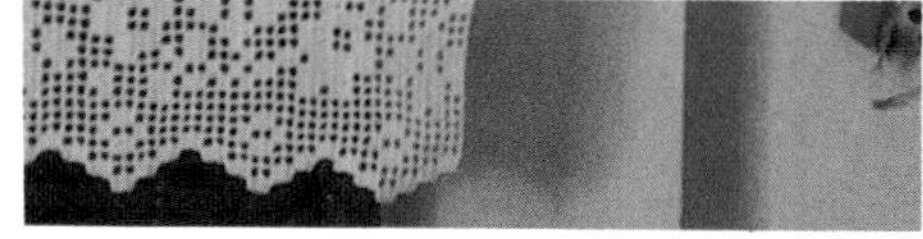

Measurements

Length – 122cm (48in)
Depth – 34cm (13½in)
Note: the length can easily be adjusted in multiples of approximately 11cm (4½in). Work from chart for required length, ending with 2nd, 14th or 26th row. To increase length allow additional yarn. 1 hank will work approximately 50cm (19¾in).

Materials

3 x 100g hanks No 2 crochet cotton
No 4 crochet hook

Gauge

10 sps and 11 rows measure 10cm (4in)

Abbreviations

ch – chain; **cont** – continue; **dc** – double crochet; **dec** – decrease; **rep** – repeat; **sc** – single crochet; **sk** – skip; **ss** – slip stitch; **sp(s)** – space(s); **st(s)** – stitch(es)
Note: work instructions in brackets the number of times given.

To Make

Make 84 ch. **1st row:** 1 dc in 4th ch from hook, 1 dc in each of next 2 ch, (2 ch, sk 2 ch, 1 dc in next ch) 5 times, 1 dc in each of next 9 ch, (2 ch, sk 2 ch, 1 dc in next ch) 3 times, 1 dc in each of next 3 ch, (2 ch, sk 2 ch, 1 dc in next ch) 4 times, 1 dc in each of next 9 ch, (2 ch, sk 2 ch, 1 dc in next ch) 3 times, 1 dc in each of next 3 ch, 5 ch, sk 5 ch, 1 dc in each of last 4 ch, turn. **2nd row:** 3 ch, sk 1st dc, 1 dc in each of next 3 dc, 5 ch, 1 dc in each of next 4 dc, (2 ch, 1 dc in next dc) twice, 2 dc in ch sp, 1 dc in each of next 7 dc, (2 ch, sk 2 sts, 1 dc in next dc) 5 times, 1 dc in each of next 3 dc, (2 ch, 1 dc in next dc) 3 times, 1 dc in each of next 6 dc, (2 ch, sk 2 sts, 1 dc in next dc) 6 times, 1 dc in each of next 2 dc, 1 dc in top of turning ch, turn. **3rd row:** 5 ch, 1 dc in 4th ch from hook, 1 dc in next ch, 1 dc in first dc – this completes the 1st block of the 3rd row – now reading chart from right to left complete row following chart. Reading all odd-numbered rows from right to left and all even-numbered rows from left to right, cont in this way, starting rows 5 and 7 as for row 3. On rows 9, 11 and 13 work 1 ss in each of 1st 3 dc, 3 ch to dec 1 block. Rep rows 1 to 36 twice, then rows 1 to 26 again. Fasten off.

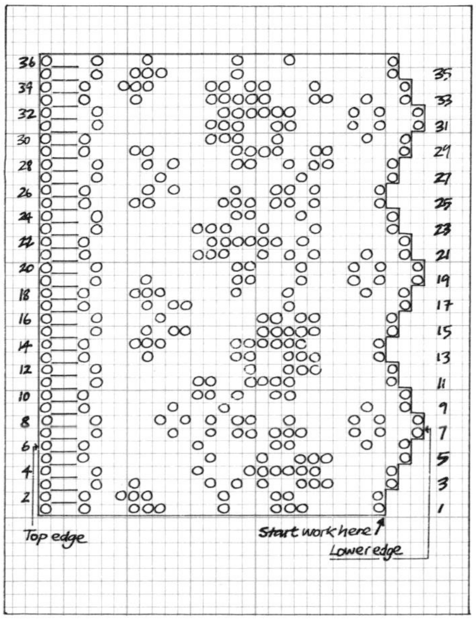

Top Edging
Join yarn to top right-hand corner, 1 sc in corner (3 ch, 1 sc in joining point of next row) to end, 3 ch, 1 sc in corner. Fasten off. Press over a damp cloth.

Lady's Mantle
Crochet Mantelpiece Cloth or Table Runner

Key
☐ Space = 1 dc in dc, 2 ch, sk 2 sts
o Block = 1 dc in dc, 2 dc in space or 1 dc in each of 3 dc

Top edge
Start work here
Lower edge

White Blossom

Crochet Cushion Cover

Measurements

40cm (15¾in) square, excluding border

Materials

4 x 100g hanks knitting worsted
8/H crochet hook
40cm (15¾in) zip fastener

Abbreviations

ch – chain; **dc** – double crochet; **lp(s)** – loop(s); **patt** – pattern; **rep,** – repeat; **sc** – single crochet; **sk** – skip; **ss** – slip stitch; **st(s)** – stitch(es); **yo** – yarn over
Note: work instructions in brackets the number of times given

To Make

The Squares
Flat Square (make a total of 4 squares)
With 8/H hook, make 29 ch. **1st row:** 1 sc in 2nd ch from hook, (1 dc in next ch, 1 sc in next ch) to last ch, 1 dc in last ch, 1 ch, turn. **2nd row:** (1 sc in dc, 1 dc in next sc) to end, 1 ch, turn. Rep 2nd row for patt until work measures 20cm (8in). Fasten off.

Pineapple Square (make a total of 4 squares)
With 8/H hook, make 28 ch. **1st row:** 1 sc in 2nd ch from hook, 1 sc in each ch to end, 1 ch, turn. 27 sts. **2nd row:** 1 sc in each sc to end, 1 ch, turn. **3rd row:** as 2nd row. **4th row:** 1 sc in each of 1st 3 sts, *insert hook into next st, yo, draw lp through, (yo, insert hook into the same st 2 rows below, yo, draw lp through, yo, draw through 2 lps) 6 times, yo, draw through all 8 lps on hook – called 1 pineapple – 1 sc into each of next 3 sc; rep from * to end, 1 ch, turn. **5th to 7th rows:** as 2nd row. **8th row:** 1 sc in each of first 2 sts, *1 pineapple in next sc, 1 sc in each of next 3 sc; rep from * to last st, 1 pineapple in last sc, 1 ch, turn. **9th to 11th rows:** as 2nd row. **12th row:** 1 sc in first sc, *1 pineapple in next sc, 1 sc in each of next 3 sc; rep from * to last 2 sts, 1 pineapple in next sc, 1 sc in last sc, 1 ch, turn. **13th to 15th rows:** as 2nd row. **16th row:** 1 pineapple in next sc, *1 sc in each of next 3 sc, 1 pineapple in next sc; rep from * to last 2 sts, 1 sc in each of next 2 sc, 1 ch, turn. These 16 rows form the patt. Rep them until work measures 20cm (8in). Fasten off.

To Finish
Join to form 2 squares, alternating the patterns as shown but do not join the front to back.

The Border
With right side of front facing, work sc evenly along each edge, working 3 sc into each corner. Each side edge should have a multiple of 4 sc plus 1 sc. Join with ss into 1st sc. Fasten off. Do not turn. Rejoin yarn to center sc at any corner. **Next row:** 4 ch, (1 dc, 1 ch) twice in corner sc, *sk next sc, leaving last lp of each dc on hook work 5 dc in next sc, yo and draw through all 6 lps, 2 ch, sk next sc, 1 dc in next sc, 2 ch; rep from * to within 3 sc before corner, sk next sc, 1 cluster in next sc, 1 ch, sk next sc, (1 dc, 1 ch) 3 times in corner sc, rep from first * all round omitting instructions in brackets at end of last rep, join with a ss into 3rd of 4 ch. Fasten off. Work sc evenly around back, join with a ss. Fasten off. Join front to back leaving border free and leaving 1 side open for zipper. Insert zipper. Press lightly.

Little Flowers *Cushions*

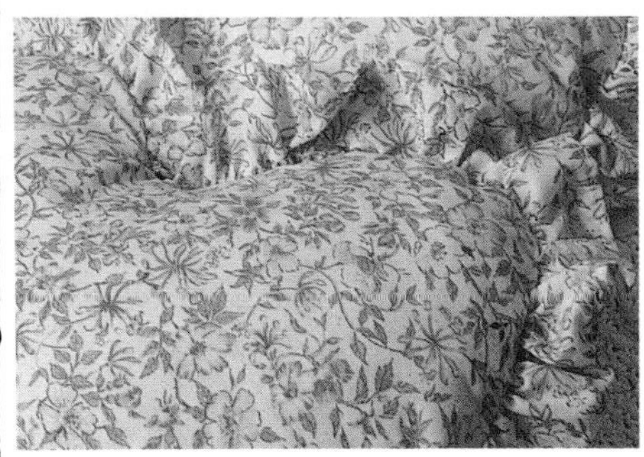

Measurements

38cm (15in) square or 38cm (15in) diameter

Materials

Fabric 85cm x 45cm (33½in x 17¾in)
Frill can be any width, within reason. Decide what looks good on the cushion size and with the chosen fabric.
Pins
Matching thread
Pillow form
Pair of compasses

To Make

SQUARE CUSHION WITH FRILL

1 From fabric cut out 2 pieces, each 41cm (16¼in) square, for cushion back and front. For frill multiply the outer cushion measurement by between 1½ and 2. Cut out as many lengths across the fabric width to achieve this measurement.

2 Pin, baste and stitch frill pieces together into a ring, with French seams. Turn a double 6mm (¼in) wide hem along outer edge of frill; pin, baste and stitch hem into place.

3 Divide the inner edge of frill into 4 equal sections, work 2 rows of gathering in each frill section on either side of 1.5cm (⅝in) stitching line.

4 Position the frill, facing inwards, to one cushion piece with right sides together, matching each frill section each side of the cushion cover. Pull up gathers evenly to fit, making sure that there is sufficient gathering round each corner. Pin, baste and stitch frill in place.

5 Place 2nd cushion piece to first with right sides together, over frill. Pin, baste and stitch together for 3 sides and for 5cm (2in) round the corner on each end of the 4th side.

6 Trim and turn cushion cover to the right side. Insert pillow form; turn in opening edges in line with the remainder of the seam. Slip stitch together with small neat stitches.

As an alternative, the frill can also be double; in this case double the finish width and add twice the seam allowance, 3cm (1¼in), for the cutting width. The frill sections need only be seamed together with plain flat seams as they are enclosed. The frill ring is then folded in half with wrong sides together and gathered as before. Stitch on to one cushion cover piece and complete as for previous cushion cover.

On a circular cushion cover, the opening should be about one third of the diameter and the cover will have to be divided up equally in the same way as the frill.

HEART CUSHION

1 Decide on the height which can be divided into 12 equal squares. On squared paper, draw a line A-B to this measurement.

2 Mark off C, 2 squares from A, and D, 3 squares from A. Mark a horizontal line through D.

3 Set a pair of compasses to 3 squares: place compass point at C and mark E and F across the horizontal line on each side of D. Place compass point on E and draw top arc. Repeat on opposite side.

4 Set compasses to 8 squares; place point where heart top crosses horizontal line at left hand side and mark H. Repeat at right hand side and mark G. Place point on G and then H to mark in base of heart.

5 Using ruler, mark straight lines from B to curved lines, if a more pointed shape is required.

6 Now draw up heart pattern to the size of cushion required, following points 1 to 5 as a guide.

7 Make up the cushion in the same way as the square cushion, adding a frill if desired.

8 Insert pillow form (or stuff with polyester fiberfill if heart-shaped form is not available).

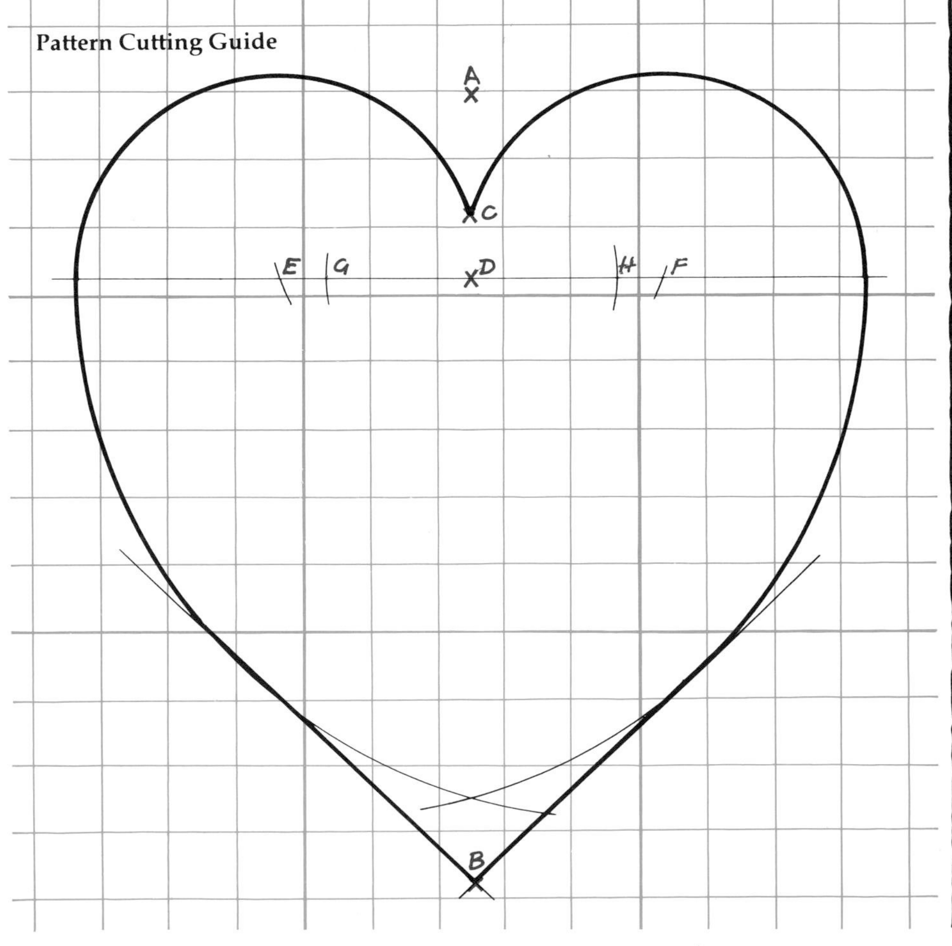

Pretty Flowers *Patchwork Cushion* *(Picture on page 57)*

Materials

One piece Pellon Quilter's Secret – 10cm (4in) square
75cm (7/8yd) floral fabric – 1.52m (60in) wide (A)
45cm (1/2yd) plain cream cotton fabric for patches and cushion cover back (B)
10cm x 40.5cm (4in x 16in) pink dotted fabric for heart shapes (C)
30.5cm (12in) square (2oz) batting
10cm x 40.5cm (4in x 16in) iron-on interfacing
3m (3¼yd) of 2cm (¾in) wide lace edging
35.5cm (14in) zipper
40.5cm (16in) square pillow form
Matching thread

To Make

Carefully read 'The Secret of Patchwork' on page 93.

To decorate the patchwork block:
1 Cut and fuse together: 5 x 10cm (4in) squares of floral fabric with 5 x 10cm (4in) squares of Quilter's Secret.

2 Cut and fuse together: 4 x 10cm (4in) squares of cream fabric with 4 x 10cm (4in) squares of Quilter's Secret.

3 Assemble squares and rows following Block Diagram A.

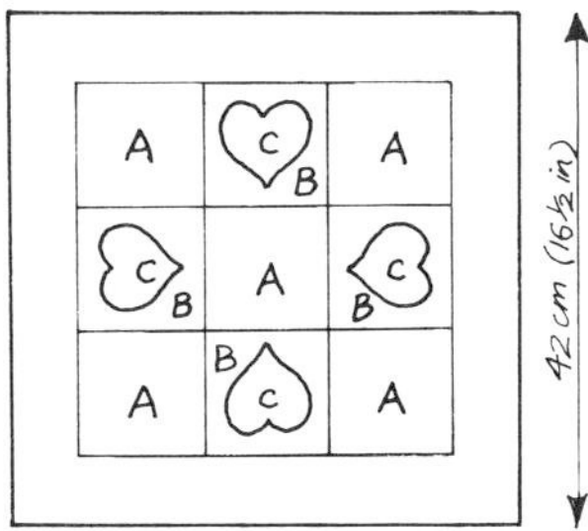

4 Make template of heart shape and cut out four hearts from pink dotted fabric.

5 Fuse heart shapes to a backing of iron-on interfacing.

6 Pin and baste heart shapes to cream squares with hearts pointing towards center. Machine or hand embroider edges of hearts to secure cream squares.

7 Gather lace edging and attach to edges of patchwork block.

8 Cut piece of floral fabric 42cm (16½in) square.

9 Place batting between patchwork block and floral fabric square insuring patchwork lies in center of fabric.

10 Machine stitch edges of patchwork block to floral fabric, securing batting between the two layers of fabric.

11 Gather lace edging. Pin, baste and machine stitch to seam line of outer edges of floral square with lace pointing away from cushion center.

12 Cut cushion back 2.5cm (1in) wider than cushion front.

13 Cut cushion back into two equal parts, each 22.25cm x 21cm (8¾ x 8¼in).

14 Turn back both vertical center seam edges 1.25cm (½in) and press.

15 Insert zipper within 2.5cm (1in) center seam allowance.

16 With right sides facing, pin, baste and machine stitch edges of cushion front to edges of cushion back.

17 Turn to right side. Insert pillow form and close zipper.

The Rose
Woven Bedside Rug

Measurements

112cm x 56cm (44in x 22in)

Materials

127cm (50in) of 56cm (22in) wide rug-making canvas
Pre-cut Rug Yarn
1 Off White – 12 balls
2 Deep Rose – 6 balls
3 Pink – 3 balls
4 Light Green – 2 balls
5 Apple Green – 1 ball
6 Dark Green – 1 ball
7 Gold – 1 ball
8 Lemon – 1 ball
9 Brown – 1 ball
10 Beige – 1 ball
11 Light Grey – 1 ball
It is advisable to buy all large amounts, such as background shades, together, to insure they are all the same dye lot
Large bodkin needle
Plastic jumbo crochet hook for working fringed edge

To Make

Note: it is important to read all instructions before beginning.
There are two methods of working cross stitch. The row-by-row method is done by working a row of half cross stitches and then, beginning with the last stitch, work back along the line to complete the second half of each cross stitch. The stitch-by-stitch method is worked by completing each cross stitch individually. The row-by-row method is mostly used to cover large areas of canvas such as the background of designs. Not only is it quicker to work than the stitch-by-stitch method, it makes it easier to maintain a regular rhythm which helps to give stitches an even tension and a regular appearance.
The stitch-by-stitch method is ideal for working small areas of stitching, such as motifs, where only a small number of stitches will be worked in any one color. Whichever method is used, it is important to insure that all the stitches cross in the same direction and that an even tension is maintained throughout the work.

Row-by-Row Method

1 Leave a long horizontal piece of wool under the row of canvas you are about to work. This will avoid having to make a knot which might work through to the front of the canvas.

2 Working row by row, work half of each stitch by bringing needle up at lower left-hand hole of the stitch to be worked and insert through the next diagonal hole. Repeat.

3 When all half cross stitches over the intended area have been worked, bring the needle out and stitch back diagonally over the last stitch to complete the cross.

4 Working backwards, row by row, complete the other half of each cross stitch. Keep the tension of the stitches as even as possible.

5 To fasten off the wool on the wrong side of work, slide the needle through the back of 3 or 4 stitches, pull wool through and cut. There is no need to backstitch.

To avoid the wool wearing thin as it is used, keep length of wool no longer than 46-51cm (18-20in).

Stitch-by-Stitch Method

1 In this method each stitch is worked individually. Begin as instruction 1 of 'Row by Row' above. The first half of a stitch is worked as in instruction 2, but do not repeat.

2 To complete the stitch, work back diagonally over the half cross just worked. The needle will be in the correct position for the next stitch.

Fasten off as instruction 5 in Row-by-Row Method.

Starting and Finishing
The first and last few inches of the raw edges of the canvas are folded under and pressed flat. The first and last few rows of stitches are worked through the double canvas.

Binding the Selvages
Selvages are covered with a binding stitch. This is a braided over-sewing which produces a very firm covering. Work as follows – following Diagram C. Thread needle, darn in end of wool, insert needle in 1st hole and bring towards you, go over to 4th hole, back to 2nd, forward to 5th, back to 3rd, forward to 6th, and so on.

In the diagram, stitches have been omitted for clarity.

Finishing Off Short (folded) Ends
Short ends are usually fringed or they are bound with crossed oversewing stitches formed by working diagonally into every hole from left to right, then working a return row from right to left.

Fringing
Take short lengths of wool (approximately 18cm/7in) fold in half and pull through folded edge of canvas with a crochet hook; bring cut ends down through loop and pull tight.

Pressing Stitched Rugs
Lay finished rug face downwards on a large padded surface and pull to shape. Using a hot iron and damp cloth, press carefully all over including the side edges.

Rug Care and Cleaning
Shake rug to release dust. Vacuum clean both sides of rug. Use a cloth or brush dampened with a liquid detergent and carefully clean the pile. Do not use much pressure.
Dry by hanging on a line or lying flat. Dry cleaning is possible. Do not attach a backing material to the rug, or put rug in a washing machine. Do not allow rug to get soaking wet. Do not use heavy shampooing machines or tumble dry.

Key ■ 2 □ 3 ■ 7 □ 8 ■ 9 □ 10 ■ 11 □ 1 ■ 6 □ 4 □ 5

The Rose *Woven Bedside Rug*

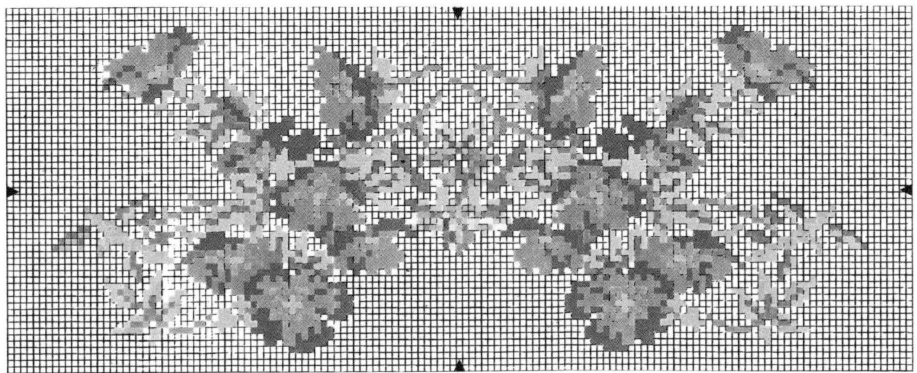

Framing Embroidery and Needlepoint Pictures

I Mounting over cardboard
When the work has been completed, remove it from the embroidery frame and pull it gently into shape. If the work is distorted, as sometimes happens, particularly with canvas work, it will have to be blocked into shape. To do this, cover a drawing board, cork or softboard with white cloth and, using an embroidery marker pen or tailor's chalk, draw the exact correct shape of the piece of work onto the white fabric. Use rust-proof pins, and with the right side of the work facing the cloth, pin the work along one outer stitched (if canvas work) edge to the drawn line. Work to one corner and down the next side. Pull the work to fit the other drawn lines exactly, dampening the back of the canvas fabric slightly to ease the stretch. Care should be taken to avoid staining the embroidery threads. Silk is particularly susceptible to water marks. Leave the work pinned to shape for twenty-four hours.

The backing
Before framing, the embroidery is stretched over a backing of thick cardboard or hardboard. For small to medium-size pieces, cardboard is adequate. When mounting canvas work the cardboard should be cut to the exact size of the stitched area. Cardboard must fit easily into the frame, and allowance must be made for the thickness of the fabric when measuring up.

Lay the embroidery face down on a clean surface and place cardboard on top. A 3.5-5cm (1⅜-2in) turning is adequate, so trim work to this size. Stretch the work over the cardboard following one of the methods shown. *Always* check that the fabric is being stretched on the straight of the grain. For this reason start gluing or lacing the work from the centers, and work out to each edge. This way it is easy to keep check on the grain. Use strong thread or fine twine for lacing, making sure to knot the ends securely. Fabric adhesive is useful for mounting embroideries, and cellophane tape or masking tape can be used to position the work before lacing. For oval shapes, start in the centers as above, working round the shape rather in the manner of slicing a cake into large

sections, and working back into the sections to make smaller slices. This way the straight grain is easier to control.

Mounting embroidery over cardboard

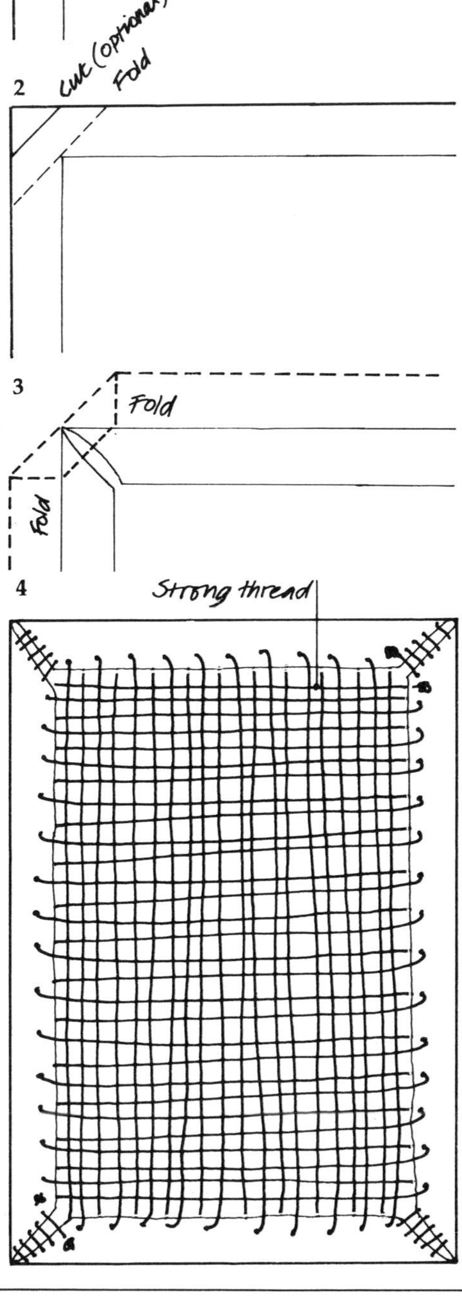

Alternative way of mounting embroidery using adhesive

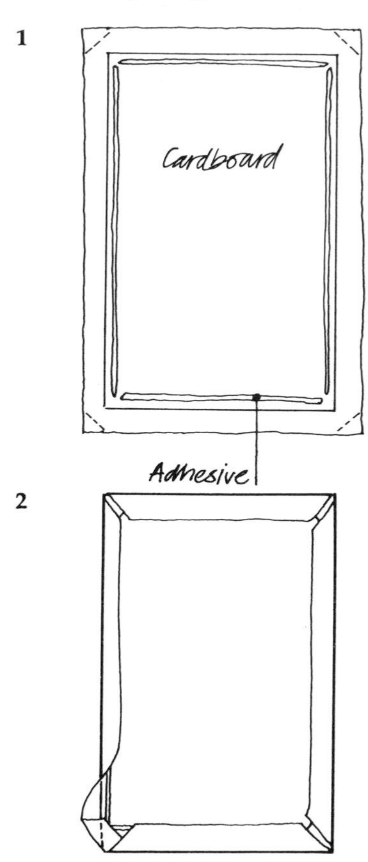

Mounting embroidery over oval cardboard

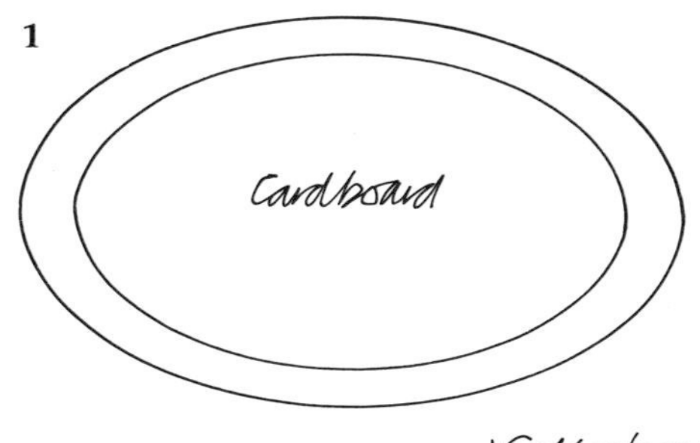

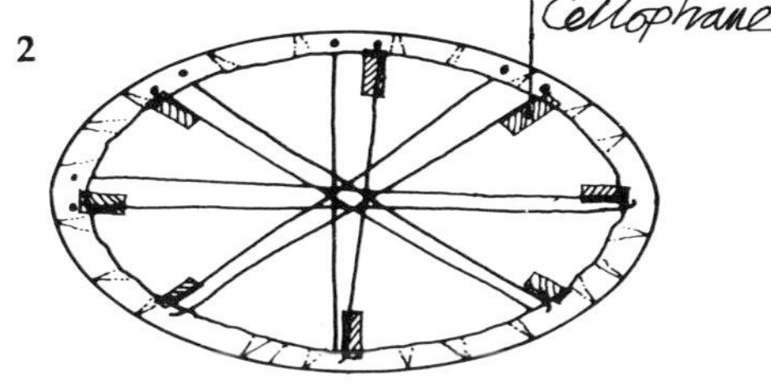

2 Putting the embroideries into frames

If the mounted work is not too thick it will be possible to fit it into an ordinary picture frame. However, some frames may not be suitable at all, if they are not deep enough to take the extra bulk of the mounted embroidery. The backing fixings may not be strong enough to hold the work in place. If you have a particularly pretty frame that you would like to use, and it is not quite deep enough, it might be possible to cheat a little. This could be done by omitting the frame backing and substituting a thinner cardboard, and simply taping this down to the frame back, or by stapling the card back to the frame. The frame can be hung by using eye hooks screwed into each side of the frame.

It is important to try to keep dust from getting into the frame and soiling the embroidery and so any short cuts should be made with this in mind. Extra thick, bulky work needs to be set into a box frame, which is a frame made with really deep sides. These can be made to measure by a professional, who will give advice on the particular piece of needlework to be framed.

3 Mats

Sometimes interest can be added to a piece of work by setting it in a cardboard mat. These can be bought ready-cut in a variety of colors and shapes, and most picture framers will cut mats to measure. When selecting a mat (or mats) choose a color that will lead the eye into the work; for instance choose a mat in one of the embroidery thread shades. For the best effect choose a shade that blends gently with the work rather than providing a contrast. Take into consideration the color of the frame and the surrounding wall color. Another way of finishing off a framed embroidery is to run a line of furnishing gimp or braid round the edge of the work, level with the inside edge of the frame. Again, choose a sympathetic color to the embroidery, or choose a color to match the background fabric, giving a subtle change of texture.

Note: The mahogany pole screen used to frame the 'Wild Roses' embroidered picture on page 65 provides an ideal way to display a beautiful example of needlework.

Midsummer Day

HEDGEROWS

Wild Roses *Embroidered Picture*

Measurements

Embroidery picture 25cm (10in) square

Materials

35cm (10in) square of even-weave linen with 28 threads to 2.5cm (1in)
Anchor Embroidery Floss: 1 skein each of 024; 025; 027; 0297; 0301; 0300; 0890; 0943; 0217; 0378; 0379; 0847; 0216; 0215; 0267; 0214; 0265; 0213; 0847; 0266; White
Tapestry needle No 24
Picture frame

To Make

Important note: read 'General Working Instructions for all Cross Stitch Embroideries' on page 16.

1 Fold fabric lightly in both directions (widthwise and lengthwise) to mark center lines. Mark center lines with basting stitches.

2 Center of chart is indicated by arrows which should coincide with basting stitches.

3 Using 2 strands of floss, work cross stitch design from 'Wild Roses' chart and key above, working as far as possible out from center. Each square on chart represents 2 double threads of fabric (2 warp and 2 weft threads) or one cross stitch.

4 Remove basting threads.

5 Follow mounting and framing instructions on page 62.

Wild Roses
Embroidered Picture

Key

ʌ	024
ǀ	025
<	027
‖	0297
●	0301
=	0300
O	0890
•	white
⊢	0943
⌶	0217
Z	0378
N	0379
+	0847
\	0216
—	0215
⊥	0267
/	0214
X	0265
>	0213
V	0847
T	0266

Shade numbers refer to Anchor Embroidery Floss.

Design 98 x 99 stitches

Design size (approx.)
14 stitches to 2.5cm (1in):
18cm (7in) square

Special instructions

1. Outline *0847*
Pink flowers and bud
027 (shown in red)
025 (shown in black)

2. Backstitch Stems
0216 (shown in black)
0266 (shown in red)

Swallows
Embroidered Picture

Measurements

Embroidery picture 24cm x 19cm (9½in x 7½in)

Materials

35cm x 30cm (13¾in x 12in) of even-weave linen with 26 threads to 2.5cm (1in)
Anchor Embroidery Floss: 1 skein each of White; Black; 0387; 5968; 0397; 0398; 0401; 0851; 0847; 0922; 0921; 0905
Tapestry needle No 24
Picture frame

To Make

Important note: read 'General Working Instructions for all Cross Stitch Embroideries' on page 16.

1 Fold linen in half in both directions (widthwise and lengthwise) and crease lightly to mark center lines. Work basting stitches along center lines.

2 Center of chart is indicated by arrows which should coincide with basting stitches.

3 Using 2 strands of floss throughout, work embroidery following chart and key for 'Swallows' design below, working as far as possible out from center.

4 Each square on chart represents 2 double threads of linen (ie 2 warp and 2 weft threads), or 1 cross stitch.

5 Remove basting stitches.

6 Follow mounting and framing details on page 62.

Swallows
Embroidered Picture

Key
• white
V 0387
● black
Λ 5968
X 0397
– 0398
\ 0401
+ 0851
= 0847
O 0922
I 0921
/ 0905

Shade numbers refer to Anchor Embroidery Floss.

Design 76 x 47 stitches

Design size (approx.)
13 stitches to 2.5cm (1in):
14cm x 8.5cm (5½in x 3⅜in)

Special instructions
Outline
Birds – *0921*
Eyes – Black

Backstitch
Beak – *0401*

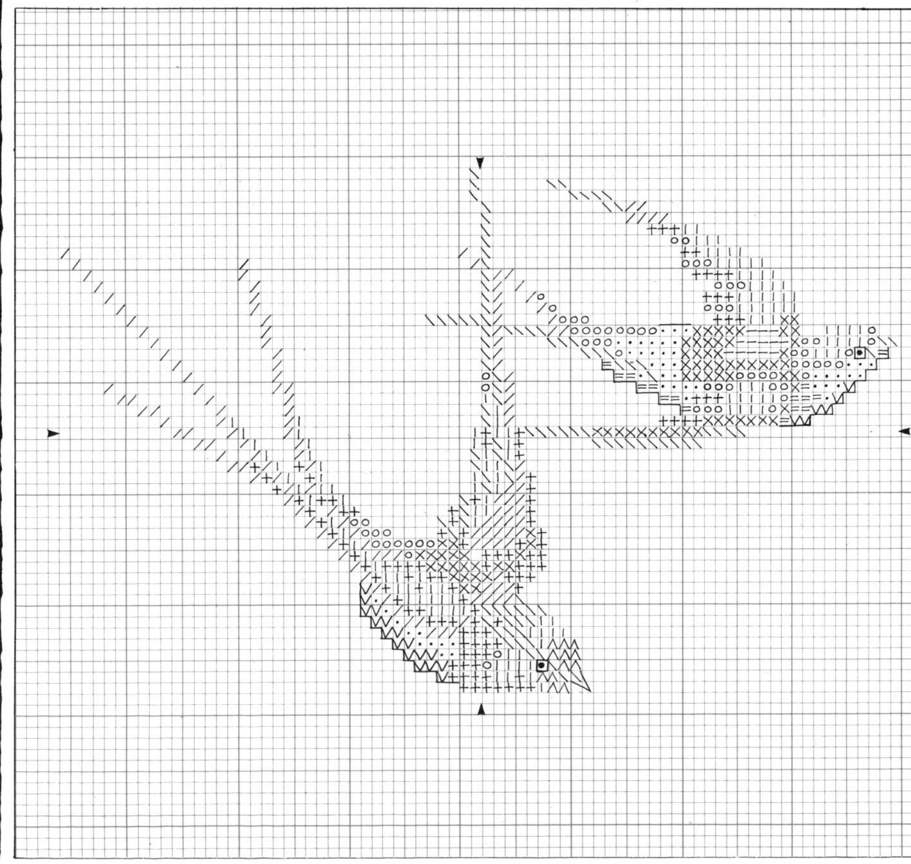

Water Lily

Needlepoint Picture

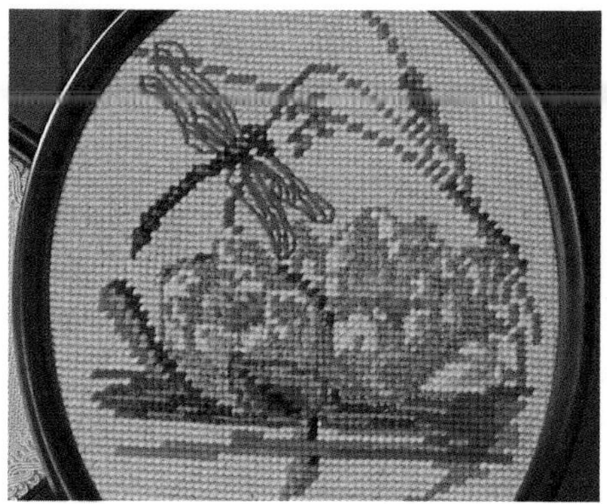

Measurements

Needlepoint picture 19cm x 25cm (7½in x 10in)

Materials

35cm (13¾in) of 58cm (23in) wide Number 10 Penelope canvas (double-threaded)
Anchor Tapestry Wool in 10m (11yd) skeins: 6 skeins 0386; 1 skein each of 0402; 0369; 0187; 0650; 0902; 0668; 0378; 0216; 3149; 3002; 0278; 3234; 0656; 0397; 0217; 3000; 3202
Tapestry needle
Oval frame

To Make

Important note: Read 'General Working Instructions for all Needlepoint on page 15.

1 Crease fabric lightly in both directions (widthwise and lengthwise) to form center lines. Work basting stitches along center lines.

2 Work needlepoint following chart and key for 'Water Lily' design on page 68, working as far as possible out from center. Each square on chart represents 1 square of double thread canvas, or 1 tapestry stitch.

3 Complete background in 0386 and work backstitch details as given on chart.

4 Remove basting stitches.

5 Mount and frame work as detailed in 'Mounting and Framing Embroideries' on page 62.

6 Model worked in traméed half cross stitch.

Water Lily
Needlepoint Picture

Key

ll	0386
–	0402
\	0369
●	0187
△	0650
l	0902
>	0668
↑	0378
=	0216
/	3149
+	3002
•	0278
X	3234
V	0656
<	0397
O	0217
⊃	3000
Λ	3202

Shade numbers refer to Anchor Tapestry wool.

Design 57 x 83 stitches

Design size (approx.)
10 stitches to 2.5cm (1in)
15½cm x 17cm (6in x 6¾in)

Special instructions
Backstitch details:
1 Outline of lilies *0817*
2 Lily centers *3002*
3 Dragonfly: top edge and back of head *0650*
4 Line through body *0187*
5 Lily petals *0397*
6 Leaf *0216*
7 Lily pads *0378*
8 Dragonfly wings *0369*

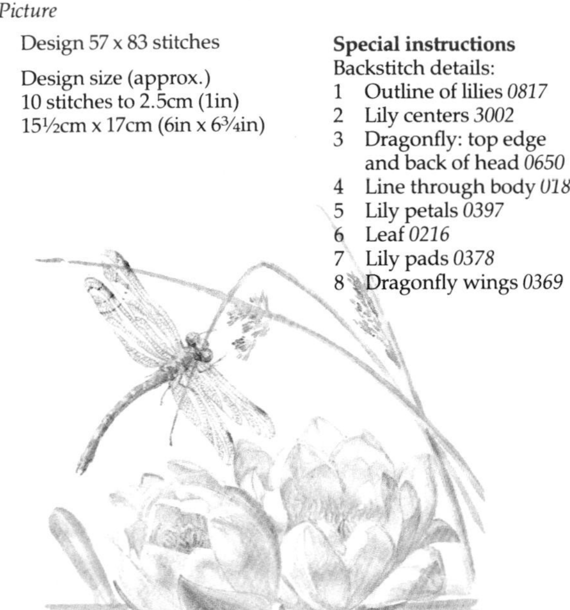

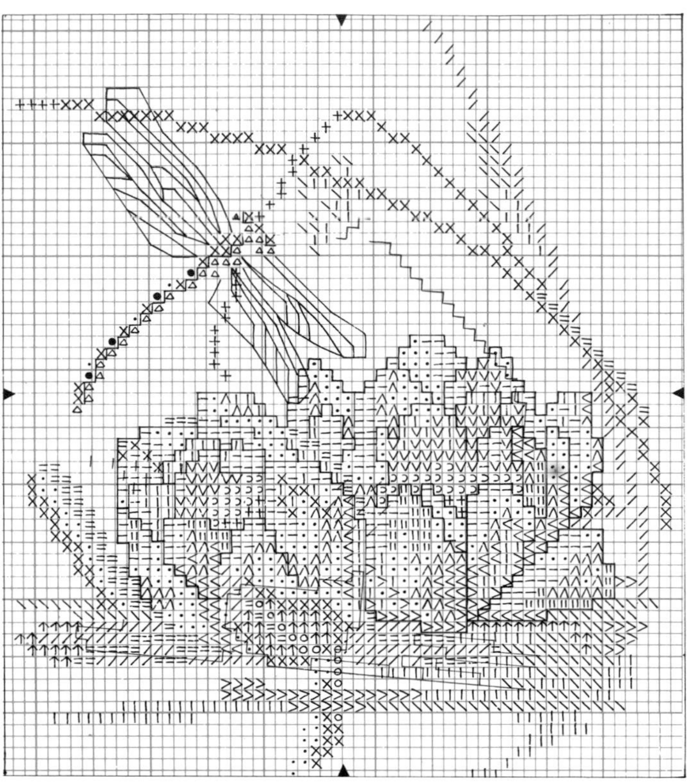

White Butterfly

Crochet Tablecloth

(Picture on page 65)

Measurements

97cm (38in) square

Materials

7 x 100g hanks No 2 crochet cotton
No 4 crochet hook

Gauge

Each square when edged measures 15cm x 15cm (6in x 6in)

White Butterfly
Crochet Tablecloth

Key
□ Space = 1 dc in dc, 2 ch, sk 2 sts
○ Block = 1 dc in dc, 2 dc in space or 1 dc in each of 3 dc

Abbreviations

beg – beginning; **ch** – chain; **cont** – continue; **dc** – double crochet; **lp** – loop; **pct** – picot; **rep** – repeat; **sc** – single crochet, **sk** – skip; **ss** – slip stitch; **st(s)** – stitch(es); **tog** – together
Note: work instructions in brackets the number of times given.

To Make

Butterfly Square (make 20)
Make 42 ch. **1st row:** 1 dc in 4th ch from hook, 1 dc in each of next 5 ch, (2 ch, sk 2 ch, 1 dc in next ch) 3 times, 1 dc in each of next 9 ch, (2 ch, sk 2 ch, 1 dc in next ch) 3 times, 1 dc in each of last 6 ch, 3 ch, turn. **Beg with 2nd row, cont from chart following key and reading even-numbered rows from left to right and odd-numbered rows from right to left.

Edging
Work 1 round of sc working 1 sc in each st along top and lower edges, 38 sc evenly along each side edge and at corners work 3 sc, ss in 1st sc. Fasten off leaving a length of yarn for sewing up.**

Floral Square (make 16)
Make 44 ch. **1st row:** 1 dc in 8th ch from hook, (2 ch, sk 2 ch, 1 dc in next ch) 3 times, 1 dc in each of next 3 ch, (2 ch, sk 2 ch, 1 dc in next ch) 5 times, 1 dc in each of next 3 ch, (2 ch, sk 2 ch, 1 dc in next ch) twice, 5 ch, turn. Complete as butterfly square from ** to **.

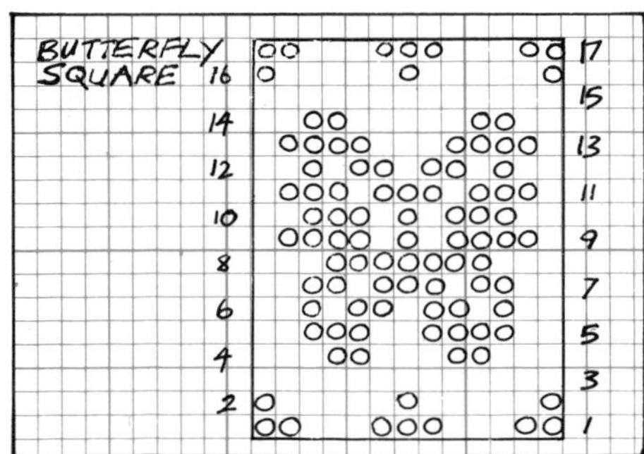

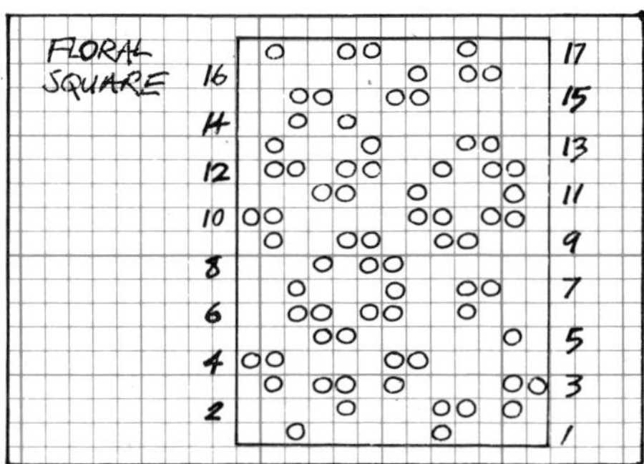

To Finish
Sew squares tog as shown on layout diagram.

White Butterfly
Layout of Squares

F	B	B	B	B	F
B	F	F	F	F	B
B	F	B	B	F	B
B	F	B	B	F	B
B	F	F	F	F	B
F	B	B	B	B	F

Key
B-Butterfly square
F-Floral square

Edging
1st round: join yarn to any corner, 2 sc in same place as join, 1 sc in each sc working 3 sc in each corner and ending with 1 sc in same place as first 2 sc, ss to 1st sc. **2nd round:** 1 sc in first sc, *5 ch, sk 2 sc, 1 sc in next sc; rep from * to end, ending 5 ch, ss to first sc. **3rd round:** ss in first lp, (3 sc, 3 ch, ss in last sc to form pct, 2 sc) in each lp, ss to first sc. Fasten off. Press over a damp cloth.

Pink Clover

Circular Tablecloth

Materials

Polyester/cotton sheeting is ideal for a floor-length cotton circular cloth as it is available 228cm (90in) wide in a variety of colors.

To Make

To make a paper pattern, join sheets of newspaper together to give the diameter required. Take a length of string and attach to a drawing pin at one end; tie a pencil to the other end so that the string is the radius of the cloth plus 2cm (¾in) for hem allowance. Place the pin in the center of the paper and draw the circle. Cut out the fabric using the paper pattern and machine-stitch hem to complete.

Tassels of Blossom *Lampshade*

Materials

Lampshade frame, 18cm (7in) high, divided into 8 sections
Spool of 1cm (⅜in) wide white cotton tape
70cm (¾yd) of 115cm (45in) wide plain cotton fabric for lining
Pins
70cm (¾yd) of 122cm (48in) wide patterned fabric for covering shade
Matching thread
2m (2¼yd) braid, 1cm (⅜in) wide
1m (1⅛yd) fringe to match braid, 2cm (¾in) wide
Fabric adhesive

To Make

1 Bind the lampshade frame. Cover each strut first. Cut a length of cotton tape about 1½ times the strut length. At the top of the first strut, tuck the tape end over the top ring and round the top of the strut. Wind the tape round the strut over the tape end, to hold it in place. Continue to wind the tape round the strut at an angle, slightly overlapping each previous layer of tape. At the bottom ring wind the tape over the bottom ring and through the back of the previous layer forming a knot on the inside of the frame. Pull tightly and trim off.

2 Bind each lampshade strut in the same way.

3 Bind the lampshade rings in the same way. Cut a length of cotton tape about twice the length of the ring. Begin at the first strut tucking the end of the tape under the working tape as before. Work round the ring at an angle, slightly overlapping previous layer of tape. At each strut end work over the end in a figure 8, covering the tape ends (at the base) to form a neat finish. Fasten off the tape at a strut into a knot, at the back, as before. If the result is too bulky, trim off the tape on the inside and turn under the tape end. Stitch to the previous tape using small stitches.

4 If the lampshade frame is very shaped, each section will have to be covered individually, firstly by the lining and then by the main fabric. In both cases the fabric will have to be cut on the bias of the fabric to provide enough 'give' to stretch tightly over the shape.

5 Begin with the lining. Cut a piece of lining on the bias of the fabric about 5cm (2in) larger than the section to be covered. Fold in half lengthwise to find the center and pin over the section, matching centers of fabric to centers of frame section at top and bottom. Continue pinning lining to taped frame, working out from the center points. Place pins inwards towards the center of the section.

6 When the lining is taut, stitch to the tape-covered struts and rings. Use a double thread and stitch down each side first, working small slanting stitches centrally over strut. Stitch lining to top and bottom rings. Make sure that the lining stays taut. Trim off excess lining down each side strut close to the stitches. At top and base leave the excess lining in place.

7 Repeat, lining each lampshade section in the same way. The lining sections will overlap at each strut.

8 Cut out and stitch the main fabric sections in place in exactly the same way as the lining, but trimming top and bottom edges close to the stitching in the same way as the sides. Center the main design of the fabric in each section.

9 Turn the excess lining over the fabric edges at top and stitch in place to the front of the top ring. Repeat at the bottom. In both cases trim the excess lining close to this stitching.

10 Stick a length of braid over each strut, covering the stitching and fabric edge. Trim braid level with top and bottom rings.

11 Stick braid round the top ring, keeping the braid level and covering the stitches and raw ends of braid. Begin and end at one side strut, turning under raw edges to neaten.

12 Stick fringe round bottom edge of the shade in the same way, beginning and ending at the same strut as the top braid. If the fringe is bulky, turn under the edges where they meet and stitch neatly together with matching thread, using small stitches. Fasten off.

CRAB-APPLE

WILLOW WARBLER

Ribbon Weaving in Miniature

Narrow ribbons can be woven in the same way as for cushions, but the result is a much smaller weave. The pincushion, pictured below, is woven from 3mm (1/8in) wide ribbons, but 7mm (1/4in) wide ribbons would produce an equally delicate effect. The techniques involved in miniature weaving are almost the same as for those used in the 'Icicles' cushion, pictured on page 18, *except that a large-eyed needle is used.* Since work is being carried out on such a small scale, a cushion can be used for a pad instead of an ironing board.

Besides sachets and pincushions, miniature weaving can be used to make decorative panels for children's clothes or for fashion garments. It also makes pretty 'soft' jewellery, hairbands, belts and bags. Worked in grosgrain ribbons, miniature weaving can be used to make book covers.

True Love

Woven Ribbon Pincushion or Lavender Sachet

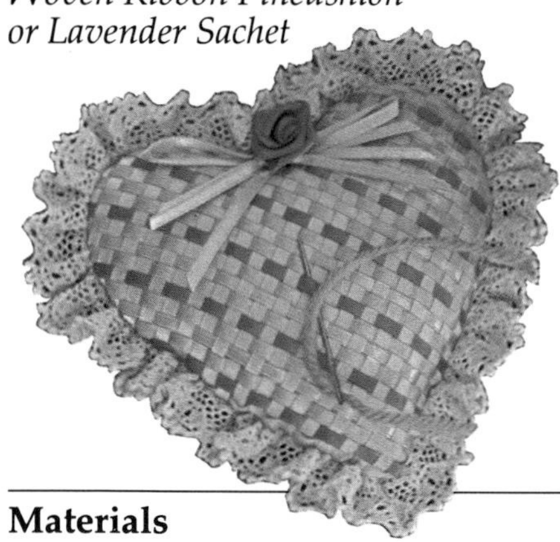

Materials

For the ribbon weaving:
3mm (1/8in) width double face Offray satin ribbon in the following colors:
Hot Pink (Code 156) – 1.85m (2yd)
Mint (Code 530) – 1.85m (2yd)
Pink (Code 150) – 3.9m (4 1/4yd)
Cream (Code 815) – 4.6m (5yd)
18cm (7in) square iron-on interfacing
Glass-headed pins
Hard board or ironing board or cushion
Tapestry needle No 6

For making up pincushion:
13cm (5in) square cream satin fabric
Matching sewing thread
13mm (1/2in) squared paper for pattern
70cm (3/4yd) 2.5cm (1in) width cream lace
Polyester batting or lavender
Offray satin ribbon: Hot Pink (Code 156) – 25cm (10in) 9mm (3/8in) width single satin. Mint (Code 530) – 51cm (20in) 3mm (1/8in) width double face satin.

To Make

WOVEN RIBBON FABRIC

1 Cut 3mm (1/8in) width weaving ribbons into 18cm (7in) lengths. Pin 18cm (7in) square iron-on interfacing onto a firm board or ironing board, with the adhesive side upwards.

2 Pin the warp ribbons (they will run from top to bottom of the weave) into place on the interfacing first by:

3 Starting at the top right hand corner of the interfacing and 2.5cm (1in) in from the right side, pin vertical lines of ribbons, edge to edge, in the following sequence: *hot pink/pink/mint/pink**. Repeat * to ** until 33 ribbons have been placed, ending with last ribbon on left hand side in hot pink. One end of the ribbons should be along the top edge of the interfacing, with the pins inserted along this edge.

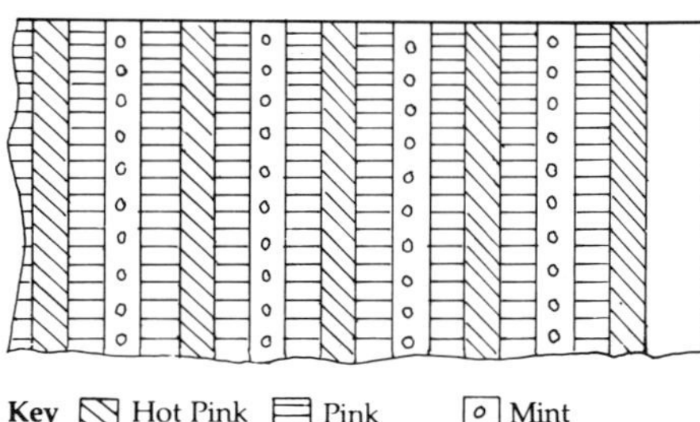

Key Hot Pink Pink Mint

4 Thread a length of the cream ribbon through the needle and weave cream ribbons (these are the weft ribbons) in and out of the warp ribbons, starting from the top right hand corner as follows:
1st row: *over 1, under 1**. Repeat * to ** to end. Pin both ends of ribbon in place.
2nd row: weave * under 1, over 1**. Repeat * to ** to end. Push ribbon up and under row (1), so that ribbon edges touch using the points of scissors. Pin ribbon ends in place. Cut off any excess ribbon.

5 Repeat these 2 rows until 13cm (5in) square of weaving is obtained, keeping the weft ribbons straight. Approximately 25 rows of cream ribbon should produce the correct size.

6 Lightly iron ribbons to hold in place. Remove pins. Turn weaving over and press back of interfacing with a damp cloth, following manufacturer's instructions. Leave to cool. The piece of ribbon weave can now be used as a piece of fabric.

Pincushion

1 Make paper pattern of heart shape, marking in grain line, seam and cutting lines. Cut out paper pattern on cutting line. Diagram A. Pin paper heart onto ribbon weaving, placing grain line of pattern on diagonal line across weaving as shown. Diagram B.

Diagram A

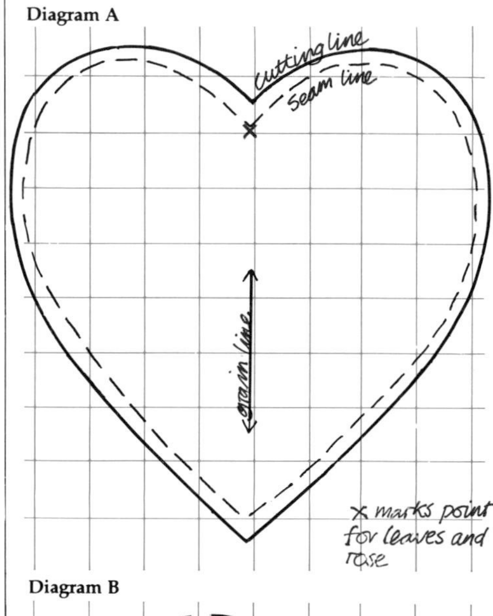

Diagram B

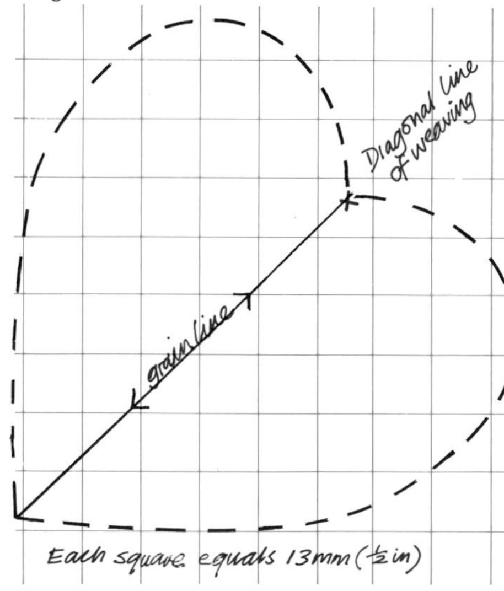

2 Trace the outline. This will be the cutting line. Run a line of small, straight machine stitches just inside the cutting line to hold the weaving in place. Cut out.

3 To make frill: join short edges of lace. Run two lines of gathering stitches along the raw edge. Pull up gathers to fit outside edge of woven ribbon heart. On the right side of the woven heart, pin gathered lace, evening out the gathers and matching baste on stitching (seam) line.

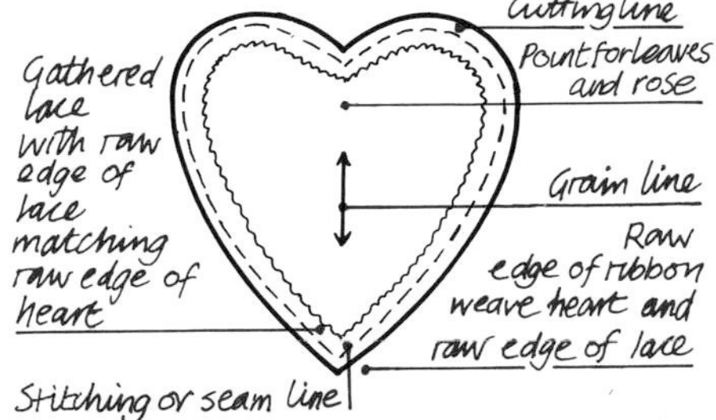

4 Place paper pattern on cream satin material, working on the straight grain of the material. Cut out. Pin right side satin heart to right side weaving/lace. Machine stitch round on seam line, leaving an opening for turning. Turn heart through to right side. Fill with polyester batting or lavender. Slip stitch opening to close.

5 To make leaves: cut 51cm (20in) mint ribbon into 3. Fold 1 length and stitch together as shown below.

Fold 2 lengths in half and baste together at center as shown.

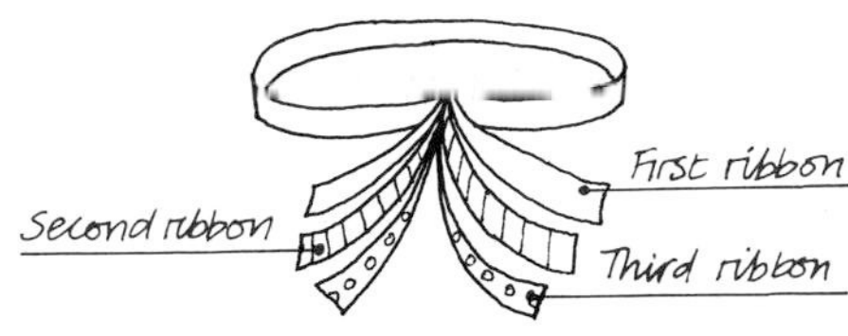

Place into position X on heart and stitch.

6 To make rose: using 9mm (3/8in) width hot pink ribbon and working from left hand side, roll end of ribbon about 6 turns to make a tight tube. Sew a few stitches at the base of the tube to hold it in place.

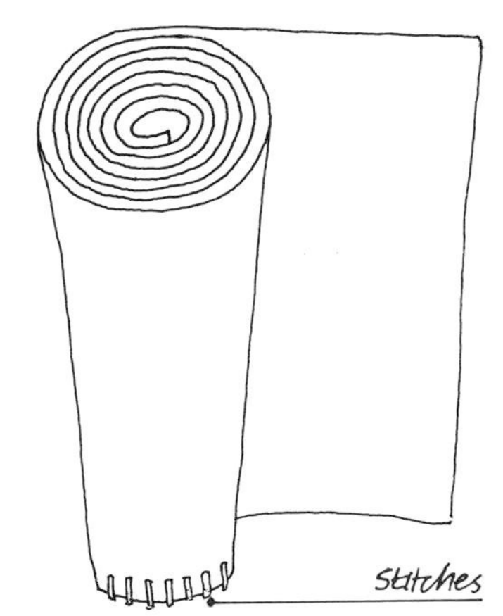

Fold top edge of ribbon behind and down (A) so that it is parallel to tube and at an angle of 45°.

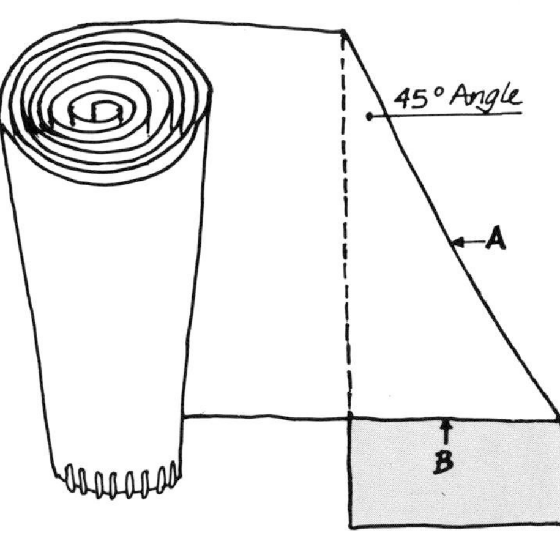

Using basted base as pivot, wind folded ribbon round tube to make cone (B). Sew in place. *Ribbon should be tight at the bottom and loose at the top.*

7 Repeat A and B for several turns, sewing in place as you go. Cut and turn under raw edge. Finish off with a few small stitches.

8 Sew rose into position over 'mint leaves'. Arrange petals on rose and trim 'leaves' to required length.

Crab-apple *Needlepoint Workbox*

Measurements

Needlepoint (approx) 28cm (11in) square

Materials

40cm (15¾in) of 58cm (23in) wide Number 10 Penelope canvas (double-sided)
Anchor Tapestry Wool in 10m (11yd) skeins: 10 skeins 0386; 1 skein each of 0402; 0366; 023; 0403; 037; 0401; 0398; 3232; 0630; 0985; 0242; 0257; 0313; 0500; 0311; 3370; 095; 0419; 3064; 0654; 0202; 0837; 0983; 0388; 3276; 0745; 0497; 3234; 3097; 024
Tapestry needle
Workbox kit

To Make

Important Note: read 'General Working Instructions for all Needlepoint' on page 15.

1 Fold canvas lightly in both directions (widthwise and lengthwise) to form center lines. Work basting stitches along center lines.

2 Center of chart is indicated by arrows which should coincide with basting stitches.

3 Work needlepoint following chart and key, working as far as possible out from center. Each square on chart represents 1 square of double thread canvas, or 1 tapestry stitch.

4 Complete background in 0386 and work backstitch details as given on chart.

5 Trim surplus canvas to within 3cm (1¼in) of stitching. Remove basting threads.

6 Mount needlepoint following instructions with workbox.

7 Model worked in traméed half cross stitch.

Crab-apple
Needlepoint Workbox

Key

•	0402
=	0366
→	023
●	0403
┐	037
L	0401
U	0398
O	3232
⊥	0630
—	0985
Λ	0242
Z	0257
↑	0313
И	0500
H	0311
⊢	3370
\	095
Δ	0419
X	3064
/	0654
+	0202
>	0837
∩	0983
V	0388
T	3276
ll	0745
<	0497
↓	3234
←	3097
|	024

Shade numbers refer to Anchor Tapestry wool.

Special instructions

back stitch details:	
bird underside	*0497*
head	*0398*
legs, feet, tail	*0419*
flowers and stems (in red)	*024*
(in black)	*037*
leaf 1	*0654*
leaf 2	*0257*
flower centers	*0500*
lettering	*0419*

Design: 98 stitches wide
93 stitches long
Approx. design sizes:
10 stitches to 2.5cm (1in):
25.5cm x 24cm (10in x 9½in)

Willow Warbler

Needlepoint Firescreen

Measurements

Area of needlepoint 38cm x 45cm (15in x 17¾in)

Materials

60cm (23½in) of 58cm (23in) wide No 10 Penelope canvas (double-threaded)
Anchor Tapestry Wool in 10m (11yd) skeins: 12 skeins of 0386; 8 skeins of 0242; 1 skein each of 0215; 0402; 0896; 0403; 037; 0216; 0240; 0638; 0647; 0278; 0401; 0424; 0398; 0397; 0735; 0734; 0306; 0305; 067; 0501; 023; 0986; 0985; 0714; 0713; 3209; 024; 0837; 3202; 0217
Tapestry needle
Firescreen kit

To Make

Important Note: read 'General Working Instructions for all Needlepoint' on page 15.

1 Fold canvas in both directions (widthwise and lengthwise) to form center lines. Work basting stitches along center lines.

2 Mark outer edges of finished needlepoint with basting stitches. This must be calculated carefully on multiples of 3 double threads in all directions, beginning at center.

3 Work needlepoint following chart and key, working out from center as far as possible. Complete background using 0386. Leave 12 double threads inside outer edge markings. Work backstitch details as given on chart.

4 Using 0242 work border of 4 rows of diagonal satin stitch blocks around all 4 sides of needlepoint design. See below.

5 Remove basting threads.

6 Mount needlepoint following instructions included with firescreen (mounting and framing instructions on page 62).

7 Model worked in traméed half cross stitch.

Willow Warbler
Needlepoint Firescreen
and
The Country Diary
Embroidered Album Cover

Design 112 x 140 stitches

Design size (approx.)
14 stitches to 2.5cm (1in):
20cm x 25cm (8in x 10in)
10 stitches to 2.5cm (1in):
28cm x 35.5cm (11in x 14in)

Needlepoint Firescreen
Special instructions

Outline:	
Birds – top	*0638*
breast	*0398*
feet	*0501*
eye	*0403*
highlight in eye	white
lettering	*0985*
Backstitch: half strand of wool	
stems	*0714*
grass (shown in black)	*0242*
grass (shown in red)	*0215*
butterflies	*0401*
beaks	*0734*
worm	*0985*
mother bird's wing, long stitch	*0424*

Embroidered Album Cover
Special instructions

Outline:	
Birds – top	*0888*
breast	*8581*
feet	*0309*
eye	black
highlight in eye	white
Backstitch: stems	*0379*
grass (shown in black)	*0214*
(shown in red)	*0215*
butterflies	*0400*
beaks	*0890*
worm	*0380*
mother bird's wing	*0905*

Key

	Tapestry Wool	*Embroidery Floss*
V	0215	0215
•	0402	white
←	0896	042
●	0403	black
Z	037	041
\	0216	0216
ll	0240	0213
+	0638	0888
Λ	0647	0906
T	0278	0889
S	0401	0400
H	0424	0905
>	0398	8581
	0397	0900
I	0735	0293
→	0734	0890
N	0306	0301
<	0305	0300
–	067	025
Δ	0217	0261
O	023	024
U	0986	0381
⊥	0985	0380
/	0714	0379
↑	0713	0378
–	3209	0376
l	024	027
∩	0837	0847
C	3202	0847
X	0242	0214

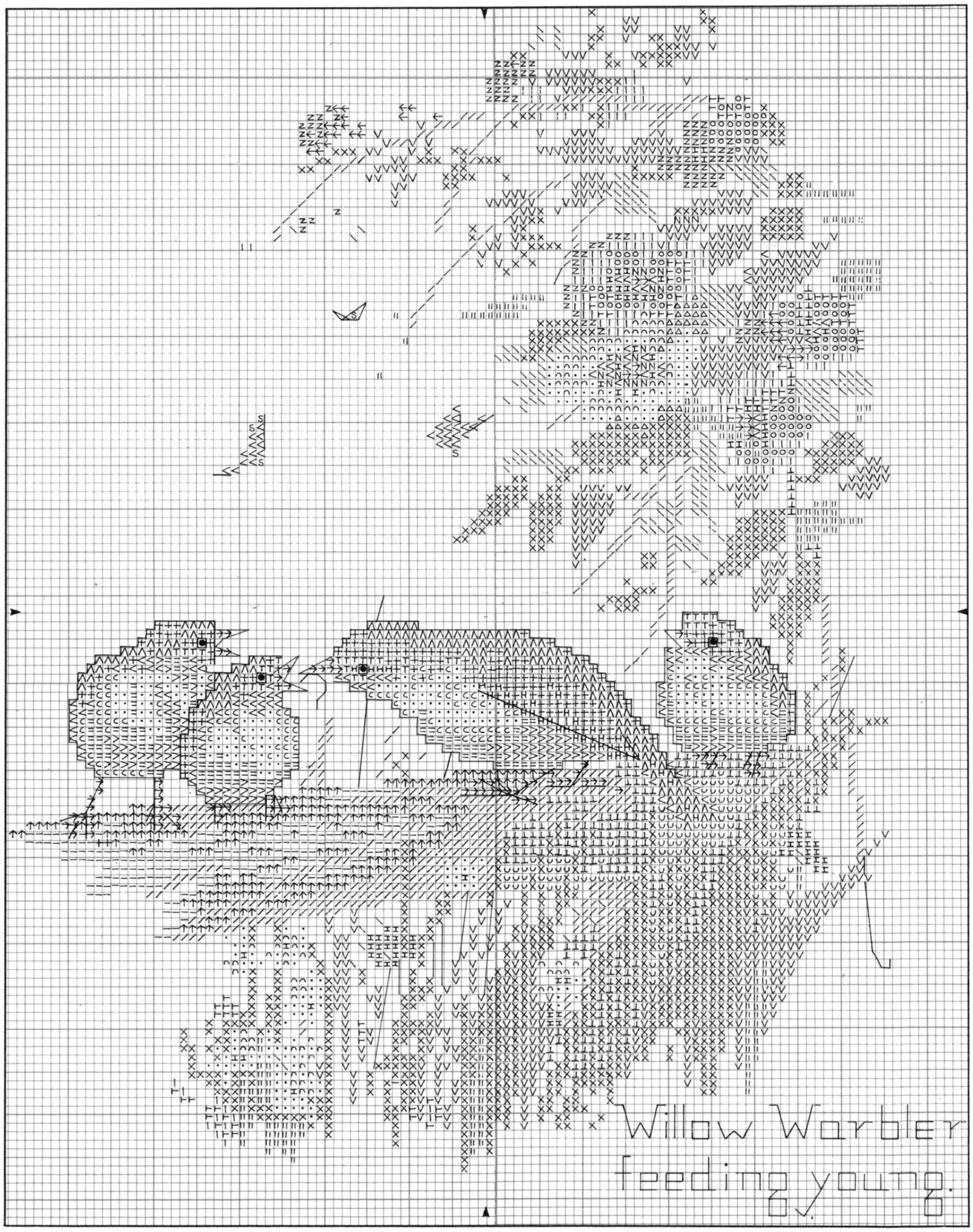

Willow Warbler
feeding young.

JUNE

"Mist in May and heat in June
Bring all things into tune."

THE COUNTRY DIARY

The Country Diary *Embroidered Album Cover*

Measurements

Embroidery design 20cm x 25cm (8in x 10in)
Finished album 28cm (11in) wide: 30cm (12in) long: 5cm (2in) deep.

Materials

80cm x 50cm (31½in x 19¾in) of even-weave linen with 28 threads to 2.5cm (1in)
Anchor Embroidery Floss: 2 skeins each of White; Black; 042; 0215; 041; 0216; 0214; 0213; 0888; 0906; 0889; 0400; 0905; 8581; 0900; 0293; 0890; 0301; 0300; 025; 0309; 024; 0381; 0380; 0379; 0378; 0376; 027; 0847; 0261
Tapestry needle No 24
Photograph album approximately 28cm (11in) wide: 30cm (12in) long: 5cm (2in) deep

To Make

Important Note: read 'General Working Instructions for all Cross Stitch Embroideries' on page 16.

1 With one long edge facing, fold linen in half to mark horizontal center line.

2 Mark second center line for design, approximately 22cm (8¾in) in from short edge of linen at right hand side. Baste center lines. Center of chart is indicated by arrows which should coincide with basting stitches.

3 Using 2 strands of floss throughout, work cross stitch design following chart and key for 'The Country Diary' design on page 75. Each square on chart represents 2 double threads of linen (2 warp and 2 weft threads), or 1 cross stitch.

4 Lettering is optional.

5 Remove basting threads.

Note: chart for 'The Country Diary' Embroidered Album Cover is exactly the same as chart for 'Willow Warbler' Firescreen. Details of key lie next to those for needlepoint design.

Covering An Album

Choose a photo album with paper pages rather than the plastic-covered type, or choose a diary, a drawing book or an address book. Many of these ready-made books will have slightly padded covers, which look good when covered with embroidery. If you are starting with a flat backed book, such as a drawing book, then line your needlework with a thin piece of polyester batting before covering the book.

Materials

Worked embroidery. Backing fabric to match color of embroidery fabric. Strong paper to line the inside covers. Choose a color to blend with the embroidery, at least as thick as cartridge paper. Fabric adhesive, white glue, masking tape, braid trim. Optional – Photo Mount adhesive for sticking paper inside cover.

To Make

1 Carefully remove the cover from the book. Remove any small traces of adhering paper from the inside and the edges of the paper spine.

2 Lay out the needlework, wrong side up and place backing fabric over. Lay open book cover on top, and fold fabric over. Adjust position of fabric so that embroidered design is well sited, and draw round edge of book onto backing fabric to mark chosen position. Cut out the fabric, leaving 4cm (1½in) all round for turnings. Clip across corners. Use a little fabric adhesive to hold the two layers of fabric together around the edges. (A)

3 Lay the book cover in position on the fabric, and smear a line of fabric adhesive on the inside edges of the book cover, and fold the fabric over. Take care with the corners, and make them as neat and flat as possible. (B)

4 Neaten the raw edges of the fabric by covering them with strips of masking tape. Fold the cover closed, and position braid along the groove made where the front cover meets the softer material of the spine. Stretch the braid over slightly, and glue in place. Repeat with back cover. (C)

5 Measure the exact size of the inside page and double the measurement (length and width). Carefully measure and cut two sheets of paper to this size, one for the front inside cover, and one for the back. Fold each sheet of paper crisply down the spine fold line. Check that the paper fits, and coat one side of one piece with white glue or Photo Mount. (D)

6 Lay the paper in place, smoothing and pressing firmly. Run a line of white glue down the inside edge of the first page, and press the lining paper firmly to this, so that the two sheets of paper hold the book together. Repeat with the back cover and back page. (E)

7 Finally, press the book closed firmly, until the adhesives are completely dry.

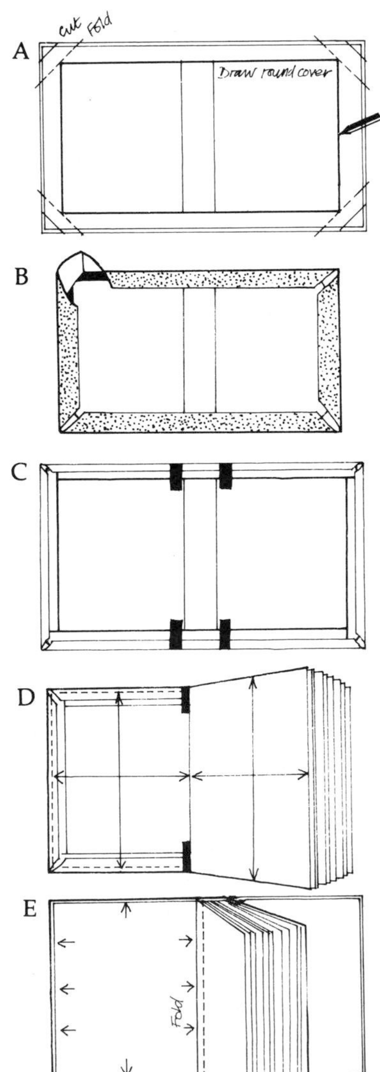

CLOVER FIELDS AND GRASS MEADOWS

Daisy *Embroidered Tablecloth with Crochet Edging*

Measurements

Tablecloth 120cm (47¼in) diameter, excluding crochet edging
Embroidered design 15cm x 17.5cm (6in x 7in)

Materials

1.3m (51in) of 130cm (51in) wide even-weave linen with 28 threads to 2.5cm (1in)
Anchor Embroidery Floss: 1 skein each of White; Black; 0387; 0895; 0894; 0970; 0969; 0215; 0214; 0213; 0400; 0397; 0265; 0391; 8581; 0303; 0301; 0300; 9575; 0968; 0256; 0860; 0847; 0264; 075; 068; 066
Tapestry needle No 24

To Make

Important Note: read 'General Working Instructions for all Cross Stitch Embroideries' on page 16.

1 Diagram. Fold fabric in half in both directions (widthwise and lengthwise) and crease lightly. These lines will form vertical center lines of designs. Mark 4 horizontal center lines at right angles to vertical lines at points approximately 27cm (10½in) from center of fabric. Baste along all center lines.

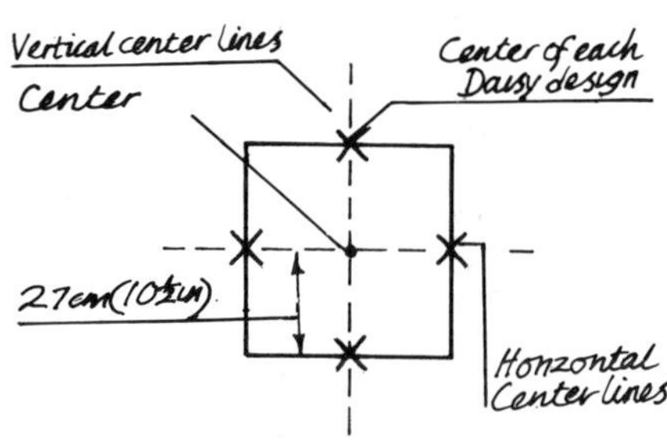

2 Using 2 strands of cotton throughout, work embroidery following chart and key for 'Daisy' design, working as far as possible out from center. Work 4 cross stitch designs centerd at points X on diagram.

3 Each square on chart represents 2 double threads of linen (2 warp and 2 weft threads or 1 cross stitch).

4 Remove basting threads.

CROCHET EDGING

Measurements

Length 416cm (169in)

Materials

10 balls of 3 ply yarn
No 4 crochet hook
Important Note: (1 ball will make 5 repeats of pattern including edging and flowers)

Gauge

10 pattern rows to 8cm (3¼in)

Abbreviations

beg – beginning; **ch** – chain; **cont** – continue; **dc** – double crochet; **hdc** – half double crochet; **pct** – picot; **prev** – previous; **r** – ring; **rep** – repeat; **sc** – single crochet; **sk** – skip; **sp(s)** – space(s); **ss** – slip stitch; **st(s)** – stitch(es)

To Make

Make 29 ch. **1st row:** 1 dc into 4th ch from hook, *** 3 ch, sk 4 ch ***, ** into next ch work 2 dc/1 ch/2 dc **, * 5 ch, sk 6 ch *, into next ch work 1 sc/3 ch/1 sc, rep from * to *, ** to ** and *** to ***, 1 dc into each of next 2 ch, turn. **2nd row:** *** 3 ch, sk 1st dc, 1 dc into next dc, 3 ch, sk 3 ch sp ***, ** into next 1 ch sp work 2 dc/1 ch/2 dc, 3 ch **, * into center ch of next 5 ch sp work 1 sc/3 ch/1 sc*, 5 ch, rep from * to *, 3 ch, rep from ** to **, 1 dc into each of last 2 sts, working last dc into top of 3 ch, turn. **3rd row:** rep from *** to *** of prev row, into next ch sp work 2 dc/1 ch/2 dc, 5 ch, rep from * to * of prev row, 5 ch, rep from ** to ** of prev row, 1 dc into each of last 2 sts, turn. **4th row:** rep 2nd row. **5th row:** rep 3rd row, ending with 6 ch, turn. **6th row:** rep 2nd row, beg with 2 dc instead of 3 ch and 1 dc. **7th row:** rep 3rd row, cont with 13 dc into 6 ch sp, ss into adjacent dc, ss up 3 ch of prev row, turn work back to front. **8th row:** 1 pct, (make 3 ch, 1 sc into 1st of 3 ch), sk 1st of 13 dc, 1 dc into next dc, * 1 pct, sk next dc, 1 dc into next dc, rep from * 4 times, 1 pct, rep 2nd row to end, turn. **9th row:** rep 3rd row, cont working along half circle, * 3 ch; sk pct; 1 dc into next dc, rep from * 5 times, 3 ch, ss into base of 1st dc, ss up 3 ch of prev row, turn. **10th row:** cont working along half circle, * 1 pct, 1 dc into 3 ch sp, 1 pct, 1 dc into next dc, rep from * 5 times, 1 pct, 1 dc into last 3 ch sp, 1 pct, rep 2nd row to end, turn. Rep 2nd to 10th row 51 times more. Join end edges to form r.

Upper Edge
Rejoin yarn in seam st along straight edge with * 3 ch, 1 sc into 1st of 3 ch, 1 sc under dc bar of next row, rep from * to end, ss into 1st sc. Fasten off.

Flower Motif (make 52)
Make 6 ch, ss into 1st ch to form a r. **1st round:** 5 ch,* 1 sc into r, 3 ch, rep from * 4 times, ss through 2nd of 5 ch. **2nd round:** into each of next ch sps work 1 sc/1 hdc/3 dc/1 hdc/1 sc, ss into 1st sc. Fasten off. Attach flowers to center of half circle.

To Finish
1 (a) Press embroidered linen with damp pressing cloth and dry iron and lay out absolutely flat. (b) Using 61cm (24in) length of string tied to pencil, pin free end of string to center of linen and draw circle to form outer edge of linen cloth. Cut just inside pencil line. (c) To prevent fraying while finishing, zigzag-stitch raw edge of linen. (d) Press a 6mm (¼in) hem on right side of fabric using steam iron or dry iron and dampened pressing cloth. (e) Machine hem in place. (f) Press again, making sure hemmed edge lies absolutely flat.

2 (a) Lay tablecloth out flat. Pin inner edge of crochet on right side of tablecloth, overlapping edge of crochet on tablecloth by about 1cm (⅜in) so that it covers hem. (b) Position 13 motifs between each embroidered design and ease in fullness of edge of crochet. (c) Baste crochet in place. (d) Stitch both edges of crochet in place by hand or machine.

3 Remove basting threads and press finished tablecloth with damp pressing cloth and dry iron.

Daisy
Embroidered Tablecloth

Key
- X white
- • 0387
- ↓ 0895
- > 0894
- ● black
- ⊃ 0970
- Λ 0969
- V 0215
- \ 0214
- O 0213
- Δ 0400
- T 0397
- ↑ 0265
- + 0391
- U 0581
- → 0301
- ∩ 0300
- ⊥ 9575
- = 0968
- < 0256
- ‖ 0860
- — 0847
- / 0265
- | 075
- ← 068
- C 066

Shade numbers refer to Anchor Embroidery Floss.

Design 68 x 98 stitches

Design size (approx.)
14 stitches to 2.5cm (1in):
15cm x 17.5cm (6in x 7in)

Special instructions
Outline –
Butterflies – *0581*
Daisy centers – *9575*
Daisies – *0397*
Backstitch: Stems
1 *0860*
2 *0895*
3 *0214*
4 *0256*
5 *0969*
Small dots in daisy centers made with *0303* by bringing needle up through hole and going back down as close as possible.
Small dots in butterfly wing made similarly with black, also dots at antennae ends with *0581*.

Garden
Embroidered Teacosy

Measurements

Total size of embroidery 30cm x 36cm (12in x 14in)
Meadow Crane's-bill design 7cm x 10cm (2⅞in x 4in)
Willow Herb design 12cm (4¾in) square

Materials

The Embroidery
40cm (15¾in) of 45cm (17¾in) even-weave linen with 26 threads to 2.5cm (1in)
Anchor Embroidery Floss:
(a) For Meadow Crane's-bill design: 1 skein each 0895; 0894; 0893; 0101; 0102; 098; 0256; 0862; 0861; 0268; 0266; 0215
(b) For Willow Herb design: 1 skein each 042; 0265; 0253; 0301; 0300; 0258; 0257; 0266; 0265; 078; 069; 068
Tapestry needle No 24

The Teacosy
Embroidered linen: 36cm x 30cm (14in x 12in)
Backing floral fabric and iron-on interfacing, each 36cm x 30cm (14in x 12in)
72cm x 30cm (28½in x 12in) of plain cotton fabric for lining
72cm x 30cm (28½in x 12in) medium weight batting
Piping cord and 2.5cm (1in) wide bias binding
Matching thread

Garden
Embroidered Tea Cosy
A 'Meadow Crane's-bill'

Key	
△	0895
⫯	0894
ℓ	0893
O	0101
•	0102
X	098
+	0256
\	0862
—	0861
/	0268
V	0266
Λ	0215

Shade numbers refer to Anchor Embroidery Floss.

Design 39 x 55 stitches

Design size (approx.)
14 stitches to 2.5cm (1in):
7cm x 10cm (2⅞in x 4in)

Special instructions
Outline:
Flowers – *0102*
Leaves – *0268*

Backstitch
Petal lines *0895*
Buds (1) – *0256*
(shown in black)
(2) – *0895*
(shown in red)

A

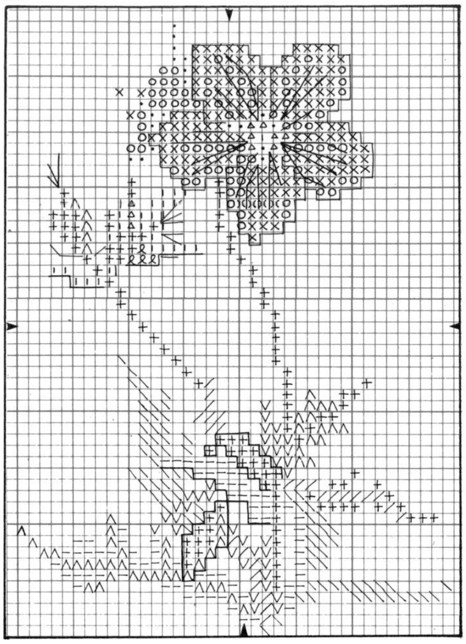

B

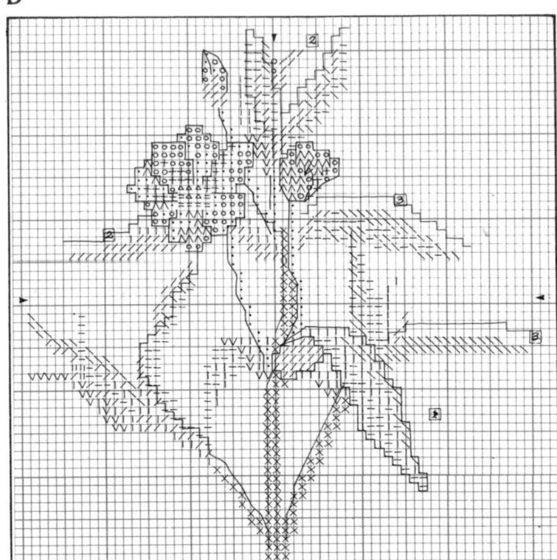

Willow Herb

Design 59 x 61 stitches

Design size (approx.)
14 stitches to 2.5cm (1in):
12cm (4¾in) square

Special instructions
Outline:
Flowers, bud and red stems – *069*
Leaves 1 *0258*
2 *0257*
3 *0266*
Green stems *0266*

Backstitch:
Flower center – *0301*
Work design in reverse if preferred

Key	
O	042
/	0265
—	0253
=	0301
△	0300
V	0258
I	0257
\	0266
X	0265
•	078
Λ	069
+	068

Shade numbers refer to Anchor Embroidery Floss.

To Make

THE EMBROIDERY

Important Note: read 'General Working Instructions for all Cross Stitch Embroideries' on page 16. Start by marking positions for motifs as follows:

1 (a) Fold linen in half in both directions (widthwise and lengthwise) to form center lines. (b) With 1 long edge facing, mark lines in top 2 corners 7cm (2¾in) above horizontal center line and 7cm (2¾in) either side of vertical center line. Baste along these lines to form center lines for Willow Herb design. (c) In lower section mark a line 7cm (2¾in) below horizontal center line and work a further 2 lines of basting stitches 10cm (4in) either side of vertical center line. The original vertical and the new horizontal lines form the center lines for the 3 Meadow Crane's-bill designs. (d) Work basting stitches along center lines for Meadow Crane's-bill designs. (e) Center of chart is indicated by arrows which should coincide with basting stitches.

2 Each square on chart represents 2 double threads of linen (2 warp and 2 weft threads), or 1 cross stitch. Using 2 strands of floss throughout, work cross stitch designs following charts and keys A and B (together with picture of teacosy on page 79), working as far as possible out from center. Remove basting stitches.

THE TEACOSY

1 Find center of embroidered fabric and mark. Measure width, passing through center mark. Measure height in same way, but allowing slightly more fabric above the embroidery than below it. Add 1.5cm (⅝in) seam allowance. Pin and baste outline of rectangular shape.

2 Make paper pattern by cutting paper to size of rectangle. Place small plate to one corner, with sides matching sides of paper. Mark curve formed across corner of paper. Fold paper in half widthways, cut along curved edge. Unfold pattern. Place pattern to embroidered fabric, matching base, side and top edges. Mark round curved top edges. Cut out, adding 1.5cm (⅝in) seam allowance beyond marked lines.

3 Cut piece of iron-on interfacing to finished size and press to wrong side of embroidered fabric inside marked line.

4 Using pattern, cut out 1 piece from backing fabric, 2 lining pieces and 2 pieces of batting, adding 1.5cm (⅝in) seam allowances round each piece.

5 Measure curved top edge of embroidered piece and cover piping cord with bias binding to same length plus 3cm (1¼in).

6 To make a tab, cut 8cm (3¼in) length of bias binding. Fold in half lengthwise. Pin, baste and stitch both ends.

7 (a) Find center top point of embroidered fabric and pin 1 short end of tab over this mark. (b) Machine stitch piping cord within center of bias binding. Pin and baste covered piping cord centrally round curved edge and over tab end. (c) Pin second short end of tab over top of piping. (d) Stitch piping in place. (e) Trim piping cord only to meet base of cosy.

8 With right sides facing, pin, baste and stitch round curved edge of backing fabric and embroidery.

9 Place batting and lining pieces together in pairs; pin and baste together. Put together with lining sides matching. Pin, baste and stitch together round curved edge, leaving opening in center top for turning. Trim.

10 Place lining and cosy pieces together with right sides facing. Pin, baste and stitch together along marked base line. Trim and turn to right side through opening in lining. Turn in opening edges and slip stitch together. Push lining up inside cosy to lie flat.

JULY

"Then came hot July, boyling like to fire,
That all his garments he had cast away:"

Purple Bells

BELL

Smocking

Smocking is an enjoyable craft and brings much satisfaction particularly when used to decorate a little girl's dress such as 'Purple Bells'. Use embroidery floss. The number of strands, used at one time, are optional and depend on the strength of the stitch and shade required.

Preparing the Fabric

Having decided the area of the fabric to be smocked, evenly space smocking dots on the wrong side of the fabric (use transfers, as specified in the little girl's dress instructions on page 88).

To gather the fabric in pleats, ready to work the smocked embroidery, thread a needle with a length of strong synthetic thread. The thread must be long enough to complete a row. Begin at the right hand side of the fabric, with the wrong side of the fabric facing. Knot the end of the thread and work a small back stitch at the first dot. Gather the fabric along the row of dots, making a small stitch at each dot. Leave the ends of thread loose.

When rows are stitched, pull up the gathering threads, in pairs, to the correct width and knot these ends together. Turn the fabric over to the right side to begin smocking. Do not remove the gathering threads until all the smocking is complete.

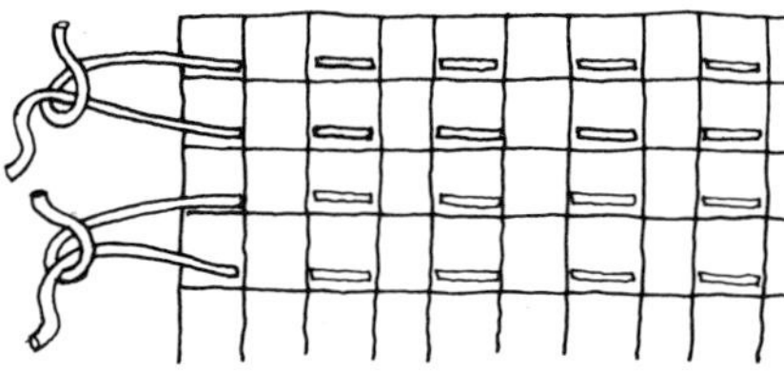

Working the Smocking

All the smocking stitches used on the child's dress and rag doll are worked from left to right across the fabric using the gathering thread lines as a guide. Each stitch is made through the fold of the pleat facing you and the needle is inserted through the fabric from right to left. Take care not to pull the thread up too tightly. Follow diagrams and instructions in conjunction with the picture of smocking on page 87.

Cable Stitch

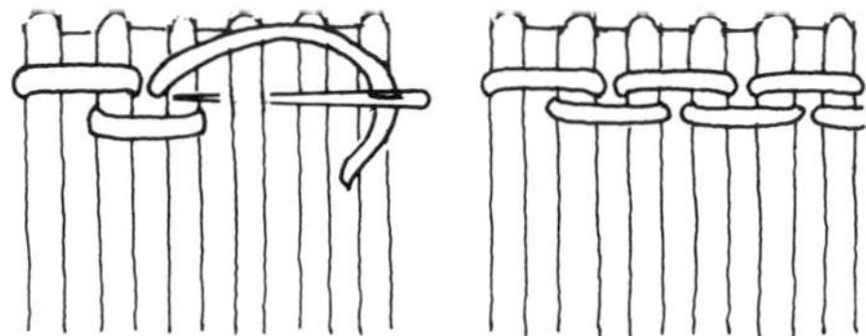

Bring the needle through from the wrong side at the left hand side of pleat 1. Keeping thread above needle, insert needle through pleat 2 from right to left. Pull up thread. Keeping thread below needle, insert needle through pleat 3 from right to left. Continue inserting needle through each pleat with the thread alternately above and below.

Double Cable Stitch

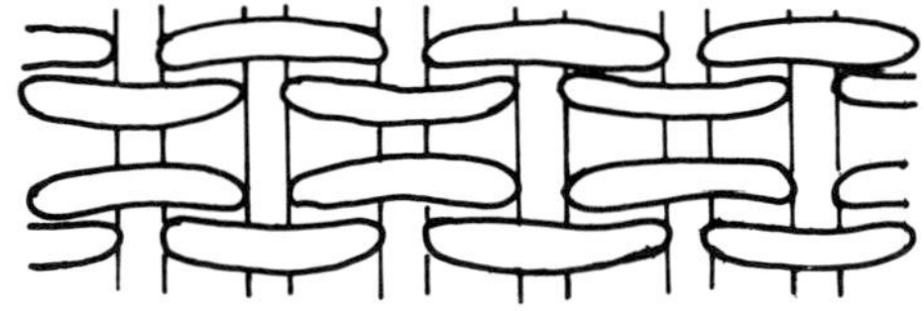

This is two rows of cable stitch worked closely together, one above the other, but where the thread was held above the needle in one row it should be held below the needle in the second row.

Stem Stitch

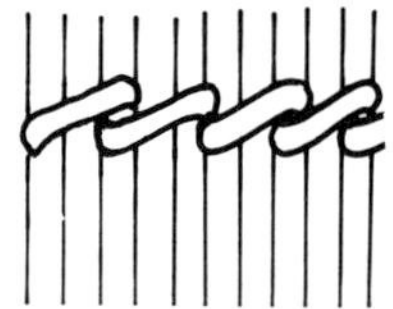

This is a version of cable stitch, but the thread is always held to the same side of the needle instead of above or below.

Trellis Stitch

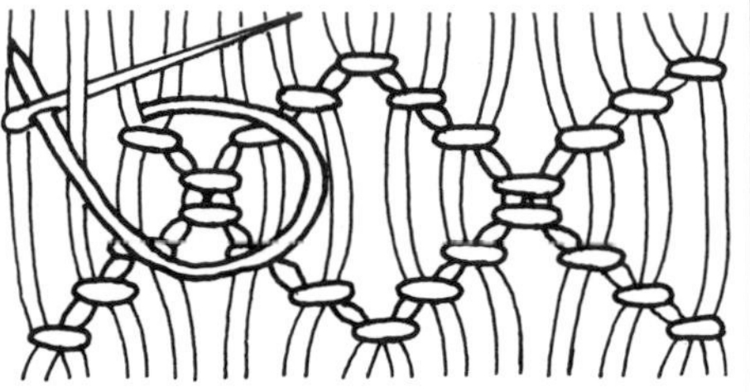

This is a version of stem stitch which travels up and down as it moves across the fabric. Starting at the upper level, work a few stitches each slightly lower than the previous one until the lower level is reached. Keep the thread above the needle. Now work the same number of stitches symmetrically until the upper level is reached again – keep the thread below the needle for these stitches. Continue working across the row in this way. When working the row below this one make sure that the upper points of the second row exactly meet the lower points of the first row to form diamond shapes.

Diamond Stitch

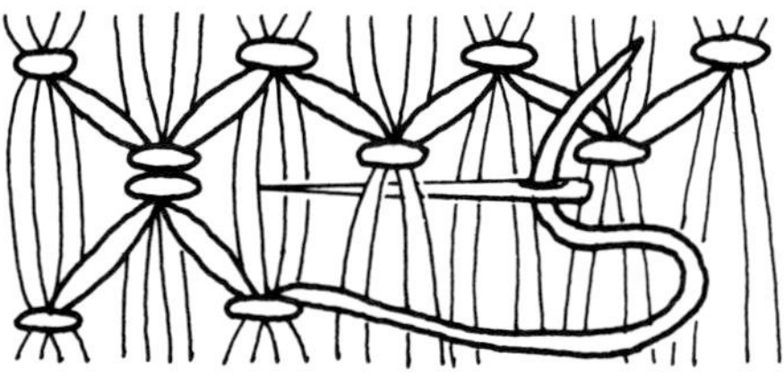

This is very similar to trellis stitch but only the points of each zigzag are worked. Start by bringing the needle from the wrong side to the left of the first pleat at the upper level. With thread above needle, take stitch through second pleat on same level. With thread above needle, take stitch through third pleat at lower level. With thread below needle, take stitch through fourth pleat at lower level. With thread below needle, take stitch through fifth pleat at upper level. Continue along row in this way. As with trellis stitch, make sure the upper points of the second row worked exactly match the lower points of the first row worked.

Purple Bells *Little Girl's Dress with Smocking*

Measurements

To fit chest 61cm (24in)
Nape to waist 28cm (11in)
Nape to hem 68.5cm (27in)
Note: 1.5cm (⅝in) seam allowance and 6cm (2⅜in) hem have been included

Materials

Tracing paper
2m (2¼yd) of 145cm (57in) wide floral fabric
10 rows of smocking dot transfer with dots 6mm (¼in) apart and rows 1.3cm (½in) apart
1 embroidery skein each of 4 different colors
Matching thread
Pins
35cm (13¾in) zipper
6mm (¼in) wide elastic for sleeves
Hook and eye

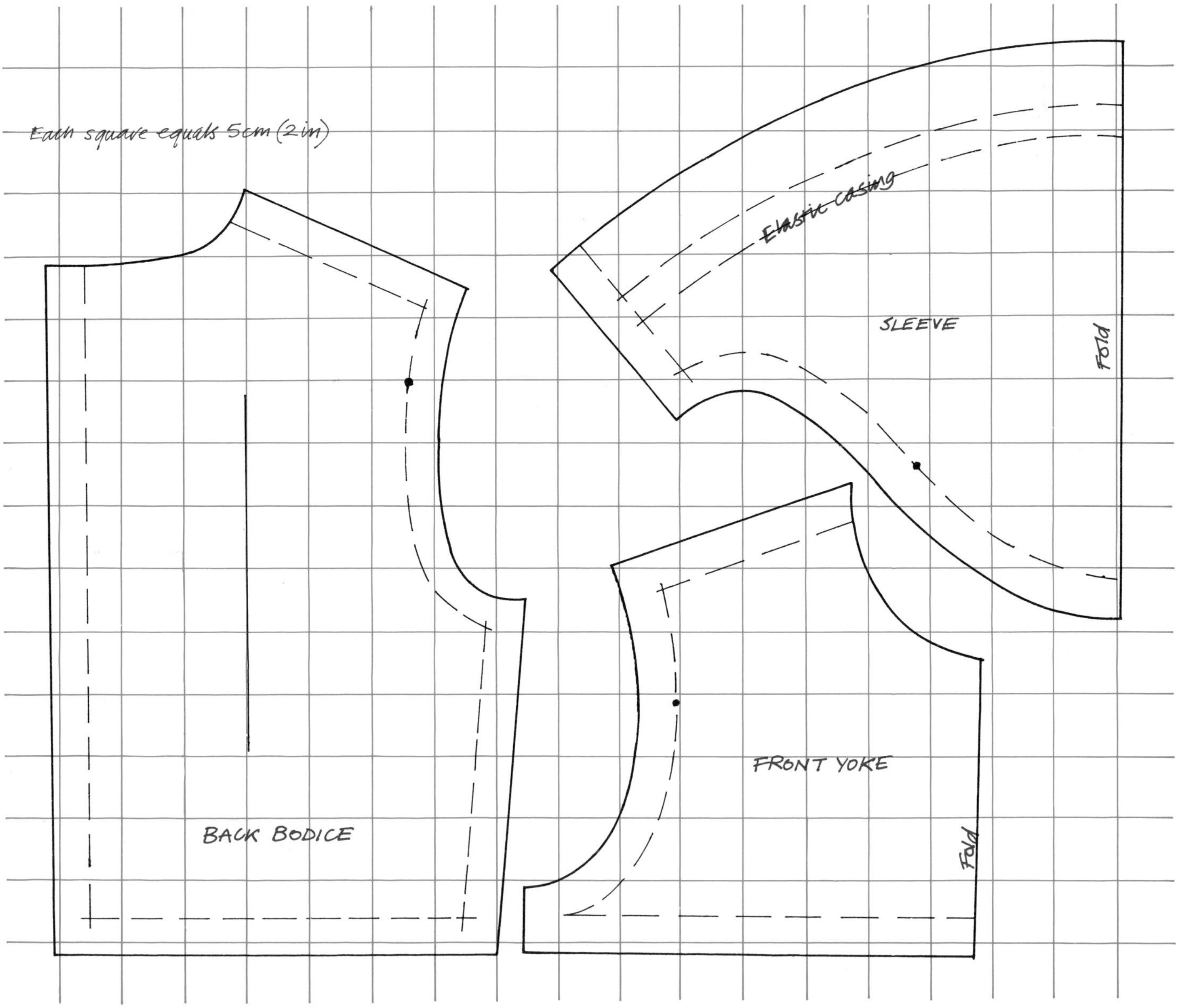

Each square equals 5cm (2in)

Elastic casing

SLEEVE

Fold

BACK BODICE

FRONT YOKE

Fold

To Make

1 Trace patterns for back bodice, front yoke and sleeve from the samples on page 85. Place center of sleeve and front yoke to fold of paper to gain complete pattern.

2 Cut out two back bodices, two sleeves and one front yoke. From remaining fabric cut out one front skirt 101.5 x 62cm (40 x 24½in), two back skirts, each 46 x 51cm (18 x 20in) and two ties each 68.5 x 12.5cm (27 x 5in).

3 Transfer smocking dots to wrong side of yoke front, 1.5cm (⅝in) from top edge.

4 Gather up smocking dots and then smock yoke with double cable, diamond and trellis stitches. Refer to page 86.

5 Place front yoke to front skirt with right sides together. Pin, baste and stitch together. Neaten seam.

6 Pin, baste and stitch center back seam of back skirt, leaving 10cm (4in) free at top of seam.

7 Work two rows of gathering stitches along top edge of each skirt back, on either side of seam line.

8 Place back skirts to back bodices with right sides together, pulling up gathers evenly to fit. Pin, baste and stitch together. Neaten seams.

9 Insert zipper into center back opening.

10 Place front yoke to back yoke with right sides together; pin, baste and stitch shoulder seams. Neaten seams.

11 Fold each tie in half with right sides together, pin, baste and stitch raw edges together, leaving one short straight edge open. Trim and turn to right side.

12 Turn a double 6mm (¼in) hem along the lower edge of each sleeve; pin, baste and stitch in place. Work two rows of gathering between marks round head of each sleeve.

13 From remaining fabric cut a 3cm (1¼in) wide bias strip for sleeve casing, following sleeve pattern for length. Turn in long raw edges for 6mm (¼in) and place to wrong side of sleeve over marked position. Pin, baste and stitch in place.

14 Measure child's arm and add 2.5cm (1in). Cut elastic to fit. Insert elastic into casing, holding both ends in place. Repeat for second sleeve.

15 Position sleeves into armholes with right sides together, pulling gathers evenly to fit. Pin, baste and stitch sleeve in place.

16 Make a small pleat in each raw end of tie and pin at waist seam of back.

17 Pin, baste and stitch side seams, catching in ties and continuing seam through sleeves, matching armhole center point.

18 From remaining fabric cut out a 5cm (2in) wide bias strip, long enough to go round neck edge. Place one long edge of strip to neck with right sides together. Pin, baste and stitch, taking 6mm (¼in) seam allowance. Turn bias strip over onto wrong side of neck edge. Turn under remaining long and short raw edges for 6mm (¼in) and hem in place. Add hook and eye to back neck.

19 Turn up hem edge; turn under raw edge of fabric. Pin, baste and hem in place.

Bell *The Rag Doll*

DOLL

Materials

1m (1⅛yd) of 90cm (36in) wide calico
Scrap of black felt
Matching thread
Polyester fiberfill
Blue, black, red and natural embroidery floss
6mm (¼in) wide fabric tape
50g of bulky wool, for hair
1cm (⅜in) wide Offray satin ribbon
Note: take 6mm (¼in) seam allowance throughout

To Make

1 Trace the patterns for the doll from the diagram marking features, darts etc.

2 From calico cut out two heads, two bodies, two pairs of legs, two pairs of arms. From black felt cut out four shoes and two soles. Transfer all pattern markings onto calico.

3 Pin, baste and stitch darts in head pieces.

4 Place each head to each body with right sides together; pin, baste and stitch together at neck seam.

5 Place arms together in pairs with right sides together; pin, baste and stitch all round, leaving top edge open. Snip into allowance at wrist and thumb and turn to right side. Fill hands lightly. Stitch along finger and thumb marks. Fill remainder of the arms to within 2.5cm (1in) of top edge.

6 With right sides facing, pin and baste the two body/head pieces together, leaving side openings for arms. Leave base edge open. Insert arms through side openings and pin and baste in place. Machine – sew following basting stitches. Turn through base. Fill head and body firmly until they are a good shape. Check neck, to prevent head from flopping over.

7 Place felt shoes over matching leg pieces and pin. Place legs in pairs with right sides together. Pin, baste and stitch front and back seams. Pin, baste and stitch felt soles onto the base of each leg. Clip curves and turn legs to the right side. Fill legs to within 2.5cm (1in) of top.

8 Position legs to front base edge of body, insuring that they are pointing in the correct direction. Stitch in place. Fill firmly. Turn in base edges of body and stitch together.

9 Embroider features, using blue satin stitch for eyes, straight black stitches for lashes, french knots for nose and red satin stitch for mouth.

10 Working with a double thread, stitch through arms and legs at marked positions to enable limbs to bend.

11 Cut a 19cm (7½in) length of 6mm (¼in) wide tape. Cut 61cm (24in) lengths of wool. Lay wool perpendicular to tape, matching centers to within 1.3cm (½in) of tape ends. Stitch in place through center of tape.

12 Turn under ends of tape and place centrally to head, with one end at mark on forehead. Catch to head through center parting. Bring hair down at each side to ear level and braid. Secure ends and trim. Turn ends of braid up under hair and catch in place at each side to form loops. Tie with ribbon bows.

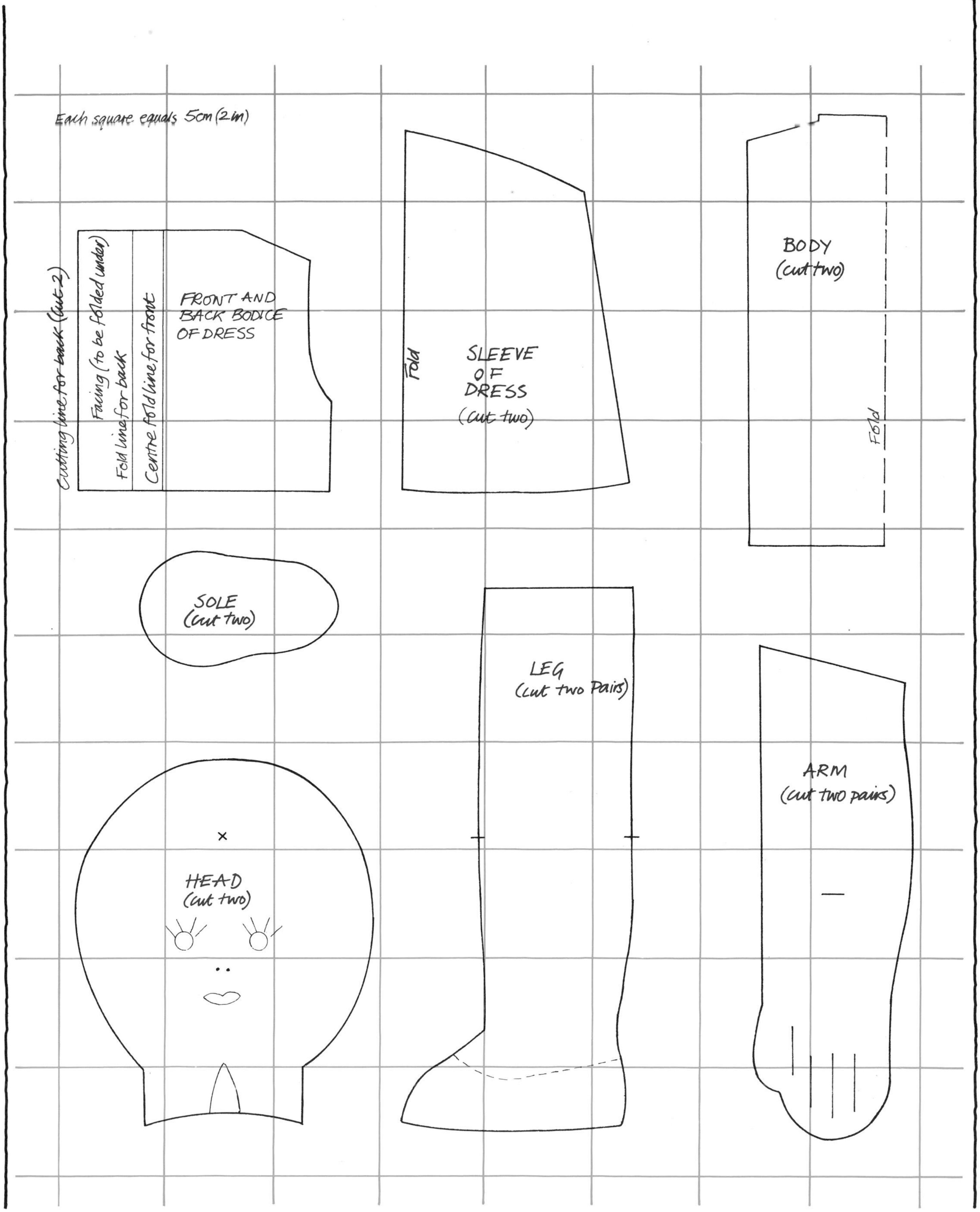

Each square equals 5cm (2in)
Cutting line for back (cut 2)
Facing (to be folded under)
Fold line for back
Centre fold line for front
FRONT AND BACK BODICE OF DRESS
Fold
SLEEVE OF DRESS
(cut two)
BODY
(cut two)
Fold
SOLE
(cut two)
LEG
(cut two Pairs)
ARM
(cut two pairs)
HEAD
(cut two)

Materials

5cm (2in) squared paper for pattern
1m (1⅛yd) of 115cm (45in) wide plain cotton fabric
Pins
Matching thread
3.2m (3⅝yd) of lace edging
Elastic
Five 8mm (⅜in) diameter buttons
50cm (⅝yd) of 145cm (57in) wide floral patterned fabric
50cm (20in) of 1cm (⅜in) wide Offray satin ribbon.
Scraps of embroidery cotton
Scrap of bias binding
Note: Take 6mm (¼in) seam allowance throughout

To Make

Pantaloons
1 From plain cotton fabric cut two pieces each 28cm (11in) by 18cm (7in).

2 Turn a narrow double hem to the right side on one short edge of each piece. Pin, baste and stitch in place. Pin, baste and stitch lace edging over hem.

3 Fold each piece in half vertically with right sides together; pin, baste and stitch from lace edging for 15cm (6in), leaving the remainder of the seam open.

4 With right sides facing, place the two pieces together. Pin, baste and stitch both seams.

5 Turn 1.5cm (⅝in) of fabric to the wrong side around waist edge. Turn under 6mm (¼in); pin, baste and stitch all round, leaving opening at one seam. Insert elastic, pull up to fit waist, overlapping ends for 2cm (¾in). Stitch together.

Petticoat
1 Trace off patterns for front and back bodice.

2 From plain cotton fabric cut out one front bodice and two back bodices. Cut out one piece for skirt 26cm (10¼in) by 64cm (25in).

3 Neaten edge of back facing on each back bodice. Turn in and press.

4 Turn under double 6mm (¼in) hems on neck edges of both front and back bodices. Pin, baste and stitch in place.

5 Place back and front bodices with right sides together; pin, baste and stitch shoulder seams.

6 Make narrow hems round armholes as for neck.

7 Pin, baste and stitch side seams.

8 Fold skirt in half with right sides together, matching raw edges. Pin, baste and stitch from hem edge for 18cm (7in), leaving remainder of the seam open. Turn a narrow double hem on either side of opening; pin, baste and stitch.

9 Make a narrow hem along bottom of skirt and add lace as for pantaloons.

10 Work two rows of gathering stitches round top of skirt on either side of seam line. Place skirt to bodice with right sides together, pulling up gathering stitches evenly to fit. Pin, baste and stitch together.

11 Fasten back opening with buttons and buttonholes.

Dress
1 Make patterns for front and back bodice and sleeve.

2 From patterned fabric cut out one front bodice and two back bodices. Cut out two sleeves, placing pattern to fabric fold. For skirt cut out one piece 20cm (8in) by 76cm (30in) and for frill one piece 9.5cm (3¾in) by 145cm (57in).

3 Place front and back bodices with right sides together; pin, baste and stitch shoulder seams.

4 Neaten edges and then fold in back facing on each back bodice and press.

5 From remaining fabric cut a piece 5cm (2in) by 16.5cm (6½in) for collar. Place one long edge along bodice neckline; pin, baste and stitch. Fold collar in half and stitch ends. Turn to right side, turn in remaining raw edges and hem in place to wrong side along previous seam line.

6 Turn under a narrow double hem along the bottom edge of each sleeve; pin, baste and stitch. Cut an 11.5cm (4½in) length of elastic; place on wrong side of sleeve 1.3cm (½in) up from neatened hem edge. Stitch in place. Repeat for second sleeve.

7 Work two rows of gathering stitches along top edge of each sleeve. Place sleeves to bodice with right sides together, pulling up gathers evenly to fit. Pin, baste and stitch sleeves to armholes.

8 Pin, baste and stitch side seams, continuing stitching down to hem edge of each sleeve.

9 Pin, baste and stitch frill pieces with right sides together to form a ring. Work two rows of gathering along top edge of frill. Turn a narrow double hem along the bottom edge of frill; pin, baste and stitch hem in place.

10 Fold skirt with right sides together; pin, baste and stitch center back seam, leaving 7.5cm (3in) open at top edge. Turn a narrow double hem on either side of opening; pin, baste and stitch.

11 Place frill to bottom edge of skirt, pulling up gathers evenly to fit. Pin, baste and stitch in place.

12 Stitch skirt to bodice, adding fastenings as for petticoat.

13 Make a ribbon sash and catch in place at each side seam.

Apron
1 From plain cotton fabric cut out one piece 76cm (30in) by 28cm (11in) for skirt, one piece 4cm (1½in) by 28cm (11in) for top band and two pieces each 4cm (1½in) by 16cm (6¼in) for straps.

2 Turn a narrow double hem down center back edges of skirt; pin, baste and stitch.

3 Smock a 2.5cm (1in) wide section across top of skirt working stem and trellis stitches as shown on page 86.

4 Turn in 6mm (¼in) on long edges of each strap then fold straps in half. Pin, baste and stitch folded edges together.

5 Place band with right side to skirt at top of smocking; pin, baste and stitch in place.

6 Pin raw ends of straps to band 1.5cm (⅝in) in from center back and center front. Turn in raw edges of band for 6mm (¼in) and stitch, catching in strap ends.

7 Make a hem along bottom edge of apron and add lace as for pantaloons.

8 Fold two 6mm (¼in) wide tucks across bottom edge of apron; pin, baste and stitch.

9 Fasten back with buttons and buttonloops.

Mob cap
1 From plain cotton fabric cut out one 30cm (12in) diameter circle.

2 Work a narrow double hem all round circle and add lace as for pantaloons.

3 Cut a length of bias binding to fit round circle, 4 cm (1½in) from hem edge. Place on wrong side; pin, baste and stitch in place, turning under raw short ends to meet together. Insert elastic and pull up to fit head; overlap ends of elastic and stitch together.

NODDING HEADS

FORGET-ME-NOT

The Secret of Patchwork

Patchwork can be applied to many different items including cushions, babies' quilt covers and teacosies. Small items like these can be fun and quick to do and are ideal for the beginner.

The choice of color and fabric play a vital role in creating a successful design. A selection of light and dark, patterned and plain fabrics, which tone well together, can be used in one of a number of design blocks. Cotton is the easiest and most successful type of fabric for patchwork. It is important to choose the correct thickness of batting; a thick lofty batting for a fluffy quilt, and a light batting for a cushion cover or teacosy.

Bias binding, piping, lace, ribbons and frills can all be used to add to the interest of the patchwork item. A border can adjust the overall size and act as a frame for design. Appliqué, as used in the 'Pretty Flowers' Patchwork Cushion, may also be worked in conjunction with patchwork.

Pellon has brought the age-old craft of patchwork up to date with a new sewing aid called Quilter's Secret which makes patchwork designs quick and easy to do. Seams can be worked by hand to remain true to traditional methods or can be machined for speed. Quilter's Secret is a non-woven, iron-on patchwork pattern with precise cut and stitch lines, eliminating the need for templates. It can be washed and pressed with a cool iron. Shapes are cut out and fused to the fabric using a warm iron and a damp pressing cloth. Design blocks of patchwork are formed by joining triangles to form squares, squares to form rows and rows to form a complete design block.

Pellon's Quilter's Secret is available from most fabric shops, and department stores.

Nodding Heads

Moses Basket

Measurements

Base of basket approximately 64cm x 37cm (25in x 14½in)

Materials

2m (2¼yd) of 150cm (59in) wide border-pattern fabric
2m (2¼yd) of 90cm (35½in) wide medium weight batting
1m (39½in) of 115cm (45½in) wide plain cotton fabric for lining
2.5m (2¾yd) of 2cm (¾in) wide satin bias binding
2.5m (2¾yd) of 3cm (1¼in) wide pre-gathered broderie anglaise
Velcro fasteners
5m (5½yd) of 1.5cm (⅝in) wide Offray satin ribbon
Pins
Matching thread
Moses basket with base approximately 64cm x 37cm (25in x 14½in)

To Make

1 To line basket: measure the basket base on the outside both ways and cut out a rectangle of patterned fabric from the center part of the fabric to this size, adding 2cm (¾in) all round. Cut a piece of batting and lining the same size as the fabric.

2 For side pieces: mark the center point of each long side. Measure from center to center round top of basket, and the height of the basket at the deepest point. Repeat to measure around base edge of sides. Cut out a rectangle of fabric to each size, plus 5cm (2in) all round. Cut out a piece of batting and piece of lining to match both pieces.

3 Place fabric and lining bases with wrong sides together, sandwiching batting between them. Pin and baste together. Quilt across the fabric in a diamond design.

4 Quilt each side piece in the same way.

5 Place the basket base centrally on the wrong side of the base fabric and trace around it.

6 Pin, baste and stitch side seams of side pieces to make up the complete side piece. Trim edges. Work two rows of gathering stitches round base edge of complete side piece.

7 Mark center of each side of base rectangle. Pin, baste and stitch side piece to base, matching centers and pulling up gathers evenly to fit. Trim and neaten base seam.

8 Place cover inside basket and check for fit. Mark around fabric 3cm (1¼in) above top edge of basket. Remove and cut along marked line.

9 Bind top edge of lining with satin bias binding: pin, baste and stitch one half of binding to right side of lining. Fold binding over raw fabric edge to wrong side. Hem remaining edge of binding in place over previous stitching line.

10 Pin broderie anglaise round top edge of lining, placing edge against bias binding. Zigzag stitch in place.

11 Cut one frill length from the border section of fabric 20cm (8in) wide and the complete length of the fabric. Pin, baste and stitch together into a ring. Turn under a double 6mm (¼in) hem along bottom edge of frill; pin, baste and stitch in place. Turn down top edge for 4.5cm (1¾in), turn under 6mm (¼in). Work two rows of gathering round frill 3cm (1¼in) and 3.5cm (1⅜in) from top edge.

12 Place lining inside basket and mark the position of each handle on each side of lining. Pin, baste and stitch frill round lining, so that it falls over basket edge. Pull up gathers evenly to fit ending stitching on each side of handle positions. Stitch frill only across these gaps to hold gathers in place.

13 Pin, baste and stitch ribbon round lining over gathered stitching, by hand. Stitch only through frill at handle positions.

14 Stitch Velcro fasteners to lining and to frill at handle positions to hold them together and to enable the lining to be removed from basket for laundering.

15 Make a bow from two lengths of ribbon and stitch to each side of the basket between handle positions.

Patchwork Quilt for Moses Basket

Measurements

41cm x 61cm (16in x 24in)

Materials

One panel each of Pellon Quilter's Secret Assortment
10cm (4in) square and 10cm (4in) right triangle
25cm (10in) of 90cm (35½in) wide pink fabric (A)
60cm (23½in) floral fabric (B)

42cm (16½in) x 62cm (24½in) floral fabric for backing
42cm (16½) x 62cm (24½in) 8 oz batting
2m (2¼yd) of 3.8cm (1½in) wide gathered cream lace
Matching thread

To Make

Carefully read 'The Secret of Patchwork' on page 93.

1 Cut and fuse together:

(i) 8 x 10cm (4in) squares floral fabric with 8 x 10cm (4in) squares Quilter's Secret.

(ii) 8 x 10cm (4in) right triangles in pink fabric with 8 x 10cm (4in) right triangles Quilter's Secret.

(iii) 16 x 10cm (4in) right triangles in floral fabric with 16 x 10cm (4in) right triangles Quilter's Secret.

(iv) 8 x 10cm (4in) quarter triangles in pink fabric with 8 x 10cm (4in) quarter triangles Quilter's Secret.

(v) 8 x 5cm (2in) right triangles pink fabric with 8 x 5cm (2in) right triangles Quilter's Secret.

(vi) 8 x 5cm (2in) right triangles floral fabric with 8 x 5cm (2in) right triangles Quilter's Secret.

2. Assemble triangles, squares and rows following block diagram.

3 Pin and baste gathered lace, placing right sides and raw edges of frill and patchwork block together.

4 Lay the backing on top, right sides together, and stitch around the edges, leaving a gap to turn.

5 Turn right side out. Press lightly.

6 Insert batting. Stitch gap.

7 Quilt by sewing through all layers with stab stitch at corners of patchwork shapes. Catch in approximately ¼ to ⅓ of corners.

For-get-me-not *Child's Crochet Pinafore*

Measurements

To fit chest	52	56	60cm
	20½	22	23½in
Length to shoulder	43	46	49cm
	17	18	19½in

Materials

Chat Botté 'Lotto'
100 mercerized cotton
Main shade 5 6 7 x 50g balls
Scrap of contrast shade (center of flowers)
No 6 steel and No 1 steel crochet hooks

Gauge

16 grids and 14 rows to 10cm (4in) measured over grid pattern using No 6 steel hook
Note: adjust hook size if necessary

Abbreviations

alt – alternate; **beg** – beginning; **ch** – chain; **cont** – continue; **dc** – double crochet; **dec** – decrease; **hdc** – half double crochet; **patt** – pattern; **rep** – repeat; **sc** – single crochet; **sk** – skip; **ss** – slip stitch; **r** – ring

To Make

Skirt – Back and Front Alike
Using No 6 hook make 168 (174, 180) ch loosely. **Foundation row:** 1 sc into 2nd ch from hook, 1 sc into each ch to end, turn. 167 (173, 179) sc. **Next row:** 1 sc into each sc to end, turn. Cont in patt: **1st row:** 4 ch, sk 1st 2 sc, *1 dc into next sc, 1 ch, sk next sc; rep from * ending 1 dc into last sc, turn. **Patt row:** 4 ch, sk 1st dc, *1 dc into next dc, 1 ch; rep from * ending 1 dc into 2nd of turning ch, turn. 83 (86, 89) grids. Patt 3 (4, 4) more rows. ****Dec row:** patt to within last grid, turn. Rep dec row once. Patt 5 (6, 6) rows **. Rep from ** to ** 3 times, then rep dec row twice. 73 (76, 79) grids. Patt straight until work measures 29 (31, 33) cm 10¼ (12¼, 13) in from beg. Fasten off securely.

Back Yoke
Using No 6 hook make 94 (100, 106) ch loosely. **Foundation row:** 1 dc into 6th ch from hook, *1 ch, sk next ch, 1 dc into next ch; rep from * to end. 45 (48, 51) grids. Cont in patt as for skirt until yoke measures 14 (15, 16) cm 5½ (6, 6¼) in from beg. Fasten off securely.

Front Yoke
Work as for back yoke until 12 fewer rows have been worked.

Neck Shaping
1st row: patt until 21 (22, 23) grids have been completed, turn. **2nd and every following alt row:** patt to end. **3rd row:** patt 18 (19, 20) grids, turn. **5th row:** patt 16 (17, 18) grids, turn. **7th row:** patt 15 (16, 17) grids, turn. **9th row:** patt 14 (15, 16) grids, turn. **11th row:** patt 13 (14, 15) grids, turn. **12th row:** patt to end. Fasten off securely.

2nd side
1st row: sk 2 (3, 4) dc after 1st side and join yarn to next dc, patt to end. 21 (22, 23) grids. **2nd and every following alt row:** patt to end. **3rd row:** ss into each st to 4th dc of last row, patt to end. **5th row:** ss into each st to 3rd dc of last row, patt to end. **7th row:** ss into each st to 2nd dc of last row, patt to end. **9th row:** as 7th. **11th row:** as 7th. **12th row:** patt to end. Fasten off securely. Join shoulders. Join skirt sections to yoke.

Side Frills
1st row: with right side facing and using No 1 hook, beg at lower edge of skirt and work 1 row of sc evenly along side edge (work a multiple of 4 sc plus 3), turn. **2nd row:** *sk 3 sc, 3 dc/3 ch/3 dc all in next sc; rep from * to last 3 sc, ss in last sc. Fasten off securely.

Flowers (make 19)
Using No 6 hook make 6 ch, ss into 1st ch to form a r. **1st round:** *3 ch, 1 sc into r; rep from * 4 times. **2nd round:** 1 sc/1 hdc/3 dc/1 hdc/1 sc in each 3 ch sp, ss into 1st sc. Fasten off securely.

To Finish
Position 7 flowers around front neck, 7 along front yoke seam and remaining 5 along back yoke seam. Using contrast yarn work a French knot in the center of each flower then secure to pinafore.

Using yarn double and No 1 hook make four 20cm (8in) lengths of ch for ties. Attach 1 to each end of yoke seam, on wrong side.

Flowers in Bloom

Embroidered Cutwork Collar

(Picture on page 92)

Measurements

To fit 31cm (12¼in) neck edge of dress

Materials

50cm (19¾in) of 91cm (36in) wide cream fine weight fabric
Anchor Embroidery Floss: 1 skein each of 06, 08, 024, 0945
Anchor Pearl Cotton No 8: one 10g ball 0386
Crewel needles, No 8 for 1 strand and No 6 for 3 strands and Pearl Cotton
9mm (⅜in) squared paper for pattern

To Make

1 Make half pattern for collar using squared paper and following diagram carefully.

2 Cut 45cm x 35cm (17¾in x 13¾in) piece from fabric. Fold in half widthwise and crease lightly.

3 Place fold of fabric against fold line of paper pattern and cut out collar as indicated on diagram.

4 Transfer outlines of flower motif onto front right corner of collar as indicated in picture on page 94.

5 Work embroidery following diagram and key, noting all parts similar to those numbered are worked in same stitch and color.

6 Use 1 strand for back stitch and French knots, and 3 strands for rest of embroidery.

7 It is important when working buttonhole stitch to have curved edge (shown on chart by a continuous black line) lying near to edges of fabric to make cutting easier once embroidery is complete.

8 When embroidery is complete, press carefully on wrong side with cool iron.

9 From wrong side, cut away surplus fabric around buttonhole stitch, taking care not to snip edges of stitches.

10 Cut enough 2.5cm (1in) wide bias strips from remaining fabric, joining where necessary, to obtain length to fit neck edge, plus allowance for ties.

11 Trim surplus fabric at neck edge and taking 6mm (¼in) turnings, bind neck edge with bias strip allowing equal amounts of bias strip at each end for ties.

12 Instructions for working embroidery stitches are on page 16.

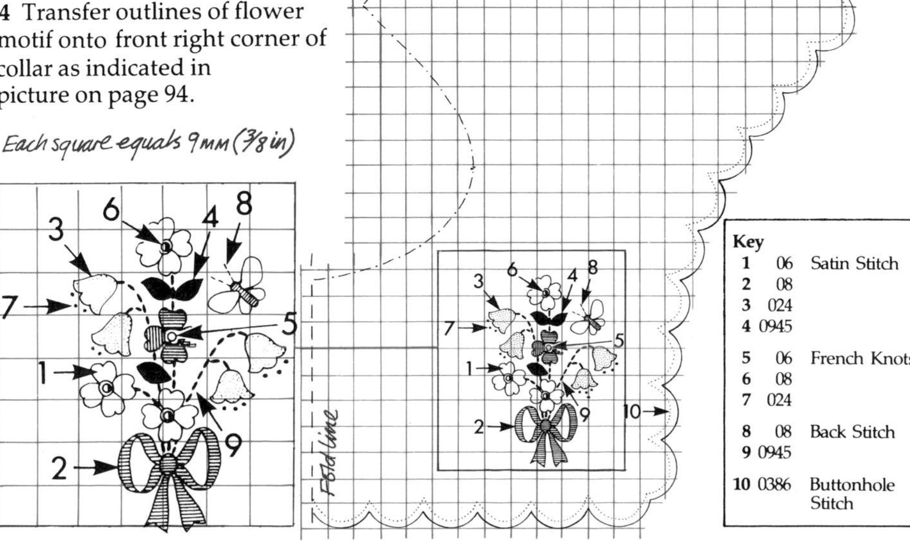

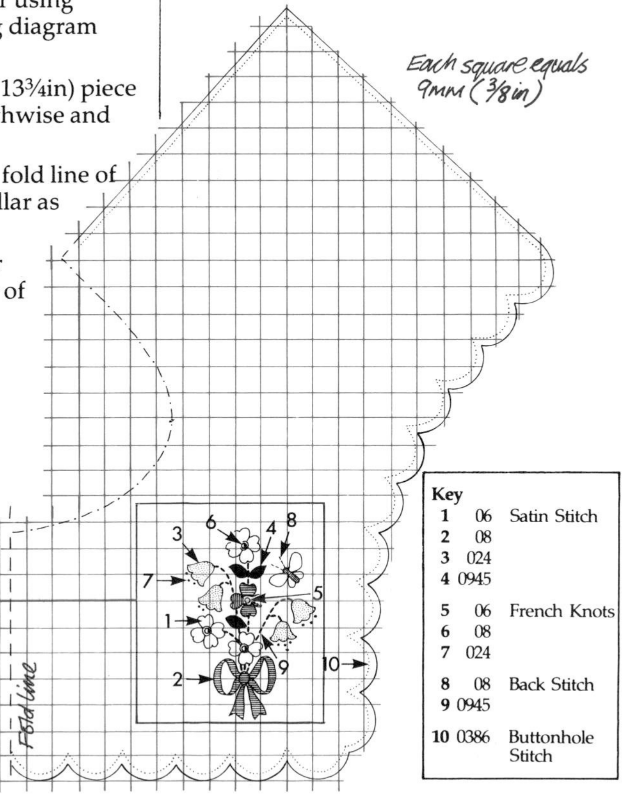

Butterfly *Crochet Pendant*

(Picture on page 92, inset)

Measurements

5cm x 3.8cm (2in x 1½in)

Materials

Anchor Mercer Crochet Cotton No 60 (10g)
1 ball selected color
No 10 steel crochet hook (if your crochet is loose, use a size finer hook; if tight use a size larger hook)
Small piece of fabric to fit frame
Gilt oval frame with top hanger, 50mm x 38mm (2in x 1½in)

Gauge

1.7cm (⅝in) from point to point

Abbreviations

ch – chain; **ss** – slip stitch; **dc** – double crochet; **hdc** – half double crochet; **sc** – single crochet; **tc** – treble crochet; **lp(s)** – loop(s)
Note: Work in conjunction with picture

To Make

Commence flower with 7 ch, join with a ss to form a ring. **1st row:** (1 sc into ring, 5 ch, 1 sc into 2nd ch from hook, 1 hdc into next ch, 1 dc into each of next 2 ch) 9 times, 1 ss into 1st sc. Fasten off.

Commence stems with 20 ch, 1 ss into 2nd ch from hook, 1 ss into each ch, 24 ch, 1 ss into 2nd ch from hook, 1 ss into each ch, 18 ch, 1 ss into 2nd ch from hook, 1 ss into each ch. Fasten off.

Stitch flower to stem.

Commence butterfly body with 7 ch. **1st row:** leaving the last lp of each on hook work 2 dc into 4th ch from hook, thread over and draw through all lps on hook, 3 ch, 2 sc into 2nd ch from hook, 1 ss into next ch. Fasten off.

Commence wing with 5 ch. **1st row:** 1 sc into 2nd ch from hook, 1 dc into each of next 2 ch, into next ch work 5 dc/3 ch/1 ss/2 ch and 3 dc, working along other side of foundation ch work 1 dc into each of next 2 ch, 1 sc into next ch. Fasten off.

To make up, overlap wings and sew to body. Sew single threads through head to form antennae. Damp and pin out flower and butterfly to shape. Sew crochet in position onto fabric, placing as shown and then secure in frame.

AUGUST

"Fairest of months! ripe Summer's Queen
The hey-day of the year
With robes that gleam with sunny sheen,
Sweet August doth appear."

HEATHER

COMMON RED POPPY

CORNFIELD AND POPPY

Heather *Knitted Sweater*

Measurements

To fit bust	81-86	89-94	97-102cm
	32-34	35-37	38-40in
Length from	58	60	61cm
shoulder	23	23½	24in

Materials

Knitting worsted,	A	5	5	5	50g balls
	B	4	4	4	50g balls
	C	4	4	4	50g balls
Bouclé Aran	D	4	5	5	50g balls

Pair of long needles each Nos 5 (4mm), 3 (3¼mm) and 8 (5½mm)

Gauge

22 sts and 40 rows to 10cm (4in) over moss stitch on No 5 (4mm) needles and Diamanté

Abbreviations

k – knit; **p** – purl; **st(s)** – stitch(es); **patt** – pattern; **inc** – increase, increasing; **dec** – decrease, decreasing; **beg** – beginning; **rep** – repeat; **cont** – continue

To Make

Left Half of Front and Back (knitted sideways)
Begin at left cuff. With No 5 (4mm) needles and D, bind on 99 (105, 111) sts. Knit 1 row. Work in patt joining on and breaking off colors as required: **1st row** (right side): in B, k. **2nd to 18th rows:** in B, k 1, (p 1, k 1) to end. **19th and 20th rows:** in D, k. **21st to 38th rows:** in C, as 1st to 18th. **39th and 40th rows:** in D, k. **41st to 58th rows:** in A, as 1st to 18th. **59th and 60th rows:** in D, k. These 60 rows form patt.
Cont in patt until sleeve measures 29cm (11½in) from beg, ending after a wrong side row.
Working extra sts into patt, shape sleeve by inc 1 st at each end of next 5 rows. Now cast on 50 sts loosely at each end of next row. 209 (215, 221) sts. Mark center of last row.
Cont in patt until work measures 15 (17, 19) cm, 6 (6¾, 7½) in from marker, ending after a wrong side row.
Shape neck thus: **Next row:** patt 105 (107, 111), bind off next 18 sts loosely, patt to end. Cont on last group for front. Dec 1 st at neck edge on next 5 rows. 81 (85, 87) sts. Work straight until front measures 27 (28, 30) cm, 10½ (11¼, 12) in from group of 50 cast-on sts. Bind off loosely using color of last row.
With wrong side facing, rejoin appropriate color and work straight on the 105 (107, 111) sts until back measures same as front. Bind off loosely using color of last row.

Right Front
With No 3 (3¼mm) needles and A, cast on 99 (107, 115) sts. **1st row:** k 2, (p 1, k 1) to last st, k 1. **2nd row:** k 1, (p 1, k 1) to end. Rep. these 2 rows for 10 cm (4 in), ending after a 1st row.** **Next row:** rib 2 (4, 6), (inc in next st, rib 4) 9 times, rib 3 (5, 7), bind off next 49 (53, 57) sts loosely in rib (**NB:** this group of sts will be stitched to side edge of left half of front).
***Cont on remaining 59 (63, 67) sts.
Change to No 5 (4mm) needles and k 2 rows in D. Now work in patt as on left half of front and back until work measures 23cm (9in) from *top* of welt, ending after a wrong-side row.
Shape sleeve by inc 1 st at side edge on next 5 rows. Now bind on 63 sts at side edge on next row. 127 (131, 135) sts.
Cont in patt on all sts until work measures 11 (13, 14) cm, 4½ (5, 5½) in from 63 cast-on sts, ending at front edge.
Shape neck thus: **Next row:** bind off 19 sts loosely, work to end. Dec 1 st at neck edge on next 5 rows. 103 (107, 111) sts.
Work straight until front measures 23 (24, 25) cm, 9 (9½, 10) in from 63 cast-on sts.
Bind off loosely.

Right Back
Work as right front to **. **Next row:** bind off 49 (53, 57) sts loosely in rib, rib 3 (5, 7) (including st on needle after binding off), (inc in next stitch, rib 4) 9 times, rib to end.
Complete to match right front working from *** to end, omitting neck shaping.

Collar (worked sideways)
With No 8 (5½mm) needles and D, cast on 12 sts. Work in garter st for 63cm (25in). Bind off loosely.

Right Sleeve Edging
First join shoulder seam on right front and back. With No 8 (5½mm) needles and D, right side facing, k up 80 (84, 88) sts evenly along sleeve edge. Knit 1 row. Bind off firmly.

To Finish
Do not press. Join center front and center back seams. Sew welt in position to left half of front and back. Join side and sleeve seams. Sew collar in a ring then stitch to neck edge. Press seams following diamanté instructions.

Common Red Poppy

Needlepoint Cushion Cover

Measurements

38cm (15in) square

Materials

50cm (19¾in) of 58cm (23in) wide No 10 Penelope (double-threaded) canvas
Anchor Tapestry Wool in 10m (11yd) skeins: 21 skeins 0386; 1 skein 0402 White; 0403 Black; 0215; 0611; 013; 010; 09; 0336; 0647; 0722; 0842; 0306; 0635; 019; 0638; 0216; 0278; 0122; 0118; 0726; 0242; 0983; 3363
Tapestry needle No 18
45cm (17¾in) square backing fabric
Matching thread
38cm (15in) square pillow form

To Make

Important Note: read 'General Working Instructions for all Needlepoint' on page 15.

1 Fold canvas lightly in both directions (widthwise and lengthwise) to form center lines. Work basting stitches along center lines.

2 Center of chart is indicated by arrows which should coincide with basting stitches. Each square on chart represents 1 square of double thread canvas, or 1 tapestry stitch.

3 Work needlepoint following chart and key for 'Poppy' design on page 109, working as far as possible out from center.

4 Complete background in 0386 and work backstitch details as given on charts.

5 Trim surplus canvas to within 2cm (¾in) of stitching and cut backing fabric to match.

6 Remove basting stitches.

7 Stitch pieces together along 3 sides, as close as possible to edge of stitching.

8 Turn right side out and insert pillow form.

9 Join remaining side.

10 Model worked in traméed half cross stitch.

Common Red Poppy
Needlepoint Cushion Cover

and

Poppy
Embroidered Place Mat

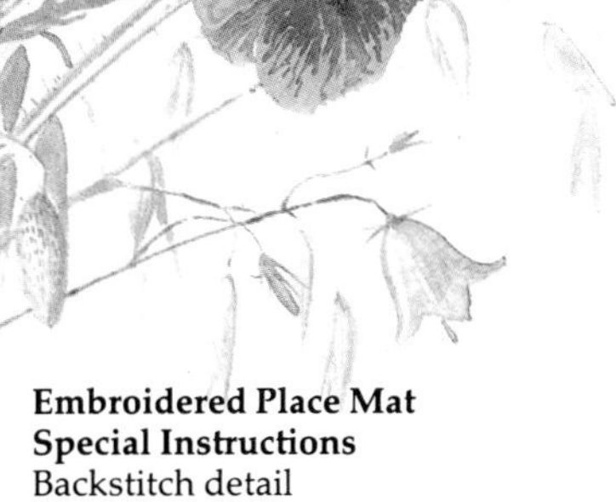

Design sizes (approx.)
14 stitches to 2.5cm (1in)
18cm x 16cm (7in x 6¼in)
10 stitches to 2.5cm (1in)
23cm x 20cm (9¼in x 8in)

Needlepoint Cushion Cover

Special Instructions

A. Background *0386*

B. Outline: backstitch details

1 Top, largest poppy	*036*
2 Two lower poppies	*019*
3 Top-most poppy bud	*019*
4 Daisy outlines	*3363*
5 Daisy centre	*0216*
6 Poppy centres dotted with ...	*040*
7 Lettering	*0983*

C. Backstitch instructions:
Petal lines and stems on daisies are back stitched. Make long stitches, using the small solid circles as guides to show where to put needle in fabric.

D. Make poppy centre dots in *0403* by bringing needle up through hole and then back down as close as possible.

Embroidered Place Mat
Special Instructions
Backstitch detail

1 Top, largest poppy	*043*
2 Two lower poppies and top-most poppy bud	*047*
3 Daisy outlines	*0398*
4 Daisy centre	*0862*

5 Make poppy centre dots in back by bringing needle up through hole and then back down as close as possible.

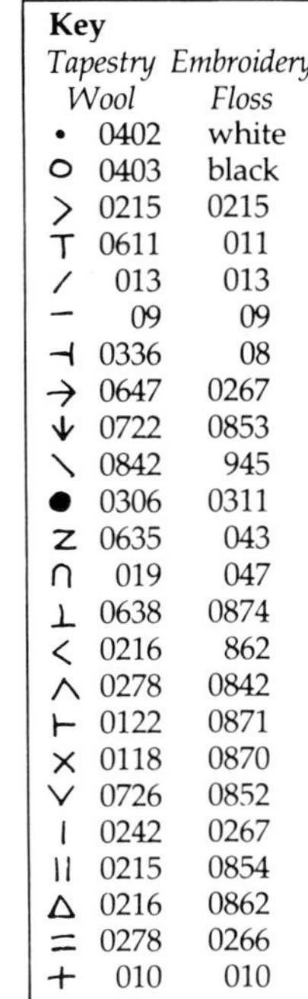

Key

	Tapestry Wool	*Embroidery Floss*
•	0402	white
O	0403	black
>	0215	0215
T	0611	011
/	013	013
−	09	09
⊣	0336	08
→	0647	0267
↓	0722	0853
\	0842	945
●	0306	0311
Z	0635	043
∩	019	047
⊥	0638	0874
<	0216	862
∧	0278	0842
⊢	0122	0871
×	0118	0870
∨	0726	0852
|	0242	0267
||	0215	0854
Δ	0216	0862
=	0278	0266
+	010	010

Corn-field and Poppy *Embroidered Tablecloth*

Measurements

Finished tablecloth 125cm (49½in) square

Materials

1.3m (51in) of 132cm (52in) wide medium weight embroidery fabric
Anchor Embroidery Floss: 5 skeins 0262; 4 skeins 0335; 3 skeins 0369; 2 skeins each of 0305 and 0381
Crewel needles, No 5 for 6 strands of cotton and No 7 for 3 strands

To Make

1 Trim fabric to 130cm (51in) square and turn back 2.5cm (1in) hems on all sides. Miter corners and stitch. Fold fabric in half in both directions (widthwise and lengthwise) and crease lightly to mark center lines. Baste along center lines. Open out and fold and crease again diagonally from corner to corner. Tablecloth is now divided into 8 sections. Work lines of basting stitches along remaining folds.

2 The 'Corn-field and Poppy' embroidery chart is shown below. Diagram shows one-eighth of completed work. Center is found by extending broken lines which should coincide with lines of basting stitches. Trace chart between each of the 8 basting lines as shown on chart. Dotted lines show positions of designs in adjacent sections.

3 Work embroidery following chart and key. All parts similar to numbered parts are worked in same color and stitch. Use 6 strands of floss for daisy stitch and French knots and 3 strands for rest of embroidery. Embroidery is worked in 7 stitches – satin stitch, chain stitch, blanket stitch, straight stitch, French knots, stem stitch and long-tailed daisy stitch with a straight stitch in the center. See 'Glossary of Embroidery Stitches' on page 156 for instructions.

4 When embroidery is completed press lightly on wrong side and remove basting stitches.

Corn-field and Poppy
Embroidered Tablecloth

Key

Section		*Stitch*
1	0305	long-tailed daisy stitch with straight stitch at center
2	0381	
3	0369 or T3817	
4	0381	satin stitch
5	0335 or T3559	satin stitch
6	0369 or T3817	satin stitch
7	0262	chain stitch
8	0262	blanket stitch
9	0262	straight stitch
10	0305	French knots
11	0369 or T3817	stem stitch

Shade numbers refer to Anchor Embroidery Floss.

continue broken line to find centre point

11
5
7
continue broken line to find centre point
4
10
9
8
3
1
6
2

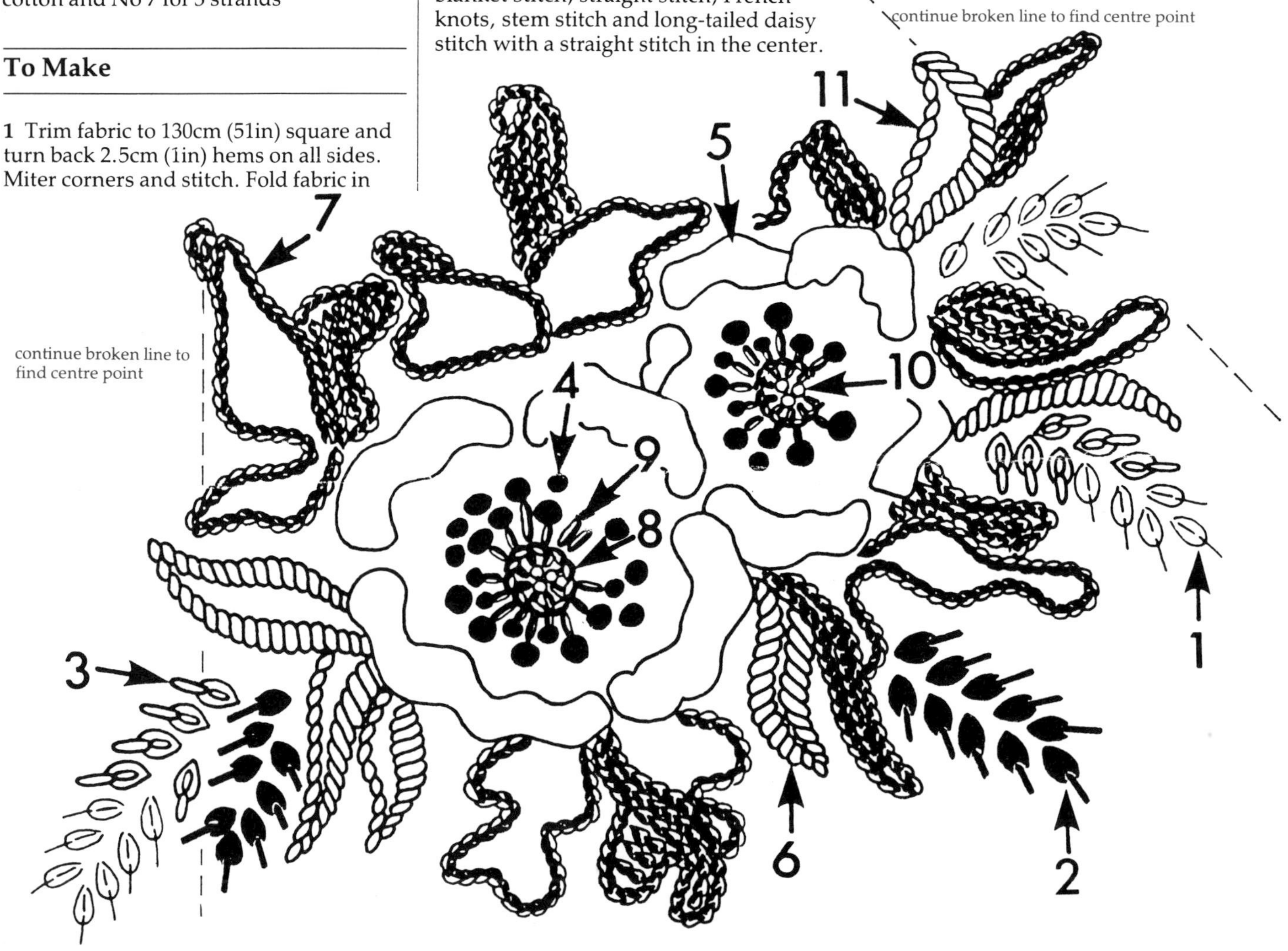

POPPY

Poppy *Tufted Hearth Rug*

Measurements

137cm x 68½cm (54in x 27in)

Materials

Pre-cut Rug Yarn:
1 Cream – 38 packs; *2* white – 2 packs; *3* Pale Red – 2 packs; *4* Light Green – 2 packs; *5* Olive Green – 2 packs; *6* Deep Red – 1 pack; *7* Gold – 1 pack; *8* Beige – 1 pack; *9* Brown – 1 pack; *10* Light Grey – 1 pack; *11* Lilac – 1 pack; *12* Lavender – 1 pack; *13* Moss – 1 pack; *14* Black – 1 pack.
Note: it is advisable to buy all large amounts of pre-cut rug yarn at one time to insure they are all the same dye lot.
3 balls Patons Turkey Binding Wool shade 203 (optional)
152cm (60in) of 68.5cm (27in) width rug-making canvas
Rug-making latchet hook
Large bodkin needle for binding edges
Note: rug making is easier to carry out if the work is done sitting at a table with one narrow end of the rug facing. The knots are then worked on the line of canvas which lies on the edge of the table. If a weight is placed on the unworked canvas, it will assist in supporting the worked part of the rug.

To Make

1 Knot the wool in the following 4 easy steps.

(a) Fold 1 piece of rug wool exactly in half around the shank of the hook. The uniformity of the pile produced depends greatly on this fold being as precise as possible.

(b) Push the hook under the weft strands of canvas where the knot is to be worked (weft strands run horizontally from left to right).

(c) Insuring the latch of the hook is free and open, place the two ends of wool over the hook and then allow the latch to close over the wool.

(d) Pull the hook through the loop of the wool and push the hook forwards. Gently pull the two ends of wool with fingers to make the knot firm. It is important to try to pull all ends of wool, which form the tufts, to exactly the same length in order to prevent errors and save time when clipping of work is carried out.

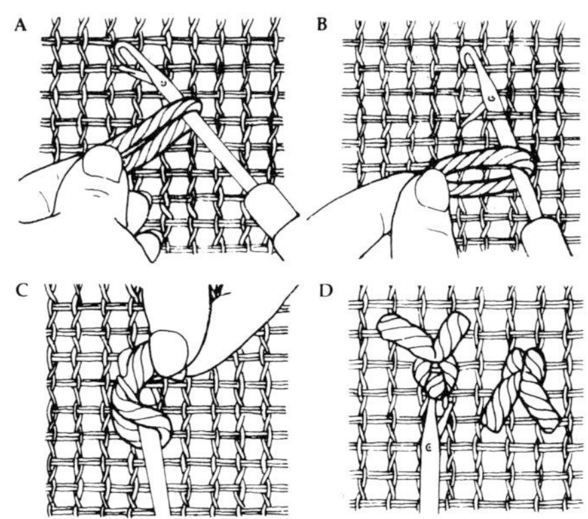

2 Fold under 4cm (1½in) of the canvas across the width of the starting edge and work through the double canvas to give a neat and strong finish.

3 Work from left to right and from selvage to selvage in rows across the width of the canvas following chart.

4 Work through every hole, taking care to knot in the correct color by following the 'Poppy' rug chart below. Do *not* work colors or blocks of pattern separately since this will result in any change of tension being more noticeable.

5 The last few rows should be worked through double canvas in the same way as the starting edge.

6 To give the rug a smooth even surface, clip any long ends with *sharp* scissors. It is well worth taking a great deal of time and trouble when clipping, since any errors of judgement may cause disappointment in the final appearance. Careful clipping, however, can give the rug a truly professional finish. Remove loose ends with a damp cloth or cellophane tape.

7 The ends of the rug where work was done through double canvas will not require any further attention. The appearance of the selvage edges can be neatened with a binding stitch.

When working binding stitch use pre-cut rug yarn in skeins, taking care to choose a shade which will match the color at the edge of the rug or the general background. Thread wool into bodkin needle and, with the wrong side facing, darn in the end of wool.

Following diagram make a few upright oversewing stitches and then insert needle up through the 1st hole. Go over to the 4th hole, back to 2nd, forward to 5th. Repeat to end, following this sequence of working stitches and diagram below.

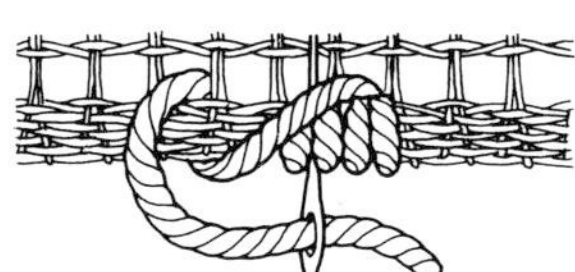

Key 1 2 6 3 7 8 9 10 11 12 4 13 5 14

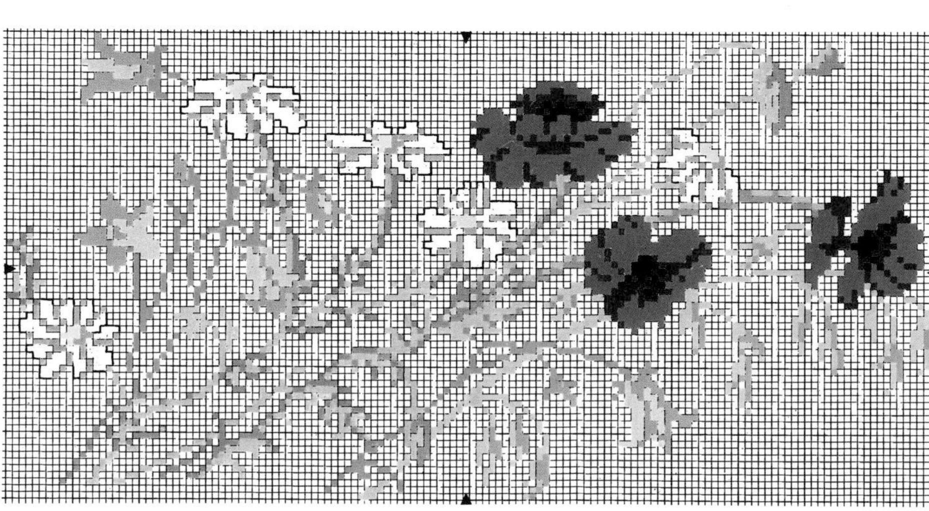

Three Methods of Rug Care and Cleaning

1 Shake off any dirt out of doors when the rug is dry and vacuum clean both sides.

2 Use a clean cloth which has been dipped in a solution of liquid detergent. Wring out cloth thoroughly before gently stroking the pile. Rugs must not be allowed to become too wet and must not be left to lie damp.

3 Professional dry cleaning.
Note: after cleaning, hang the rug on a line where plenty of air can get to the pile.

POPPY

POPPY

POPPY

Poppy *Knitted Jacket*

Measurements

To fit bust	81	86	91	97	102cm
	32	34	36	38	40in
Length from shoulder, *approx.*	61	62	62	63	63cm
	24	24½	24½	25	25in
Sleeve seam	47	47	47	47	47cm
	18½	18½	18½	18½	18½in

Materials

Mohair yarn (weights vary; check gauge)
Main Shade (M)
14 15 15 16 16 25g yarns
Green
2 2 2 2 2 25g yarns
1 yarn each in Orange, Dark Red, Lilac, Beige and White (25g)
Pair of needles each Nos 7 (5mm) and 5 (4mm)
8 buttons
A skein each of black and yellow embroidery floss

Gauge

16 sts and 22 rows to 10cm (4in) over plain stockinette stitch on No 7 (5mm) needles

Abbreviations

k – knit; **p** – purl; **st(s)** – stitch(es); **inc** – increase, increasing; **dec** – decrease; **beg** – beginning; **alt** – alternate; **rep** – repeat; **st st** – stockinette stitch

To Make

Right Front
With No 5 (4mm) needles and M, cast on 33 (35, 37, 39, 41) sts. **1st row:** k 2, (p 1, k 1) to last st, k 1. **2nd row:** k 1, (p 1, k 1) to end. Work 16 more rows in rib inc 7 sts evenly on last row. 40 (42, 44, 46, 48) sts. Change to No 7 (5mm) needles and st st working from chart thus: (**NB:** do not carry yarn across back of work over more than 3 sts at a time. Use a separate ball of yarn for each color area.) **1st row:** k, 3 (4, 5, 6, 7) M, work 1st row of chart reading from right to left, k 3 (4, 5, 6, 7) M. **2nd row:** p, 3 (4, 5, 6, 7) M, work 2nd row of chart reading from left to right, p 3 (4, 5, 6, 7) M. **3rd to 92nd rows:** rep the last 2 rows 45 times but working rows 3 to 92 of chart.
Keeping chart correct, shape neck by binding off 7 (8, 8, 9, 9) sts at beg of next row. Now dec 1 st at neck edge on next 4 rows. 29 (30, 32, 33, 35) sts.
Work straight until front measures 7 (9, 9, 10, 10) cm, 3 (3½, 3½, 4, 4) in from beg of neck shaping, noting that when chart is complete M only should be used and ending at side edge.
Shape shoulder by binding off 9 (10, 10, 11, 11) sts at beg of next and following alt row. Work 1 row. Bind off.

Left Front
Work as right front but working 1 row fewer before shaping neck and reversing chart, thus 1st row placing chart will be: k, 3 (4, 5, 6, 7) M, work 1st row of chart reading from left to right, k 3 (4, 5, 6, 7) M.

Back
With No 5 (4mm) needles and M, bind on 71 (75, 79, 83, 87) sts. Work 18 rows in rib as on right front but inc 11 sts evenly on last row. 82 (86, 90, 94, 98) sts.
Change to No 7 (5mm) needles and st st working from chart thus: **1st row:** k, 3 (4, 5, 6, 7) M, work 1st row of chart reading from left to right, k 8 (10, 12, 14, 16) M, work 1st row of chart reading from right to left, k 3 (4, 5, 6, 7) M. **2nd row:** p, 3 (4, 5, 6, 7) M, work 2nd row of chart reading from left to right, p 8 (10, 12, 14, 16) M, work 2nd row of chart reading from right to left, p 3 (4, 5, 6, 7) M. **3rd to 103rd rows:** rep the last 2 rows 50 times, then 1st row again but working rows 3 to 103 of chart.
Work straight in M until back measures same as fronts to shoulder shaping, ending after a p row.
Shape shoulders by binding off 9 (10, 10, 11, 11) sts at beg of next 4 rows, then 11 (10, 12, 11, 13) sts at beg of next 2 rows. Slip final 24 (26, 26, 28, 28) sts on a spare needle.

Sleeves
With No 5 (4mm) needles and M, cast on 31 (33, 33, 35, 37) sts. Work 17 rows in rib

Poppy
Knitted Flower Motif Jacket

Key
□ Main
X Green
/ Beige
Δ Lilac
○ White
• Orange
V Dark Red

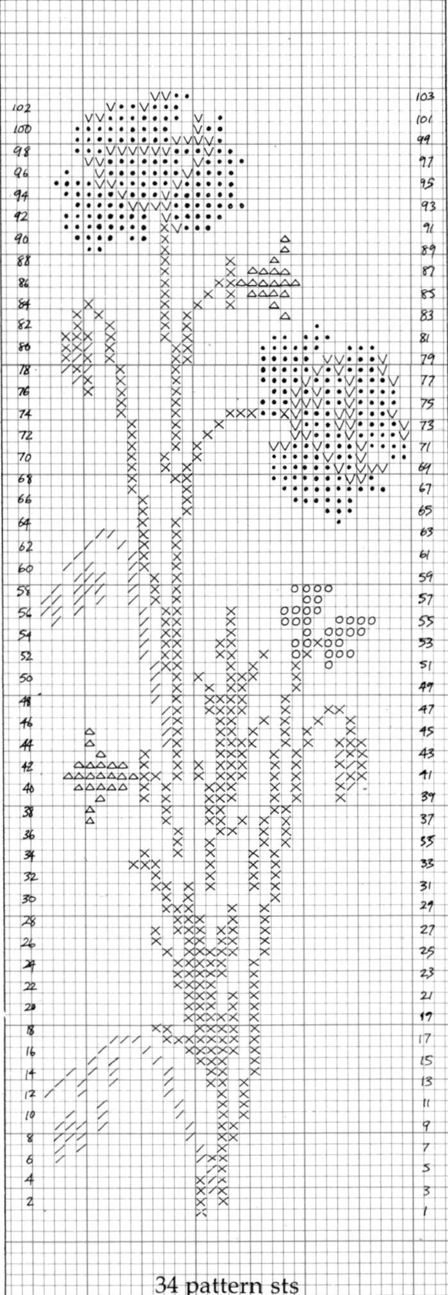

as on right front. **Next row:** rib 3 (4, 4, 3, 2), *inc in next st, rib 3 (2, 1, 1, 1); rep from * to last 4 (5, 5, 4, 3) sts, inc in next st, rib to end. 38 (42, 46, 50, 54) sts. Change to No 7 (5mm) needles and beg k row work in st st shaping sleeve by inc 1 st at each end of 7th row, then on every following 6th row until there are 58 (62, 66, 70, 74) sts, then on every following 4th row until there are 66 (70, 74, 78, 82) sts. Work straight until sleeve measures 47cm (18½in) at center. Bind off loosely.

Neckband
First join shoulders. With no 5 (4mm) needles and M, right side facing, k up 65 (67, 71, 75, 79) sts evenly round neck. Beg 2nd row work 7 rows in rib as on welt. Bind off in rib.

Borders
With No 5 (4mm) needles and M, cast on 7 sts. Work a strip in rib as on welt to fit, when slightly stretched, up left front to top of neckband. Bind off firmly in rib. Mark position on strip for 8 buttons, 1st to be in 3rd and 4th rows, last in 3rd and 4th rows from top and remaining 6 spaced evenly between. Work 2nd border as first but working holes to match markers thus: **1st row:** rib 2, bind off 3 sts, rib to end. **2nd row:** in rib, casting on 3 sts over those bound off.

To Finish
First embroider poppy centers in black and daisy centers in yellow. Omitting ribbing, press following pressing instructions. Allowing approximately 21 (23, 24, 25, 27) cm, 8½ (9, 9½, 10, 10½) in for armhole, stitch bound-off edge of sleeves to yoke. Join side and sleeve seams. Sew on borders and buttons. Press seams.

Poppy *Embroidered Place Mats and Napkins*

PLACE MATS

Measurements

Finished place mat 45cm x 30cm (17¾in x 12in)
Embroidered design 19cm x 15cm (7½in x 6in)

Materials

(Information given for one place mat only) 55cm x 40cm (21¾in x 15¾in) evenweave linen with 28 threads to 2.5cm (1in)
Anchor Embroidery Floss: 1 skein each of White; Black; 0215; 013; 011; 010; 09; 08; 0267; 0398; 0898; 0853; 945; 0311; 0359; 043; 047; 0874; 0847; 862; 0854; 0842; 0871; 0870; 0852; 0862; 0267; 0266
Tapestry needle No 24
55cm x 40cm (21¾in x 15¾in) iron-on interfacing
55cm x 40cm (21¾in x 15¾in) heavy weight floss for backing

To Make

Important Note: read 'General Working Instructions for all cross stitch embroideries, on page 16.

1 Fold linen lightly in both directions (widthwise and lengthwise) to form center lines. Work basting stitches along center lines.

2 Center of chart is indicated by arrows which should coincide with basting stitches. Each square on chart represents 2 double threads of linen (2 warp and 2 weft threads), or 1 cross stitch.

3 Using 2 strands of floss throughout, work embroidery following chart and key for 'Poppy' design on page 110, working as far as possible out from center.
Notes: (i) Place Mat worked without lettering. (ii) Chart is also used for 'Common Red Poppy' Tapestry Cushion Cover pictured on page 98.

4 Remove basting stitches.

5 With embroidered design positioned centrally, mark outline of finished mat onto fabric with basting stitches.

6 Trim surplus fabric, 2cm (¾in) beyond basting stitches.

7 Cut out 1 piece of iron-on interfacing and 1 piece of backing fabric to same size as finished mat. Place interfacing to wrong side of embroidered fabric, matching edges to basting stitches. Press in place, following instructions included with Vilene interfacing.

8 Position backing fabric inside basting stitches, pin and baste in place.

9 Fold edges of embroidered linen over edges of backing and interfacing with double 1cm (⅜in) deep hem. Neaten corners ensuring each corner is folded in same direction.

10 Pin, baste and stitch hem close to outer edges. Repeat close to inside edges.

NAPKINS

Measurements

Finished napkin 40cm (15¾in) square
Embroidered design (approx) 8cm (3¼in) square

Materials

Information below is for 1 napkin only
50cm (19¾in) square evenweave linen with 28 threads to 2.5cm (1in)
Anchor Embroidery Floss: 1 skein each of 013; 011; 010; 08; 945; 043; 047; 862
Tapestry needle No 24

To Make

Important Note: read 'General Working Instructions for all Cross Stitch Embroideries' on page 16.

1 Crease linen lightly in both directions (widthwise and lengthwise) to form center lines. Work basting stitches along center lines. Fold crease lines in both directions to form center lines of top left quarter section of linen. These are the lines on which to center 'Poppy' napkin design. Mark center lines of this section with basting stitches.

2 Center of chart is indicated by arrows which should coincide with basting stitches. Each square on chart represents

2 double threads of linen (2 warp and 2 weft threads), or 1 cross stitch.

3 Using 2 strands of floss throughout, work embroidery following chart and key for 'Poppy' design below, working as far as possible out from center.

4 Complete embroidery and remove basting stitches.

5 Trim linen to 43cm (17in) square, keeping design centered in one quarter.

6 Fold double 6mm (¼in) deep hems to wrong side. Pin, baste and stitch.

Poppy
Embroidered Napkin

Key	
ǀ	011
—	013
>	043
^	047
<	09
+	010
●	black
\	945
/	0842
X	0854
V	862
▲	0266
O	0874
•	white
△	0311

Design size (approx.)
14 stitches to 2.5cm
8cm (3¼in) square

For special instructions see chart for 'Poppy' Embroidered Place Mat

Shade numbers refer to Anchor Embroidery Floss.

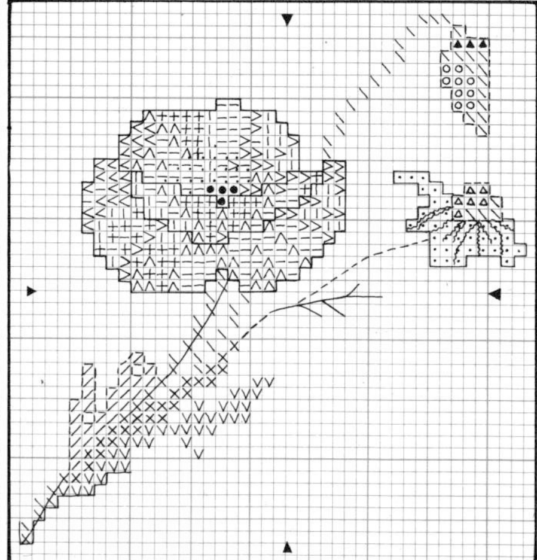

Poppy *Patchwork Tea Cosy*

Measurements

Approximately 34cm x 26cm (13½in x 10in)

Materials

50cm x 122cm (19¾in x 48in) poppy or other floral-patterned fabric (A)
Pellon Quilter's Secret
15cm (6in) plain red cotton fabric (B)
35cm (13¾in) 2oz batting
Matching thread
1.50m (1⅝yd) of 4cm (1½in) wide bias binding to match

To Make

Carefully read 'The Secret of Patchwork' on page 93.

1 Cut and fuse together:

(a) Ten 5cm (2in) squares of floral fabric with ten 5cm (2in) squares of Quilter's Secret.

(b) Five 5cm (2in) squares of red fabric with five 5cm (2in) squares of Quilter's Secret.

(c) Ten 5cm (2in) right triangles of floral fabric with ten 5cm (2in) right triangles of Quilter's Secret.

(d) Eight 5cm (2in) right triangles of red fabric with eight 5cm (2in) right triangles of Quilter's Secret.

2 Assemble triangles, squares and rows following block diagram below.

3 Cut a piece of floral fabric for backing, 34.5cm x 27cm (13½in x 10½in). Cut two pieces of lining and two of batting to same size.

4 Cut two border strips of floral fabric 5.6cm x 22cm (2¼in x 8¾in). Sew to both sides of patchwork block using 6mm (¼in) seam.

5 Sandwich one piece of batting between patchwork front and lining.

6 Machine quilt patchwork block around all edges of design. The quilting stitch line follows the seam 'ditch' between two patchwork pieces.

7 Sandwich one piece of batting between floral fabric back and lining. Baste.

8 Machine quilt in diagonal rows to form diamond design, 3.8cm (1½in) apart.

9 Trim top corners to curved shape.

10 Place front and back together, wrong sides together. Baste. Pin loop into position at top.

11 Neatly bind curved raw edges with red bias binding.

12 Neatly trim bottom edge with red bias binding.

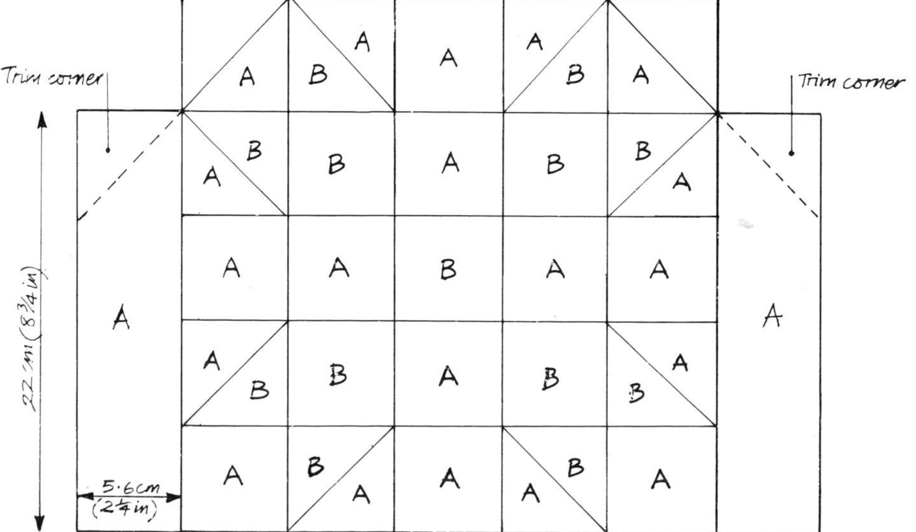

Poppy *Patchwork Cushion Cover*

Measurements

40.5cm (16in) square – without frill

Materials

(for 1 cushion cover)
75cm (29½in) poppy or other floral-patterned fabric 122cm (48in) wide (A)
Pellon Quilter's Secret 10cm (4in) squares and 10cm (4in) quarter triangles
75cm (29½in) plain red furnishing fabric (B)
Matching thread
40.5cm (16in) square pillow form

To Make

Carefully read 'The Secret of Patchwork' on page 93.

1 Cut and fuse together:

(a) Four 10cm (4in) squares of floral fabric with four 10cm (4in) squares of Quilter's Secret.

(b) Ten 10cm (4in) quarter triangles of floral fabric with ten 10cm (4in) quarter triangles of Quilter's Secret.

A

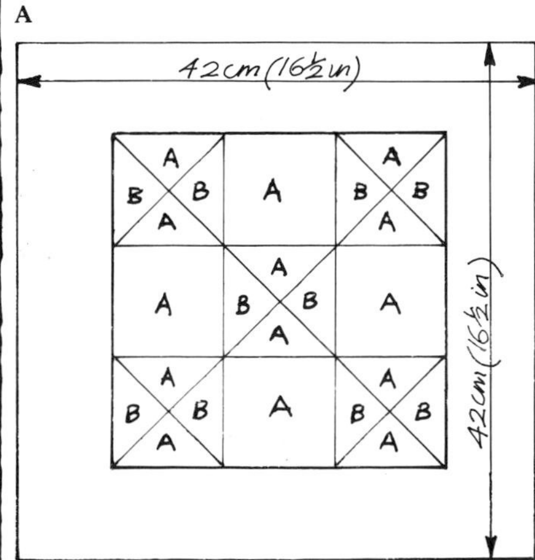

(c) Ten 10cm (4in) quarter triangles red fabric with ten 10cm (4in) quarter triangles Quilter's Secret.

2 Assemble triangles, squares and rows following block diagram A.

3 Following diagram B cut front cushion cover borders as follows:

(a) 2 strips of floral fabric 6.3cm x 42cm (2½in x 16½in)

(b) 2 strips of floral fabric 6.3cm x 32cm (2½in x 12½in)

B

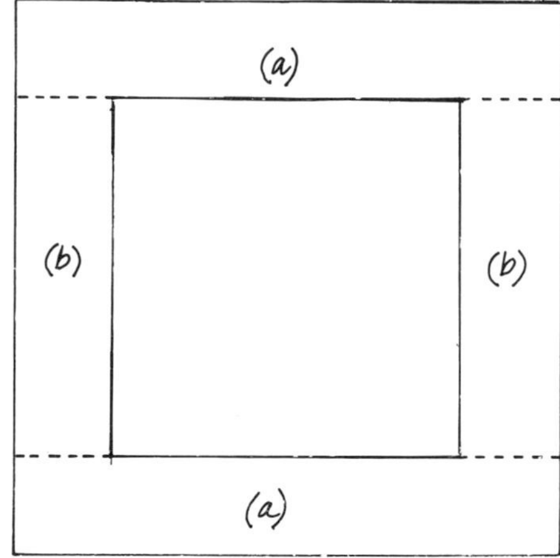

4 Pin, baste and stitch 1 strip (a) to either side of patchwork block.

5 Pin, baste and stitch 1 strip (b) to top and bottom of block. Press carefully.

6 Cut out 2.40m (2⅝yd) strip, 10cm (4in) wide, in red fabric.

7 Gather strip.

8 With right sides and raw edges of frill and patchwork block together, pin, baste and stitch frill to edges of patchwork block.

9 Ties:

(a) Cut 2 strips of plain red fabric each 5cm x 76cm (2in x 30in). Fold in half lengthwise, with right sides facing.

(b) Stitch seam along length of double fabric, 6mm (¼in) in from raw edges.

(c) Turn through to right side.

(d) Press and finish open ends.

10 Measure width between 2 bars on chair back and center same width measurement on top edge of cushion cover front. Fold each tie in half and baste into place on inside edge of patchwork block.

11 (a) Cut piece of floral fabric 29cm x 42cm (11½in x 16½in). Make a narrow hem along one long side. (b) Cut piece of floral fabric 29cm x 42cm (11½in x 16½in). Make a 5cm (2in) hem along one long side.

12 Place right sides of back cover and patchwork block together. Place side (b) to overlap the hemmed edge of side (a). This forms a slip opening through which pillow form is inserted. Diagram C.

C

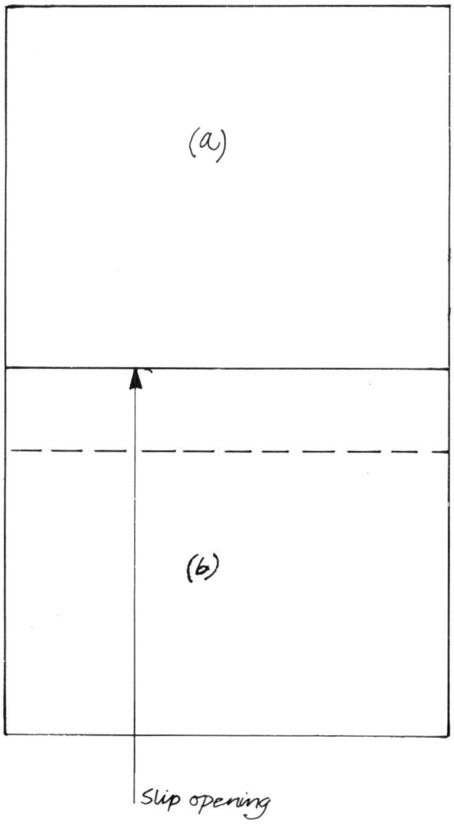

(a)

(b)

Slip opening

13 Pin, baste and stitch all sides. Turn to right side. Press. Insert pillow form overlapping back slip opening.

SEPTEMBER

"September blows soft,-
Till the fruits' in the loft."

SUNDEW

GOLDFINCH

BLACKBERRIES

LEAF *(below)*

Sundew *Knitted Lacy Sweater*

Measurements

To fit bust	86	91	97	102cm
	34	36	38	40in
Length from	60	61	62	63cm
shoulder	23½	24	24½	25in
Sleeve length	42	42	42	42cm
at center	16½	16½	16½	16½in

Materials

4 ply yarn
15 15 16 16 25g balls
Pair of No 3 (3¼mm) and No 1 (2¾mm) needles, set of four No 1 (2¾mm) needles, cable needle

Gauge

28 sts and 36 rows to 10cm (4in) over stockinette stitch on No 3 (3¼mm) needles

Abbreviations

k – knit; **p** – purl; **st(s)** – stitch(es); **patt** – pattern; **sl** – slip; **yfwd** – yarn forward; **inc** – increase(d), increasing; **dec** – decrease(d), decreasing; **beg** – beginning; **alt** – alternate; **rep** – repeat; **psso** – pass slipped stitch over; **cont** – continue; **CB** – slip next 3 sts on cable needle to back of work, k 1, now p 3 from cable needle; **CF** – slip next st on cable needle to front of work, p 3, now k 1 from cable needle; **MB** – make bobble by (k 1, p 1, k 1) all into front of next st; **tog** – together

To Make

Cable Panel (worked over 8 sts)
1st row: p 3, k 2, p 3. **2nd row:** k 3, p 2, k 3. **3rd row:** CB, CF. **4th row:** p 1, k 6, p 1. **5th row:** k 1, p 6, k 1. **6th row:** p 1, k 6, p 1. **7th row:** k 1, p 6, k 1. **8th row:** p 1, k 6, p 1. **9th row:** CF, CB. **10th row:** k 3, p 2, k 3. These 10 rows form cable panel.

Leaf Panel (worked over 9 sts)
(**NB:** sts are increased on 1st, 3rd, 5th, 7th and 9th rows and decreased on 11th, 13th, 15th, 17th and 19th rows. However, when sts are quoted at armhole shaping and sleeve tops, count sts in leaf panel as 9 only per leaf panel.) **1st row:** p 4, inc twice in next st, p 4. **2nd row:** k 4, p 3, k 4. **3rd row:** p 4, k 1, (yfwd, k 1) twice, p 4. **4th row:** k 4, p 5, k 4. **5th row:** p 4, k 2, yfwd, k 1, yfwd, k 2, p 4. **6th row:** k 4, p 7, k 4. **7th row:** p 4, k 3, yfwd, k 1, yfwd, k 3, p 4. **8th row:** k 4, p 9, k 4. **9th row:** p 4, k 4, yfwd, k 1, yfwd, k 4, p 4. **10th row:** k 4, p 11, k 4. **11th row:** p 4, sl 1, k 1, psso, k 7, k 2 tog, p 4. **12th row:** k 4, p 9, k 4. **13th row:** p 4, sl 1, k 1, psso, k 5, k 2 tog, p 4. **14th row:** k 4, p 7, k 4. **15th row:** p 4, sl 1, k 1, psso, k 3, k 2 tog, p 4. **16th row:** k 4, p 5, k 4. **17th row:** p 4, sl 1, k 1, psso, k 1, k 2 tog, p 4. **18th row:** k 4, p 3, k 4. **19th row:** p 4, sl 1, k 2 tog, psso, p 4. **20th row:** k 4, p 1, k 4. These 20 rows form leaf panel.

Front
With No 1 (2¾mm) needles, cast on 124 (132, 140, 148) sts. **1st row:** k 3, (p 2, k 2) to last st, k 1. **2nd row:** k 1, (p 2, k 2) to last 3 sts, p 2, k 1. Rep these 2 rows for 5cm (2in), ending after a 1st row. **Next row:** rib 2 (6, 10, 14), (inc in next st, rib 3) 30 times, inc in next st, rib to end. 155 (163, 171, 179) sts.
Change to No 3 (3¼mm) needles and patt thus: **1st row (right side):** p 2 (6, 10, 14), k 1, yfwd, sl 1, k 2 tog, psso, yfwd, k 1, p 4, work 1st row of cable panel, p 4, k 1, p 8, k 1, p 4, k 1, yfwd, sl 1, k 2 tog, psso, yfwd, k 1, p 4, work 1st row of cable panel, work 1st row of leaf panel, k 1, p 8, k 1, p 2, k 1, yfwd, sl 1, k 2 tog, psso, yfwd, k 1, p 2, k 1, p 8, k 1, work 1st row of leaf panel, work 1st row of cable panel, p 4, k 1, yfwd, sl 1, k 2 tog, psso, yfwd, k 1, p 4, k 1, p 8, k 1, p 4, work 1st row of cable panel, p 4, k 1, yfwd, sl 1, k 2 tog, psso, yfwd, k 1, p 2 (6, 10, 14). **2nd row:** k 2 (6, 10, 14), p 5, k 4, work 2nd row of cable panel, k 4, p 1, (p 3 tog, MB) twice, p 1, k 4, p 5, k 4, work 2nd row of cable panel, work 2nd row of leaf panel, p 1, (p 3 tog, MB) twice, p 1, k 2, p 5, k 2, p 1, (p 3 tog, MB) twice, p 1, work 2nd row of leaf panel, work 2nd row of cable panel, k 4, p 5, k 4, p 1, (p 3 tog, MB) twice, p 1, k 4, work 2nd row of cable panel, k 4, p 5, k to end. **3rd row:** p 2 (6, 10, 14), k 2 tog, yfwd, k 1, yfwd, sl 1, k 1, psso, p 4, work 3rd row of cable panel, p 4, k 1, p 8, k 1, p 4, k 2 tog, yfwd, k 1, yfwd, sl 1, k 1, psso, p 4, work 3rd row of cable panel, work 3rd row of leaf panel, k 1, p 8, k 1, p 2, k 2 tog, yfwd, k 1, yfwd, sl 1, k 1, psso, p 2, k 1, p 8, k 1, work 3rd row of leaf panel, work 3rd row of cable panel, p 4, k 2 tog, yfwd, k 1, yfwd, sl 1, k 1, psso, p 4, k 1, p 8, k 1, p 4, work 3rd row of cable panel, p 4, k 2 tog, yfwd, k 1, yfwd, sl 1, k 1, psso, p to end.
4th row: k 2 (6, 10, 14), p 5, k 4, work 4th row of cable panel, k 4, p 1, (MB, p 3 tog) twice, p 1, k 4, p 5, k 4, work 4th row of cable panel, work 4th row of leaf panel, p 1, (MB, p 3 tog) twice, p 1, k 2, p 5, k 2, p 1, (MB, p 3 tog) twice, p 1, work 4th row of leaf panel, work 4th row of cable panel, k 4, p 5, k 4, p 1, (MB, p 3 tog) twice, p 1, k 4, work 4th row of cable panel, k 4, p 5, k to end. **5th to 8th rows:** rep 1st to 4th rows once but working rows 5 to 8 of panels. **9th and 10th rows:** as 1st and 2nd but working 9th and 10th rows of panels. **11th and 12th rows:** as 3rd and 4th but working 1st and 2nd rows of cable panel and 11th and 12th rows of leaf panel. **13th to 20th rows:** rep 1st to 4th rows twice but working 3rd to 10th rows of cable panel and 13th to 20th rows of leaf panel.
These 20 rows form patt.
Cont in patt until work measures 37cm (14½in) from beg, ending after a wrong-side row.
Keeping patt correct, shape armholes by binding off 9 (10, 11, 12) sts at beg of next 2 rows. Dec 1 st at each end of next 5 rows, then on every following alt row until 121 (125, 129, 133) sts remain.
Work straight until front measures approximately 51cm (20in) from beg, ending after a 20th patt row.
Shape neck thus: **Next row:** patt 39 (40, 41, 42) turn. Cont on this group. Dec 1 st at neck edge on next 5 rows. 34 (35, 36, 37) sts. Work straight until front measures 9 (10, 11, 13) cm, 3½ (4, 4½, 5) in from beg of neck shaping, ending at armhole edge.
Shape shoulder by binding off 11 (12, 12, 12) sts at beg of next and following alt row. Work 1 row. Bind off.
With right side facing, slip next 43 (45, 47, 49) sts on a spare needle. Rejoin yarn to remaining sts and patt 1 row. Complete as first half.

Back
Cast on and work in rib for 5cm (2in) as on front, ending after a 1st row. **Next row:** rib 2 (6, 10, 14), (inc in next st, rib 6) 17 times, inc in next st, rib to end. 142 (150, 158, 166) sts.
Change to No 3 (3¼mm) needles and beg p row work in reversed st st until back measures same as front to armhole shaping, ending after a k row. Shape armholes by binding off 9 (10, 11, 12) sts

at beg of next 2 rows. Dec 1 st at each end of next 5 rows, then on every following alt row until 110 (114, 118, 122) sts remain. Work straight until back measures same as front to shoulder shaping, ending after a k row. Shape shoulders by binding off 10 (11, 11, 11) sts at beg of next 4 rows, then 11 (10, 11, 12) sts at beg of next 2 rows. Slip final 48 (50, 52, 54) sts on a spare needle.

Sleeves

With No 1 (2¾mm) needles, cast on 56 (60, 60, 64) sts. Work in rib as on front for 11 cm (4½in), ending after a 1st row.

Next row: rib 2 (3, 0, 1), inc once in next 51 (53, 59, 61) sts, rib to end. 107 (113, 119, 125) sts.

Change to No 3 (3¼mm) needles and patt thus: **1st row:** p 30 (33, 36, 39), k 1, yfwd, sl 1, k 2 tog, psso, yfwd, k 1, p 4, k 1, p 8, k 1, work 1st row of leaf panel, k 1, p 8, k 1, p 4, k 1, yfwd, sl 1, k 2 tog, psso, yfwd, k 1, p 30 (33, 36, 39). **2nd row:** k 30 (33, 36, 39), p 5, k 4, p 1, (p 3 tog, MB) twice, p 1, work 2nd row of leaf panel, p 1, (p 3 tog, MB) twice, p 1, k 4, p 5, k to end. **3rd row:** p 30 (33, 36, 39), k 2 tog, yfwd, k 1, yfwd, sl 1, k 1, psso, p 4, k 1, p 8, k 1, work 3rd row of leaf panel, k 1, p 8, k 1, p 4, k 2 tog, yfwd, k 1, yfwd, sl 1, k 1, psso, p 30 (33, 36, 39). **4th row:** k 30 (33, 36, 39), p 5, k 4, p 1, (MB, p 3 tog) twice, p 1, work 4th row of leaf panel, p 1, (MB, p 3 tog) twice, p 1, k 4, p 5, k to end. **5th to 20th rows:** rep 1st to 4th rows 4 times but working 5th to 20th rows of leaf panel. Cont in patt as on these 20 rows until sleeve measures 42cm (16½in), ending after a wrong-side row.

Shape top by binding off 9 (10, 11, 12) sts at beg of next 2 rows. Dec 1 st at each end of every right-side row until 55 sts remain, then on every row until 37 sts remain. Bind off.

Neckband

First join shoulders. With set of No 1 (2¾mm) needles, right side facing, k across sts of back dec 5 sts, k up 28 (31, 34, 37) sts evenly down left front neck, k across center front sts dec 8 sts evenly, finally k up 28 (31, 34, 37) sts up right front neck. 134 (144, 154, 164) sts.

Purl 16 rounds. Bind loosely.

To Finish

Omitting ribbing, press lightly using a warm iron and damp cloth. Join side and sleeve seams. Sew in sleeves. Fold neckband in half to wrong side and hem in position. Press seams.

Goldfinch *Embroidered Picture*

Measurements

Embroidered area 41cm x 52cm (16in x 20½in)

Embroidered area plus fabric mount 56cm x 72cm (22in x 28½in)

Materials

Fabric dye: tan or soft brown
Piece of natural linen or heavy cotton 124cm x 78cm (49in x 30¾in)
Gütermann silk thread (spool = 50 meters): 2 spools each 334 Light Grey: 34 Dark Grey: 336 Leaf Green. 1 spool each 46 Red: 800 White: 194 Pale Blue: 421 Buff: 904 Blue: 396 Dark Leaf Green: 915 Turquoise: 100 Eau de Nil: 000 Black: 104 Yellow: 453 Light Brown: 446 Dark Brown: 694 Darker Brown: 697 Very Dark Brown; or use Elsa Williams silk thread
2 washable fabric markers (contrasting shades)
Tracing paper
Ruler/yardstick, Crewel needle No 6

To Make

1 Cut fabric into 2 equal pieces, each approximately 62cm x 78cm (24½in x 30¾in)

2 Following manufacturer's instructions make up dye solution. Wet and dip one piece of fabric in dye. Remove immediately. Wash and rinse.

3 Using a fabric marker, mark rectangle A 56cm x 72cm (28½in x 22in) on the undyed fabric. Center rectangle using straight of grain as a guide. Within rectangle A mark rectangle B as shown in diagram 1.

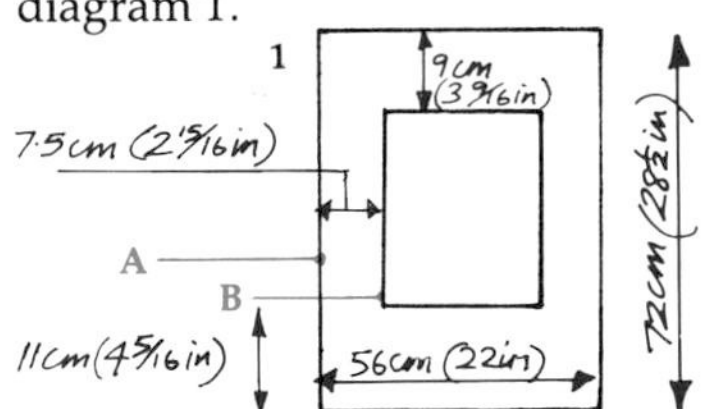

4 Mark rectangle C 2.5cm (1in) in from each side of rectangle B. Diagram 2. Cut our rectangle C and snip carefully into corners of rectangle B. Fold snipped edges to lie flat on wrong side to form a window.

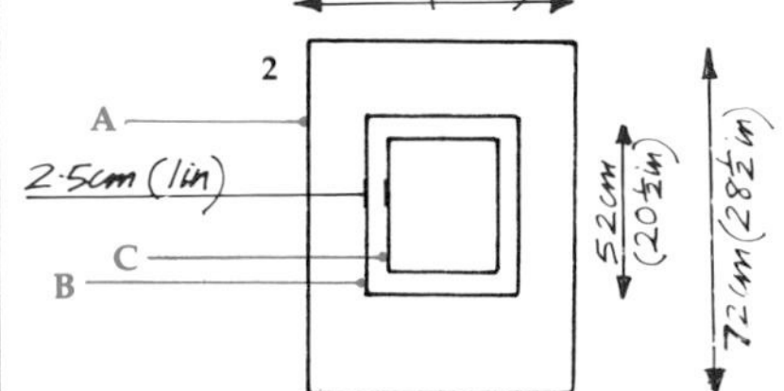

5 Press the dyed fabric with a damp cloth and warm iron.

6 On dyed fabric mark out rectangle D 41cm x 52cm (16in x 20½in). Mark rectangle E 2.5cm (1in) outside each side of rectangle D. Diagram 3.

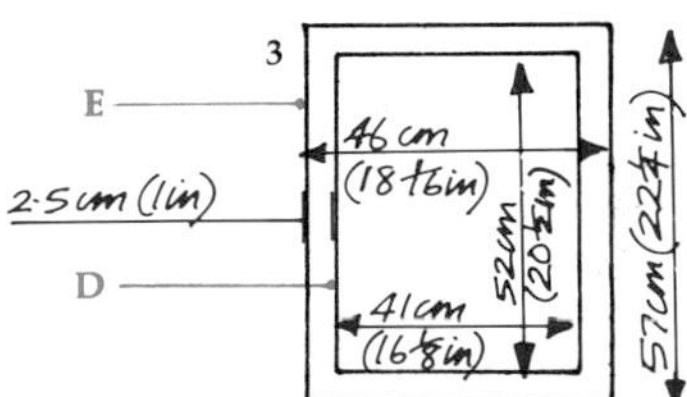

7 Center the fabric under the natural fabric matching the two 41cm x 52cm (16in x 20½in) rectangles.

8 Pin, baste and stitch window edge neatly into position. Neaten raw edges lying on wrong side.

9 Press on wrong side.

10 Following illustration from page 124 of 'The Country Diary of an Edwardian Lady' (page 118) draw a free-hand interpretation of the design onto the dyed window area of fabric. Alternatively, transfer the design onto squared paper, and, using a ruler and fabric marker, divide copy of design into sections following the diagram.

4

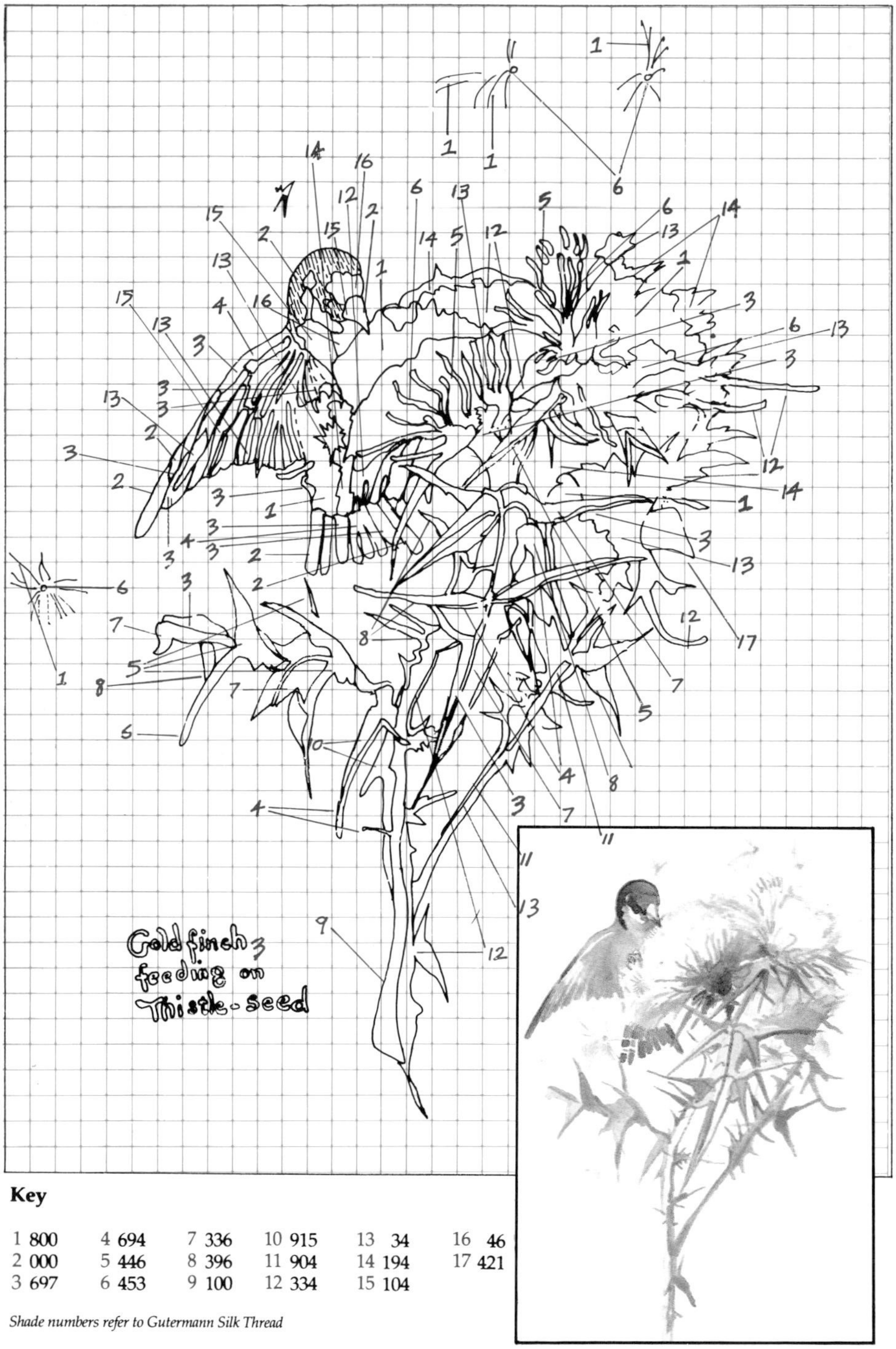

Goldfinch feeding on Thistle-seed

Key

1 800	4 694	7 336	10 915	13 34	16 46
2 000	5 446	8 396	11 904	14 194	17 421
3 697	6 453	9 100	12 334	15 104	

Shade numbers refer to Gutermann Silk Thread

11 Using a ruler or yardstick, transfer diagram 4 onto window area of fabric, each section of the paper onto the identical section on the fabric. Begin by indicating general outlines of shapes and then complete each detail in turn.

12 Work in single thread throughout following chart and key above. Three basic stitches are used: satin stitch, stem stitch, long and short stitch (refer to Glossary of Embroidery Stitches on page 156 for details).

13 Begin with black and white stitches to establish the two extremes of shading.

14 When work is complete, wash out all fabric pen markings.

15 Turn to page 62 for details of blocking, mounting and framing finished work.

Blackberries

Needlepoint Drum Stool

Measurements

Needlepoint panel 45cm (17¾in) diameter

Materials

60cm (23½in) of 58cm (23in) wide No 10 mono canvas
Crewel wool by Appleton Bros Ltd: 4 hanks 882; 1 hank each of 694; 695; 355; 402; 354; 401; 765; 766; 767; 334; 251; 692; 256; 406; 254; 934; 935; 125; 951; 965; 998; 106; 967; 953; 914; 338; 913; 209; 866; 865; 624; 861; 841
Tapestry needle No 18
Drum stool
Upholstery tacks

To Make

Important Note: read 'General Working Instructions for all Needlepoint' on page 15.

1 Lightly fold canvas in both directions (widthwise and lengthwise) to form center lines. Work basting stitches along center lines.

2 Center of chart is indicated by arrows which should coincide with basting stitches.

3 Using 5 strands of crewel wool throughout, work needlepoint following chart and key for 'Blackberries' design opposite, working as far as possible out from center.

4 Each square on chart represents 1 square of single thread canvas, or 1 tapestry stitch.

5 Complete background using 882.

6 Remove basting threads.

7 Model worked in tent stitch.

Fixing finished canvas to circular stool:
1 Thread tapestry needle with length of strong thread and work running stitches

around canvas 2cm (¾in) beyond edge of stitching to form drawstring.

2 Place canvas face down on table, center padded top onto canvas. Press downwards in center of plywood base and pull both ends of drawstring, to draw canvas edges over plywood base. Tie.

3 Ease out gathers to obtain even finish around edge.

4 Leave top for 24 to 48 hours to allow canvas to stretch.

5 Nail 2 rows of upholstery tacks, 2cm (¾in) apart, to underside edge of plywood base to secure needlepoint in place.

6 Trim surplus canvas 2cm (¾in) out from edge of drawstring.

7 Place padded top into recess of stool base. Turn upside down and secure with screws.

Blackberries
Needlepoint Drum Stool

Design size (approx.) 10 stitches to 2.5cm (1in)

Needlepoint panel 45cm (17¾in) diameter

Background *882*

Key

←	694
Λ	695
—	355
Z	402
>	354
\	401
U	765
Γ	766
T	767
•.•	334
II	251
∧	692
=	256
|	406
┘	254
V	934
X	935
┐	125
O	951
L	965
⁒	998
∀	106
⊥	967
И	953
+	914
•	338
→	913
⁙	209
●	866
↑	865
<	624
I	861
A	841
C	407
↓	691
/	253
÷	251a

Shade numbers refer to Crewel Wool by Appleton Bros. Ltd.

Leaf *Crochet Cushion Cover and Shelf Edgings*

Measurements

Cushion cover 40cm (15¾in) square
Small edgings 46cm (18in) wide by 8cm (3¼in)
Width of shelf edgings can be adjusted by varying number of leaves

Materials

8 (25g) balls 3 ply yarn
No 4 crochet hook
40cm (16in) pillow form

Gauge

3 repeats of net pattern measure 5cm (2in) wide

Abbreviations

ch – chain; **cont** – continue; **dc** – double crochet; **hdc** – half double crochet; **lp(s)** – loop(s); **patt** – pattern; **prev** – previous; **rep** – repeat; **sc** – single crochet; **sk** – skip; **ss** – slip stitch; **st(s)** – stitch(es); **tc** – treble crochet; **yo** – yarn over

Note: Work instructions in brackets the number of times given. Single leaves or leaf sprays could be used to decorate sheer curtains. Shelf edgings would make an attractive edging for a plain tablecloth.

To Make

CUSHION COVER WITH LEAF SPRAYS

Cover (make 2)
Make 102 ch. **1st row:** 1 sc in 10th ch from hook, 3 ch, 1 sc in same ch, (5 ch, sk 3 ch, 1 sc/3 ch/1 sc all in next ch) to last 4 ch, 5 ch, sk 3 ch, 1 sc in last ch, 5 ch, turn. **2nd row:** (1 sc/3 ch/1 sc all into 3rd of 5 ch, 5 ch) to end, 1 sc into turning ch, 5 ch, turn. Rep 2nd row until work measures 40cm (15¾in), ending 5 ch, turn. **Next row:** (1 sc into 3rd of next 5 ch loop, 3 ch) to end, ending last rep, 1 sc into 3rd of turning ch. Fasten off.

Leaf Sprays (make 4)
Note: work into back lps only throughout.
1st and 2nd leaves (worked alike) Make 16 ch. **1st row:** 1 sc in 2nd ch from hook, 1 sc into each of next 13 ch, 3 sc in next ch, cont along other side of foundation ch, 1 sc into each of next 14 ch, 1 ch, turn. **2nd row:** 1 sc in each of next 11 sc, turn with 1 ch. **3rd row:** 1 sc in each of 11 sc, 3 sc in space between 1st 2 rows, 1 sc in each of 11 sc along other side, 1 ch, turn. **4th row:** 1 sc in each of 12 sc, 3 sc in next sc, 1 sc in each of 8 sc, 1 ch, turn. **5th row:** 1 sc in each of 9 sc, 3 sc in next sc, 1 sc in each of 9 sc, 1 ch, turn. **6th row:** 1 sc in 10 sc, 3 sc in next sc, 1 sc in each of 6 sc, 1 ch, turn. **7th row:** 1 sc in each of 7 sc, 3 sc in next sc, 1 sc in each of 7 sc. Fasten off.

Center Leaf
Make 16 ch and work 1st row as 1st and 2nd leaves. **2nd row:** 1 sc in each of next 13 sc, 1 ch, turn. **3rd row:** 1 sc in each of 13 sc, 3 sc in space between 1st 2 rows, 1 sc in each of next 13 sc, 1 ch, turn. **4th row:** 1 sc in each of next 14 sc, 3 sc in next sc, 1 sc in each of next 11 sc, 1 ch, turn. **5th row:** 1 sc in each of next 12 sc, 3 sc in next sc, 1 sc in each of next 11 sc, turn. **6th row:** 1 sc in each of next 12 sc, 3 sc in next sc, 1 sc in each of next 10 sc, 1 ch, turn. **7th row:** 1 sc in each of next 11 sc, 3 sc in next sc, 1 sc in each of next 10 sc, 1 ch, turn. **8th row:** 1 sc in each of next 11 sc, 3 sc in next sc, 1 sc in each of next 9 sc. Fasten off.

Stalk
Make 25 ch. **1st row:** 1 sc in 2nd ch from hook, 1 sc in each ch to end, working 2 more sc in last ch, turn and work 1 sc in each ch along other side to end, 1 ch, turn. **2nd row:** 1 sc in each of 6 ch, 1 ch, turn, 1 sc in each of next 6 sc, work 3 sc in space between 1st 2 rows, work 1 sc in each of 6 sc along other side, 1 ch, turn. **3rd row:** 1 sc in each of 7 sc. Fasten off.

To Finish
Join center of center leaf to top of stalk and sew remaining 2 leaves between the center leaf and the stalk. Sew 2 leaf sprays to each piece of cover. Join 3 sides of cover, insert pillow form and join remaining side.

CROCHET SHELF EDGINGS
Leaves (Make 11 leaves for each piece of edging)
Note: work into back lps only throughout.
Make 16 ch. **1st row:** 1 sc in 2nd ch from hook, 1 sc in each of next 13 ch, 3 sc into last ch, cont along other side of ch, omit last ch and work 1 sc into each ch to end, 1 ch, turn. **2nd row:** 1 sc into each of next 12 sc, 1 ch, turn. **3rd row:** 1 sc in each of 12 sc, 3 sc into space between 1st 2 rows, 1 sc into each of next 12 sc along other side to 3 sc before next 3 sc group, 1 ch, turn. **4th row:** 1 sc in each sc to within last 3 sc of last row, working 3 sc into center sc of top 3 sc group, 1 ch, turn. **5th, 6th and 7th rows:** as 4th row. **8th row:** 1 sc in each sc to center of 3 sc group at top, ss into top sc. Fasten off. After first leaf, work remaining leaves to 7th row. **8th row:** 1 ss in corresponding sc on prev leaf, then complete as 8th row on 1st leaf. Fasten off.

Heading
1st row: Join yarn to center sc at top of 1st leaf at right hand end, 1 sc into same place, *7 ch, keeping the last lp of each st on hook, work 1 tc into center sc along side of this leaf, then 1 tc into center sc along side of next leaf, yo and draw through all 3 lps on hook – called joint dc – 7 ch, 1 sc in center sc at top of this leaf; rep from * to end, 4 ch, turn. **2nd row:** *(sk 1 ch, 1 dc into next ch, 1 ch) 3 times, sk 1 ch, 1 dc into top of joint dc, 1 ch, (sk 1 ch, 1 dc into next ch, 1 ch) 3 times, sk 1 ch, 1 dc into sc; rep from * to end. Fasten off.

To Finish
Block out into shape and press.
Make 2 more shelf edgings in the same way or as many as required making sure to increase amounts of Twilley Lyscordet accordingly.

OCTOBER

"Then came October, full of merry glee."

APPLE

BERRIES

WOODLAND

Apple *Needlepoint Cushion Cover*

Measurements

42cm x 30cm (16½in x 12in)

Materials

40cm (15¾in) of 68cm (26¾in) wide No 10 Penelope (double-threaded) canvas
Anchor Tapestry Wool in 10m (11yd) skeins: 6 skeins of 0436; 3 skeins each of 0278; 0280; 013; 2 skeins each of 0638; 0963; 010; 0412; 0650; 1 skein 0402 White
Tapestry needle No 10
40cm x 122cm (15¾in x 48in) wide matching medium weight upholstery fabric for backing
Matching thread
Pillow form to fit

To Make

Important Note: read 'General Working Instructions for all Needlepoint' on page 15.

1 Fold canvas lightly in both directions (widthwise and lengthwise) to form center lines. Work basting stitches along center lines.

2 Design is worked throughout in tent stitch. See page 157.

Apple
Needlepoint Cushion

Key
- • 0278
- ╲ 0280
- X 0638
- ╱ 0963
- — 010
- V 0412
- O 013
- + 0402
- Λ 0436
- | 0650

Shade numbers refer to Anchor Tapestry wool.

Approx. design size:
10 stitches to 2.5cm (1in)
42cm x 30cm (16½in x 11¾in)

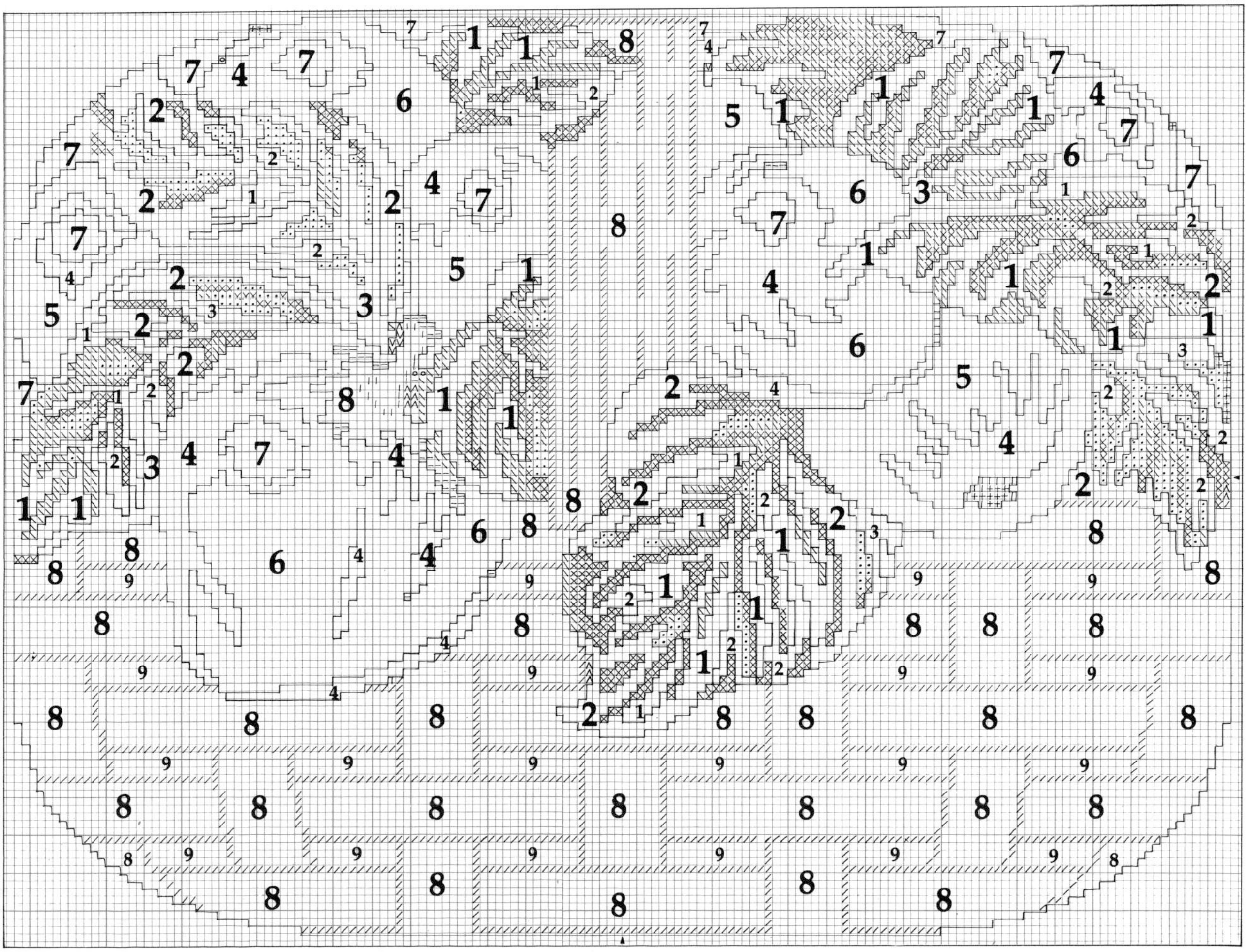

3 Work needlepoint following chart and key for 'Apple' design on page 125, working as far as possible out from center. Center of chart is indicated by black arrows which should coincide with basting stitches. Each background square on chart represents 1 intersection of double threads of canvas, or 1 tapestry stitch.

4 Remove basting threads.

5 Trim canvas to within 2cm (¾in) of stitching.

6 Cut backing fabric to same size as front.

7 With right sides together, baste and stitch close to needlepoint on 3 sides.

8 Turn to right side, insert pillow form and join remaining side.

Berries

Lady's Knitted Sweater

Measurements

To fit bust	81	86	91	97cm
	32	34	36	38in
Length from	62	63	63	65cm
shoulder	24½	25	25	25½in
Sleeve seam	47	47	47	47cm
	18½	18½	18½	18½in

Materials

Knitting worsted					
Dark (D)	2	2	2	2	50g balls
Medium (M)	8	8	8	9	50g balls
Light (L)	1	1	2	2	50g balls

Pair of needles each Nos 5 (4mm) and 3 (3¼mm)
Set of four No 3 (3¼mm) needles

Gauge

Instructions are based on a standard stockinette stitch tension of 24 sts and 30 rows to 10cm (4in) on No 5 (4mm) needles

Abbreviations

k – knit; **p** – purl; **st(s)** – stitch(es); **patt** – pattern; **inc** – increase, increasing; **dec** – decrease, decreasing; **beg** – beginning; **alt** – alternate; **rep** – repeat; **cont** – continue; **tog** – together; **D** – dark shade; **L** – light shade; **M** – medium shade; **m 3** – make 3 by increasing 3 sts in next st, now k across the 3 sts and the original st; **tw 3** – twist 3 by slipping next 2 sts, k 1, pass 2nd st on right needle over st just knitted and k into back of it, now pass 3rd st on right needle over next 2 sts and k into back of it; **MB** – make bobble thus: k into front, back, front, back of next st, thus making 4 out of 1, turn, p 4, turn, k 4, turn, p 4, turn, (k 2 tog) twice, slip 2nd st on right needle over 1st; **tbl** – through back of loops

Patt A

1st row: p 8, (k 1, m 3, p 8) to end. **2nd row:** k 8, (p 5, k 8) to end. **3rd row:** p 8, (k 5, p 8) to end. **4th row:** as 2nd. **5th row:** p 8, (k 2 tog tbl, k 1, k 2 tog, p 8) to end. **6th row:** k 8, (p 3, k 8) to end. **7th row:** p 8, (k next 3 sts tog, do not slip off left needle, now k the 1st of these sts again slipping all sts off left needle, p 8) to end. **8th row:** k 8, (p 2, k 8) to end. **9th row:** p 3, (k 1, m 3, p 8) to last 5 sts, k 1, m 3, p 3. **10th row:** k 3, (p 5, k 8) to last 8 sts, p 5, k 3. **11th row:** p 3, (k 5, p 8) to last 8 sts, k 5, p 3. **12th row:** as 10th row. **13th row:** p 3, (k 2 tog tbl, k 1, k 2 tog, p 8) to last 8 sts, k 2 tog tbl, k 1, k 2 tog, p 3. **14th row:** k 3, (p 3, k 8) to last 6 sts, p 3, k 3. **15th row:** p 3, (twist 3 as on 7th row, p 8) to last 6 sts, twist 3, p 3. **16th row:** k 3, (p 2, k 8) to last 5 sts, p 2, k 3. These 16 rows form patt A.

Patt B

1st row: p 4, (k 3, p 3) to last st, p 1. **2nd row:** k 4, (p 3, k 3) to last st, k 1. **3rd row:** p 4, (tw 3, p 3) to last st, p 1. **4th row:** as 2nd row. **5th row:** as 1st row. **6th row:** p. **7th row:** p 1, (k 3, p 3) to last 4 sts, k 3, p 1. **8th row:** k 1, (p 3, k 3) to last 4 sts, p 3, k 1. **9th row:** p 1, (tw 3, p 3) to last 4 sts, tw 3, p 1. **10th row:** as 8th row. **11th row:** as 7th row. **12th row:** p. These 12 rows form patt B.

To Make

Front
With No 3 (3¼mm) needles and D, cast on 92 (100, 104, 112) sts. **1st row** (right side): k 3, (p 2, k 2) to last st, k 1. **2nd row:** k 1, (p 2, k 2) to last 3 sts, p 2, k 1. Rep these 2 rows for 10cm (4in), ending after a 2nd row. **Next row:** rib 4 (2, 10, 8), *inc in next st, rib 5 (7, 5, 7), rep from * to last 4 (2, 10, 8) sts, inc in next st, rib to end. 107 (113, 119, 125) sts. Break D. Change to No 5 (4mm) needles and divide work thus: **Next row (wrong side):** in M, p 39 (45, 41, 47), slip these sts on a length of yarn, now using D, p across remaining 68 (68, 78, 78) sts. Cont on last group. Work in patt A until front measures approximately 19cm (7½in) from *top* of rib, ending after a 7th or 15th patt row. Slip sts on a spare needle. Return to group of sts in M and slip them onto a No 5 (4mm) needle, point facing center of work.
Work in *all-over patt* in M thus: **1st row** (right side): p. **2nd row:** k 1, (p 1, k 1) to end. Rep these 2 patt rows until work measures same as D section, ending after a 1st row. Break M. **Next row:** in D, p to end, now p across the first 26 (26, 30, 30) sts on spare needle, then in L, p across remaining 42 (42, 48, 48) sts on spare needle. Cont on the last group of 42 (42, 48, 48) sts in L. **1st row:** p 42 (42, 48, 48) sts, turn, slip remaining 65 (71, 71, 77) sts on a length of yarn. **2nd row:** (k 1, p 1) to end. Rep these 2 rows until work measures 37 cm (14½in) from top of rib, ending after a p row. Break L. Slip sts on a spare needle. Return to group of sts in D and slip them onto a No 5 (4mm) needle, point facing center of work. Using D work in patt B until work measures 37cm (14½in) from top of welt, ending after a 5th or 11th row. Break D. **Next row:** in M, p to end, now p across sts on spare needle.
Change to *bobble patt* and work thus: **1st row:** p. **2nd row:** k. **3rd row:** p 2, (MB, p 5) to last 3 sts, MB, p 2. **4th row:** k. **5th to 10th rows:** rep 1st and 2nd rows 3 times. **9th row:** p 5, (MB, p 5) to end. **10th row:** k. **11th to 14th rows:** rep 1st and 2nd rows twice. These 14 rows form bobble patt.
Cont in patt until work measures 54cm (21½in) from beg, ending after a wrong-side row.

Shape neck thus: (**NB:** do not work bobbles on edge sts) **Next row:** patt 43 (45, 47, 49), turn. Cont on this group. Dec 1 st at neck edge on next 5 rows. 38 (40, 42, 44) sts. Work straight until front measures 62 (63, 63, 65) cm, 24½ (25, 25, 25½) in from beg, ending at side edge. Shape shoulder by binding off 9 (10, 10, 11) sts at beg of next and 2 following alt rows. Work 1 row. Bind off.
With right side facing, slip center 21 (23, 25, 27) sts on a spare needle. Rejoin M to remaining sts and work 1 row. Complete as first half.

Back
Omitting neck shaping work as front to shoulder shaping, ending after a wrong-side row. Shape shoulders by binding off 9 (10, 10, 11) sts at beg of next 6 rows, then 11 (10, 12, 11) sts at beg of next 2 rows. Slip final 31 (33, 35, 37) sts on a spare needle.

Sleeves
With No 3 (3¼mm) needles and M, cast on 44 (48, 48, 52) sts. Work in rib as on front for 10cm (4in), ending after a 1st row. **Next row:** rib 5 (6, 3, 4), inc once in next 33 (35, 41, 43) sts, rib to end. 77 (83, 89, 95) sts.
Change to No 5 (4mm) needles and all-over patt as on front, shaping sleeve by inc 1 st at each end of 3rd row, then on every following 12th row until there are 89 (95, 101, 107) sts, taking extra sts into patt.
Work straight until sleeve measures 34cm (13½in) at center, ending after a wrong-side row.
Change to bobble patt as on front yoke until sleeve measures 47cm (18½in) at center. Bind off loosely.

Neckband
First join shoulders. With set of No 3 (3¼mm) needles and M, right side facing, k up 100 (108, 112, 120) sts evenly round neck, including sts on spare needles. Work 9 rounds in k 2, p 2 rib. Bind off in rib.

To Finish
Omitting ribbing, press lightly following pressing instructions. Join inner seams of front and back. Allowing approximately 21 (22, 23, 24)cm, 8¼ (8¾, 9¼, 9¾) in for armhole, sew bound-off edges of sleeves to yoke. Join side and sleeve seams. Press seams.

Berries

Man's Knitted Sweater

Measurements

To fit chest	97	102	107	112cm
	38	40	42	44in
Length from	65	66	67	69cm
shoulder	25½	26	26½	27in
Sleeve seam	52	52	52	52cm
	20½	20½	20½	20½in

Materials

Knitting worsted

Dark (D)	10	10	10	11	50g balls
Medium (M)	5	5	5	5	50g balls
Light (L)	1	1	2	2	50g balls

Pair of needles each Nos 5 (4mm) and 3 (3¼mm)
Set of 4 No 3 (3¼mm) needles

Gauge

21 sts and 35 rows to 10cm (4in) over moss stitch on No 5 (4mm) needles

Abbreviations

k – knit; **p** – purl; **st(s)** – stitch(es); **patt** – pattern; **inc** – increase, increasing; **dec** – decrease, decreasing; **beg** – beginning; **alt** – alternate; **rep** – repeat; **cont** – continue; **D** – dark shade; **L** – light shade; **M** – medium shade; **mst** – moss stitch; **tw3** – twist 3 thus: slip next 2 sts, k 1, pass 2nd st on right needle over st just knitted and k into back of it, now pass 3rd st on right needle over next 2 sts and k into back of it

To Make

Front
With No 3 (3¼mm) needles and M, cast on 108 (112, 120, 124) sts. **1st row (right side):** k 3, (p 2, k 2) to last st, k 1. **2nd row:** k 1, (p 2, k 2) to last 3 sts, p 2, k 1. Rep these 2 rows for 10cm (4in), ending after a 2nd row. **Next row:** rib 4 (2, 10, 8), (inc in next st, rib 3, inc in next st, rib 4) 11 (12, 11, 12) times, rib to end. 130 (136, 142, 148) sts.
Change to No 5 (4mm) needles and divide work thus: **Next row (wrong side):** in M, p 77 (83, 83, 89), slip these sts on a length of yarn, now using D, p across remaining 53 (53, 59, 59) sts. Cont on last group.
Work in patt B as for lady's version until front measures approximately 18cm (7in) from *top* of rib, ending after a 6th or 12th patt row. Break D. Join in M and k 1 row. Slip sts on a spare needle.
Return to group of sts in M and slip them onto a No 5 (4mm) needle, point facing center of work.
Work in *all-over* patt in M thus: **1st row (right side):** k. **2nd row:** k 2, (p 1, k 2) to end. **3rd and 4th rows:** k. Rep these 4 patt rows until work measures same as D section, ending after a 3rd row. Break M. **Next row:** in L, p 53 (53, 59, 59), slip these sts on a length of yarn, in M, k to end, now still using M, k across sts on spare needle. Beg with 1st patt row work in all-over patt in M on the group of 77 (83, 83, 89) sts until work measures approximately 36cm (14in), from *top* of rib, ending after a 3rd patt row. Break M. Slip sts on a spare needle. Return to group of 53 (53, 59, 59) sts in L and slip them onto a No 5 (4mm) needle, point facing center of work. Using L, beg with 1st patt row, work in patt B until work measures approximately 36cm (14in) from beg, ending after a 5th or 11th patt row. Break L. **Next row:** in D, p to end dec 5 sts evenly, then still using D, p across sts on spare needle dec 8 sts evenly. 117 (123, 129, 135) sts.
Change to mst over all sts and using D for remainder work until front measures 46cm (18in) from *top* of rib, ending after a wrong-side row.
Shape neck thus: **Next row:** mst 47 (49, 51, 53), turn. Cont on this group. Dec 1 st at neck edge on next 5 rows. 42 (44, 46, 48) sts. Work straight until front measures 65 (66, 67, 69) cm, 25½ (26, 26½, 27) in from beg, ending at side edge. Shape shoulder by binding off 10 (11, 11, 12) sts at beg of next and 2 following alt rows. Work 1 row. Bind off.
With right side facing, slip center 23 (25, 27, 29) sts on a spare needle. Rejoin D and mst 1 row. Complete as first half.

Back
Omitting neck shaping, work as front to shoulder shaping, ending after a wrong-side row.
Shape shoulders by binding off 10 (11, 11, 12) sts at beg of next 6 rows, then 12 (11, 13, 12) sts at beg of next 2 rows. Slip final 33 (35, 37, 39) sts on a spare needle.

Sleeves
With No 3 (3¼mm) needles and D, bind on 48 (52, 52, 56) sts. Work in rib as on front for 10cm (4in), ending after a 1st row. **Next row:** rib 4 (6, 2, 0), *inc in next st, rib 4 (3, 2, 2); rep from * to last 4 (6, 2, 2) sts, inc in next st, rib to end. 57 (63, 69, 75) sts.
Change to No 5 (4mm) needles and mst, shaping sleeve by inc 1 st at each end of

3rd row, then on every following 6th row until there are 103 (109, 115, 121) sts, taking extra sts into mst. Work straight until sleeve measures 52cm (20½in) from beg. Bind off loosely.

Neckband
First join shoulders. With set of No 5 (3¼mm) needles and D, right side facing, k up 108 (116, 128, 136) sts evenly round neck including sts on spare needles. Work 24 rounds in k 2, p 2 rib. Bind off loosely.

To Finish
Work as for lady's version but allowing 24 (26, 27, 28) cm, 9¾ (10¼, 10¾, 11¼) in for armholes and noting that neckband should be folded in half to wrong side and hemmed in position all round.

Woodland

Crochet Patchwork Jacket and Sweater

Measurements

To fit bust	81/86	91/97cm
	32/34	36/38in
Jacket length	63	68cm
	24¾	26¾in
Sweater length	60	65cm
	23½	25½in
Sleeve length	42	43cm
	16½	17in

Materials

Fisherman wool

Jacket	27	29	50g balls
Sweater	24	26	50g balls

No 5/F and 8/H crochet hooks for 1st size
No 5/F and 9/I crochet hooks for 2nd size
7 buttons for jackets

Gauge

Each square should measure 10cm x 10cm, (11cm x 11cm), 4in x 4in (4¼in x 4¼in). Over main patt of sleeve 28 sts and 28 rows measure 20cm (8in) using No 8/H hook; 26 sts and 26 rows measure 20cm (8in) using No 9/I hook.

Abbreviations

beg – beginning; **ch** – chain; **cont** – continue; **dc** – double crochet; **hdc** – half double crochet; **inc** – increase(d), increasing; **lp(s)** – loop(s); **patt** – pattern; **rtc** – raised treble crochet (inserting hook from front work 1 tc around stem of st); **rep** – repeat; **rdc** – raised double crochet (inserting hook from front work 1 dc around stem of st); **sc** – single crochet; **sk** – skip(ped); **sp(s)** – space(s); **st(s)** – stitch(es); **tog** – together; **tc** – treble crochet; **yo** – yarn over
Note: All sts worked around stems of sts must be worked to the height of the remaining sts of the new row. Figures or hook sizes in brackets are for larger size.

To Make

JACKET
Square A (make 14)
With 8/H (9/I) hook, make 21 ch. **1st row:** 1 sc in 5th ch from hook, *1 ch, sk 1 ch, 1 sc in next ch; rep from * to end. **2nd row:** 1 ch, *1 sc in ch sp, 1 ch; rep from * ending 1 sc in sp formed by turning ch, 1 sc in 3rd of 4 ch (note on subsequent rows end 1 sc in 2nd of 2 ch). **3rd row:** 2 ch, *1 sc in ch sp, 1 ch; rep from * ending 1 sc in turning ch. Rep 2nd and 3rd rows until square measures 10 (11) cm, 4 (4¼) in. Fasten off.

Square B (make 14)
With 8/H (9/I) hook, make 14 ch loosely. **1st row:** 1 dc in 3rd ch from hook, *1 puff st (yo, insert hook in st, yo and pull lp through and up to 1cm (½in) 4 times, yo and draw through all lps, 1 ch to complete puff st) in next ch, 1 dc in each of next 3 ch; rep from * to last 3 ch, 1 puff st in next ch, 1 dc in each of last 2 ch. **2nd row:** 2 ch, sk 1st dc, 1 dc in next dc, *1 dc in puff st, 1 dc in next dc, 1 puff st in next dc, 1 dc in next dc; rep from * ending 1 dc in puff st, 1 dc in next dc, 1 dc in top of turning ch. **3rd row:** 2 ch, sk 1st dc, *1 dc in next dc, 1 puff st in next dc, 1 dc in next dc, 1 dc in puff st; rep from * ending 1 dc in next dc, 1 puff st in next dc, 1 dc in next dc, 1 dc in top of turning ch. Rep 2nd and 3rd rows until square measures 10 (11) cm, 4 (4¼) in. Fasten off.

Square C (make 10)
With 8/H (9/I) hook, make 16 ch loosely. **1st row:** 1 dc in 3rd ch from hook, 1 dc in each ch to end. **2nd row (right side):** 2 ch, sk 1st dc, 1 hdc in next dc, *1 rdc around stem of each of next 4 dc*, 1 hdc in each of next 3 dc, rep from * to * once, 1 hdc in last dc, 1 hdc in top of turning ch. **3rd row:** 2 ch, sk 1st hdc, 1 dc in each st to end, 1 dc in top of turning ch. **4th row:** 2 ch, sk 1st dc, 1 hdc in next dc, *working around sts of 2nd row sk first 2 rtc and work 1 rdc around stem of each of next 2 rdc, 1 rtc around stem of each of 2 sk rtc*, 1 hdc in each of next 3 dc, rep from * to * once, 1 hdc in last dc, 1 hdc in top of turning ch. **5th row:** as 3rd row. Rep 2nd to 5th rows once, then 2nd row again. Fasten off.

Square D (make 10)
With 8/H (9/I) hook, make 16 ch loosely. **1st row:** 1 dc in 3rd ch from hook, 1 dc in each ch to end. 15 sts. **2nd, 4th, 6th and 8th rows:** 2 ch, sk 1st st, 1 dc in each st, 1 dc in top of turning ch. 15 sts. **3rd row (right side):** 2 ch, sk 1st dc, 1 dc in each of next 2 dc, *leaving last lp of each st on hook work 1 tc around stem of 2nd st of 1st row, 1 tc around 6th st of 1st row and 1 dc in top of 4th st of last row, yo and draw through all 4 lps – JST worked, 1 dc in each of next 3 dc*, rep from * to * once working 1st tc around 6th st of 1st row, 2nd tc around 10th st and dc in 8th st, rep from * to * again working 1st tc around 10th st, 2nd tc around 14th st and dc in 12th st, at end of rep work last dc in top of turning ch. **5th row:** 2 ch, sk 1st 2 dc, *leaving last lp of each st on hook work 1 tc around stem of 1st JST of 3rd row and 1 dc in 2nd st of last row, yo and draw through all 3 lps*, **1 dc in each of next 3 dc, work JST working 1st tc around 1st JST of 3rd row, 2nd tc around 2nd JST of 3rd row and dc in next st of last row**, rep from ** to ** once working 1st tc around 2nd JST of 3rd row, 2nd tc around 3rd JST of 3rd row and dc in next dc of last row, rep from * to * again working tc around 3rd JST of 3rd row and dc in last dc of last row, 1 dc in top of turning ch. **7th row:** 2 ch, sk 1st dc, 1 dc in each of next 2 dc, *1 JST working 1st tc around 1st tc of 5th row, 2nd tc around 1st JST of 5th row and dc in next st of last row, 1 dc in each of next 3 dc*, rep from * to * once working 1st tc around 1st JST of 5th row, 2nd tc around 2nd JST of 5th row and dc in next dc of last row, rep from * to * again working 1st tc around 2nd JST of

5th row, 2nd tc around last tc of 5th row and dc in next dc of last row, at end of rep work last dc in top of turning ch. **9th row:** as 5th row but working into JSTs of 7th row. **10th row:** as 2nd. Fasten off. Following diagram oversew squares tog. Join squares marked * tog and squares marked ** tog.

Neck Shaping
Round off each of the 4 neck corners thus: place pins 2cm (¾in) to each side of any corner. **1st row:** with 8/H (9/I) hook and right side facing, join yarn at 1st pin, work 4 sc evenly from pin to just before corner, insert hook in work just before corner, yo and draw lp through, insert hook in work just after corner, yo and draw lp through, yo and draw through all lps, 4 sc evenly to next pin, turn. **2nd row:** sk 1st sc, 1 sc in each of next 3 sc, sk corner st, 1 sc in each of next 3 sc, ss in last sc. Fasten off.

Sleeves
Cuff: worked from side to side. With 5/F hook, make 10 ch. **1st row:** 1 sc in 2nd ch from hook, 1 sc in each ch to end. 9 sc. **Patt row:** 1 ch, 1 sc in back lp of each sc to end. Rep patt row until cuff measures 19 (20) cm, 7½ (8) in. Fasten off. **Main part:** change to 8/H (9/I) hook. **Next row:** join yarn to corner of one long edge, 3 ch, 50 dc evenly along edge, turn. Cont in patt: **1st row:** 1 ch, 1 sc in each dc, 1 sc in top of turning ch. **2nd row (right side):** 2 ch, sk 1st sc, *sk next sc, 1 rdc around stem of dc 1 row below sk st, 1 dc in next sc; rep from * to end. These 2 rows form sleeve patt. Cont in patt inc 1 st at each end of next row and every following 4th row until there are 71 sts, working inc sts into patt. Patt straight until sleeve measures 47 (48) cm, 18½ (19) in from beg of cuff, ending with a 2nd row. Fasten off.

Hem
Work as for cuff but make 16 ch not 10 and work to 91 (102) cm, 36 (40) in. Fasten off.

Collar
With wrong side of jacket facing and using 8/H (9/I) hook, join yarn to top corner of left front, 3 ch, 70 dc evenly around neck. Rep 1st and 2nd patt rows of main part of sleeves until collar measures 19cm (7½in), ending with a 2nd row. Fasten off.

Left Front Band
1st row: with right side of jacket facing and 5/F hook, join yarn to corner of collar, work 123 (129) sc evenly along edge of collar and down left front. Work into back lps only throughout. **2nd row:** 1 ch, 1 sc in each sc to end. **3rd row:** 1 ch, 1 sc in each of 1st 3 sc, 3 ch, sk 3 sc, 1 sc in each sc to end. **4th row:** as 2nd working 1 sc in each ch of buttonhole. **5th row:** as 2nd. Fasten off.

Right Front Band
With right side of jacket facing and 5/F hook, join yarn to lower corner of right front. Work 1st and 2nd rows as left front band. **3rd row:** 1 ch, 1 sc in each of 1st 3 sc, *3 ch, sk 3 sc, 1 sc in each of next 16 (17) sc; rep from * 5 times, 1 sc in each sc to end. Work 4th and 5th rows as left front band. Fasten off.

To Finish
Join sleeve seams leaving last 5cm (2in) open. Set in sleeves sewing open rows at top to underarm squares. Sew on buttons to correspond with buttonholes.

SWEATER
Work as jacket to end of sleeves but join center front seam when joining squares.

Hem
Work as for cuff on sleeves for 91 (102) cm, 36 (40) in. Fasten off. Join short ends and sew to lower edge of sweater.

Neckband
Work as for cuff but make 5 ch and work until neckband will fit around neck. Join short ends and sew in place.

To Finish
As for jacket omitting buttons.

		* *							*		
		D							C		
				*	*		*				
	A	B		B	A	B	A		A	B	
	D	C		C	D	C	D		D	C	
	B	A	B	A	B	A	B	A	B	A	
Centre Front	C	D	C	D	C	D	C	D	C	D	Centre Front
	A	B	A	B	A	B	A	B	A	B	

NOVEMBER

" He lingers for a moment in the west,
With the declining sun sheds over all
A pleasant, fare-well smile
And so returns to God"

DRIED FLOWERS

Drying Flowers

Many garden flowers dry extremely well – particularly Alchemilla mollis, achillea, solidago, nigella, peonies and gypsophila. It is also a good idea to grow pink and white rhodanthe, daisies, acrolinium, helichrysum and statice from seed.

Seed heads, mosses and grasses can be collected from fields and hedgerows. Many garden herbs, including rosemary, santolina, lavender and heads of marjoram, also dry well. Hydrangea heads are very useful for flower arrangements as they add bulk to a display. They should not be picked, however, until they have turned to a paper-like texture which usually happens in August or September.

It is best to cut most flowers used for drying just before they reach full bloom since they continue to open as they dry. Pick the flowers on a dry day after the dew has dried. Strip the leaves from the stalks and tie them together in small bunches with rubber bands. In order to avoid crushing, do not put more than five or six stems in a bunch. Hang the bunches upside down from a rail or line in an airy place, but avoid direct sunlight which will cause the flowers to fade. It takes between one to three weeks for flowers to dry, depending on how fleshy they are. Soft flowers such as larkspur, delphinium and small floribunda roses are best dried quickly in a very warm place such as an airing cupboard.

Dried Flower Arrangements

There are many ways to arrange dried flowers which are fun and easy to do. 'Meadows' and 'Violet Wood' are fine examples. 'Melodies' and 'Poppies' are fairly simple table arrangements. Progress to 'Bright Sunshine' and 'Briar Rose' once experience has been gained.

Meadows *Hanging Flowers*

Meadows could not be easier to do or more stunning. Hang bunches of dried flowers upside down from a hanging clothes drier (or pot rack) to achieve this glorious transformation.

Flowers used in 'Meadows' are: blue cornflowers, pink and white rhodanthe, buttercups, gypsophila, peonies, pink and blue larkspur, xeranthemum and limonium.

Violet Wood *Cupboard*

The country garden theme can be continued in the kitchen by simply filling the shelves of a glass fronted cupboard with bunches of dried flowers and grasses.

Flowers used in 'Violet Wood' are: sea lavender, white and pink rhodanthe, achillea, anaphalis and yellow cotton candytuft.

Fairy-cupped
Ideas for Children

Children love helping! Encourage them to make their own small arrangements, using empty food containers and florist's clay. Containers can be decorated with gummed paper shapes or wallpaper before starting. Old egg cups, sugar basins and milk jugs also make attractive containers and take little stock to fill.

Extra bulk can be added in the form of pressed flowers, grasses and leaves as well as small artificial decorations – birthday cake decorations are perfect!

Add a little extra excitement on a country or seashore walk, especially on a chilly day, by collecting old weathered logs or driftwood. These make naturally beautiful containers for dried flowers. The children will enjoy filling the hollows with florist's clay as well as arranging scattered posies in the nooks and crannies of the wood.

Melodies and Poppies
Baskets

'Melodies' and 'Poppies' are examples of arrangements which can be viewed from more than one angle. They can both be made by referring to the pictures of the displays and by carefully reading the following instructions:

1 Choose a fairly shallow container such as a pretty basket or bowl – many culinary dishes are also ideal.
2 Place a suitably shaped block of florist's clay or Styrofoam inside container. A piece of florist's clay will hold the block firmly in place.
3 Place one of the longest flower stems vertically through the center. This stem defines the center of the arrangement and its highest point. The length of this stem depends on the size and shape of the container. Try to avoid a top heavy, unbalanced shape.
4 Place a few stems of the same length, horizontally at right angles to the center stem. This will divide the total area into four equal parts.
5 Diagonally insert four shorter stems at an angle which will divide each right angle in half. Outline the shape of the base with horizontally placed stems around the top edge of the container.

Use further stems to outline the curve of the overall shape. This completes the frame of the design and acts as a guide to placing all remaining flower stems, grasses or foliage.
Flowers used in 'Melodies' are: pink and white acrolinium, helichrysum, hydrangea, blue larkspur, gypsophila, ammobium and lonas.

Flowers used in 'Poppies' are: cotton buttercups, dandelion, candytuft and poppies, dried alchemilla, hornbeam and poppy seed heads.

Bright Sunshine
Hearth Display

'Bright Sunshine' is an example of a large dried flower arrangement which can be seen both from the front and sides but not from the back. Its instructions apply, therefore, to any display which will be placed against a wall.

Clay or Styrofoam block should be placed inside a suitably sized container in exactly the same way as described in 'Melodies' Basket. Mark the central point securely, using the tallest stem which should measure approximately one and a half times the height of the container. Use several more long stems to map out the height and width of the design. Work symmetrically forwards and backwards insuring softly curved side views.

Fill in gaps with varying lengths of stems. 'Bright Sunshine' used: hydrangea, white rhodanthe, solidago, sea lavender, echinops, achillea, alchemilla, nigella and cotton candytuft.

Briar Rose *Wall Bouquet*

The base of this arrangement is made with a 'bouquet holder' available from any florist. Cover the bare holder with reindeer moss, found in woodland parts of the countryside, or buy sphagnum moss from a florist. Hold the moss in place by inserting hairpin-shaped wire through the moss and into the holder. Add sprigs of sea lavender and small pieces of hydrangea heads to give a good general indication of shape. Place small bunches of flowers into the holder, using spiky flowers to soften the outline. Save any special flowers until last. Assemble the arrangement on the wall where it will hang so that the correct line and fall of each flower can be clearly seen.

Flowers used in 'Briar Rose': cotton zinnias, dried rhodanthe, acrolinium, nigella, poppy heads, hydrangea heads and santolina.

DRIED FLOWERS

CHRISTMAS GIFTS

Toadstool

Christmas Gifts

Christmas *Garland and Wreath*

Tie evergreen foliage to base of thin rope or wire. Working in from outer edges, point the bunches of greenery frontward and attach to base rope with thick green garden string or florist's reel wire. When the garland has reached the required length make sure that each end is finished off with sufficient greenery to cover ends. Hang garland in position on a staircase or wall and continue to decorate with ribbons, cones, bows and decorations. Secure all with florist's wire.

A Christmas wreath can be attached to the garland at regular intervals to add even further interest to this festive decoration. A single wreath can also be hung on a door or wall and will make a lovely centerpiece when used flat.

Small branches of yew and holly, sprigs of Skimmia japonica and hebe were used to make the garland and wreath. Further decoration was added in the form of ribbons, fir cones and artificial berries.

1 Styrofoam block

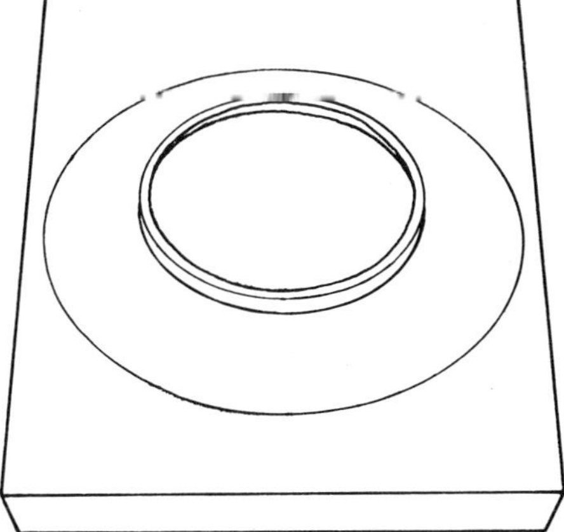

2 Use a plate to help cut out shape with knife.

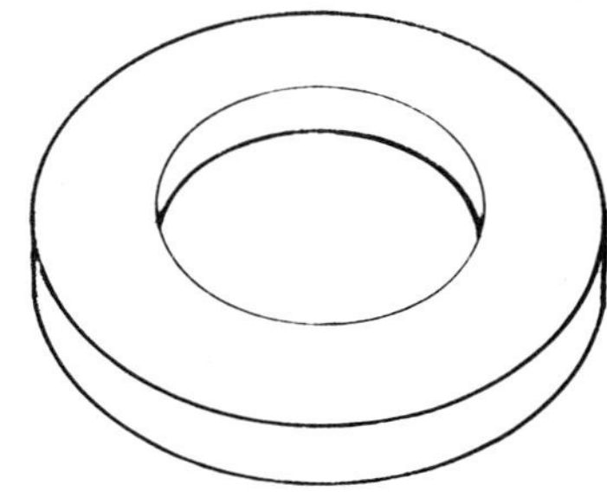

3 Use a smaller plate to cut out inner circle.

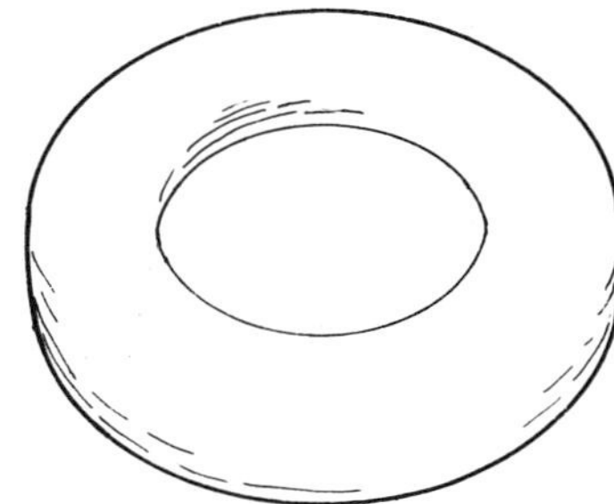

4 Smooth edges with knife.

5 Use reindeer moss or sphagnum moss to cover Styrofoam and secure with florist's wire or staples

Angel *Boxes*

The beautiful mahogany and elm boxes shown above are made by craftsmen wood turners. The mahogany box has been colored with rosewood stain, both inside and out, to show the grain of the wood to its best advantage. The elm box has been given a natural finish to highlight the wood's light, open grain pattern.

The dried-flower and petal designs for the boxes are easily made. Smear tiny drops of glue on the back of the flowers and petals, and carefully arrange inside the gilded metal lid with a pair of tweezers. A fine brush will dust away any unwanted bits.

Flowers used in 'Angel' are: hydrangea, gypsohila, fern and white acrolinium.

Boxes like these make ideal gifts and can equally well contain samples of crochet, tatting or embroidery.

Sunlit Fountain *Teapot*

Never throw out a teapot with a broken lid. Put it to good use by turning it into an eye-catching container for a small arrangement of dried flowers. If possible, use a teapot with a wide neck. Insert a piece of Styrofoam to fit tightly inside. Allow 2.5cm (1in) of Styrofoam to overflow from the rim in order to take flowers in all directions. A fairly tight arrangement suits this type of container, leaving the shape of the spout and handle clearly visible. Flowers used in 'Sunlit Fountain' are: pink floribunda roses and pink and white acrolinium.

Seed-vessels *Jars*

Use empty glass coffee jars or candy jars. Clean well and fill with dried flower heads and petals which can be arranged in stripes of color for further interest.

Flowers used in 'Seed-vessels' are: hydrangea, larkspur, peony, anaphalis, lavender and white rhodanthe petals.

Scattering Flowers
Printer's Boxes

Any suitable container, divided into sections and covered with glass, will produce an attractive collage of dried flowers to hang on a wall. Tie small bunches of flowers, add ribbons for extra color, and arrange within sections according to color, texture and shape. Small sea shells or sunflower seeds can also be included.

Flowers used in model are: blue larkspur; hydrangea; pink helichrysum heads; anaphalis and pink and white rhodanthe.

Flowers *Wall Picture*

Use a picture frame with at least 2.5cm (1in) between the glass and the backing to allow for the depth of the arrangement. Cut cardboard to form the backing of the flower design and another piece, slightly larger, to cover the back of the frame once the flower design has been put in place.

A posy design is a good subject for this type of dried-flower arrangement. Use different kinds of dried herbs, grasses, small fern leaves and leaves to form the back of the design. Smear glue sparingly onto the backs of the stems and, with the help of tweezers, place into position on backing cardboard.

Add flower heads last of all and cover any stalks in evidence with sprigs of dried herbs or greenery. Cotton or silk flowers can also be included. Replace the glass in the frame, and tape the flower design carefully in place at the back of the frame. Another piece of cardboard can be placed over the top of this to give extra protection and strength if desired. Flowers used in this picture are: cotton buttercups, blue larkspur, *Alchemilla mollis*, santolina and pink and white heads of acrolinium.

Sunset *Centerpiece*

This exquisite centerpiece will make an ideal gift for someone very special. A smaller version will be just as pretty. It is made in the same way as the two basket arrangements 'Melodies' and 'Poppies'

Flowers used in 'Sunset' are: peonies, hydrangeas, sea lavender, pink and white acrolinium, statice and achillea.

Spring *Basket*

There are lots of lovely woven baskets available which are reasonably cheap to buy and make excellent containers for dried flowers. Choose a fairly deep woven basket, such as a waste-paper basket, for this display.

Fill with bunches of long dried grasses and flowers to create a truly country feel for this very natural looking arrangement. Flowers used in 'Spring' are purple xeranthemum and white ammobium.

Toadstool *Crochet Pot Holder or Oven Mitt*

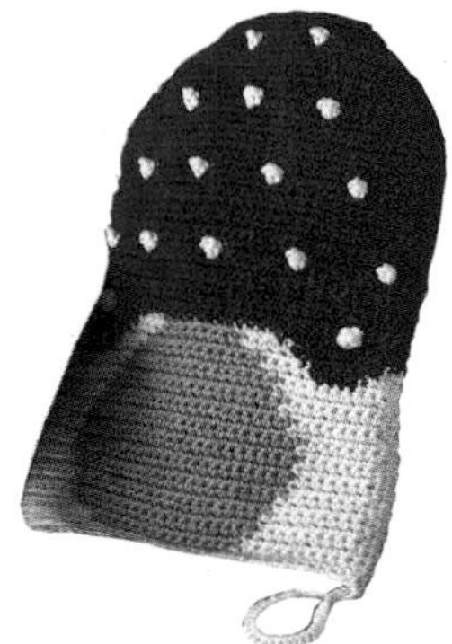

Measurements

one size

Materials

2 balls of 4 ply yarn (M) (Pampas)
1 ball of 4 ply yarn (C1) (Café au Lait)
1 ball of 4 ply yarn (C2) (Fire)
Nos 4 and 4/E crochet hooks
30cm (12in) batting (by commercial width)

Gauge

Worked on 4/E hook – 11 sc and 13 rows of sc to 5cm (2in)

Abbreviations

C1(2) – contrast shades; **ch** – chain; **hdc** – half double crochet; **lp(s)** – loop(s); **M** – main shade; **patt** – pattern; **pc st** – popcorn stitch (**Note:** to make pc st work 4 hdc into the same st, remove lp from hook, insert from front to back through 1st of 4 hdc and pull lp from 4th hdc through tightly); **prev** – previous; **r** – ring;

rep – repeat; **ss** – slip stitch; **st(s)** – stitch(es); **tog** – together; **work 2 sc tog** – work 2 sc together (**Note:** insert hook into each of the next 2 sc, yarn over and draw through all lps)

To Make

Inner Part (make 2)
With 4/E hook and M make 36 ch. **Foundation row:** 1 sc into 2nd ch from hook, 1 sc into each of next ch to end, turn. 35 sc made. **2nd row:** 1 ch, 1 sc into each of next sc to end, turn. Rep prev row 45 times more. ***Dec row:** 1 ch, work 2 sc tog, 1 sc into each of next sc to within last 2 sts, work 2 sc tog, turn. 2 sts dec. Work 1 row of sc*. Rep from * to * 3 times more. Work 7 more dec rows, last row 13 sc. Fasten off.

Outer Parts (make 2)
Note: when changing colors, complete last st of 1st shade in the new shade, ie pull up lp of last sc and complete the st with the new shade. Leave prev shade attached at the back, ready for use on next row. Use 2 separate amounts of M for each side next to stalk and first few rows of C2 (upper part of toadstool). When working pc sts leave yarn attached, working over it with the new shade, while M stays at the base of the row to within next pc st.
With 4 hook and M make 38 ch. Work foundation row as for inner part. 37 sts made. Working sc throughout, complete outer part according to graph and dec as for inner part; last row 15 sts.

To Finish
With M and C2 (as required) and No 4 hook work 140 sc, evenly spaced, along side/upper edges of all 4 parts. Place each of the inner parts on a double layer of batting. Cut out shape, leaving pins attached. Layer all parts in following order: 1st outer part (wrong side facing); 2 layers of batting; inner 2 parts; 2 layers of batting; outer part (right side facing). Join all parts along side/upper edges, using appropriately colored yarns. Join inner to outer parts along lower edge.

Tag
Rejoin M at one side seam st. Make 30 ch, ss into 1st ch to form a r. Work 40 sc into r, ss into 1st sc. Fasten off.

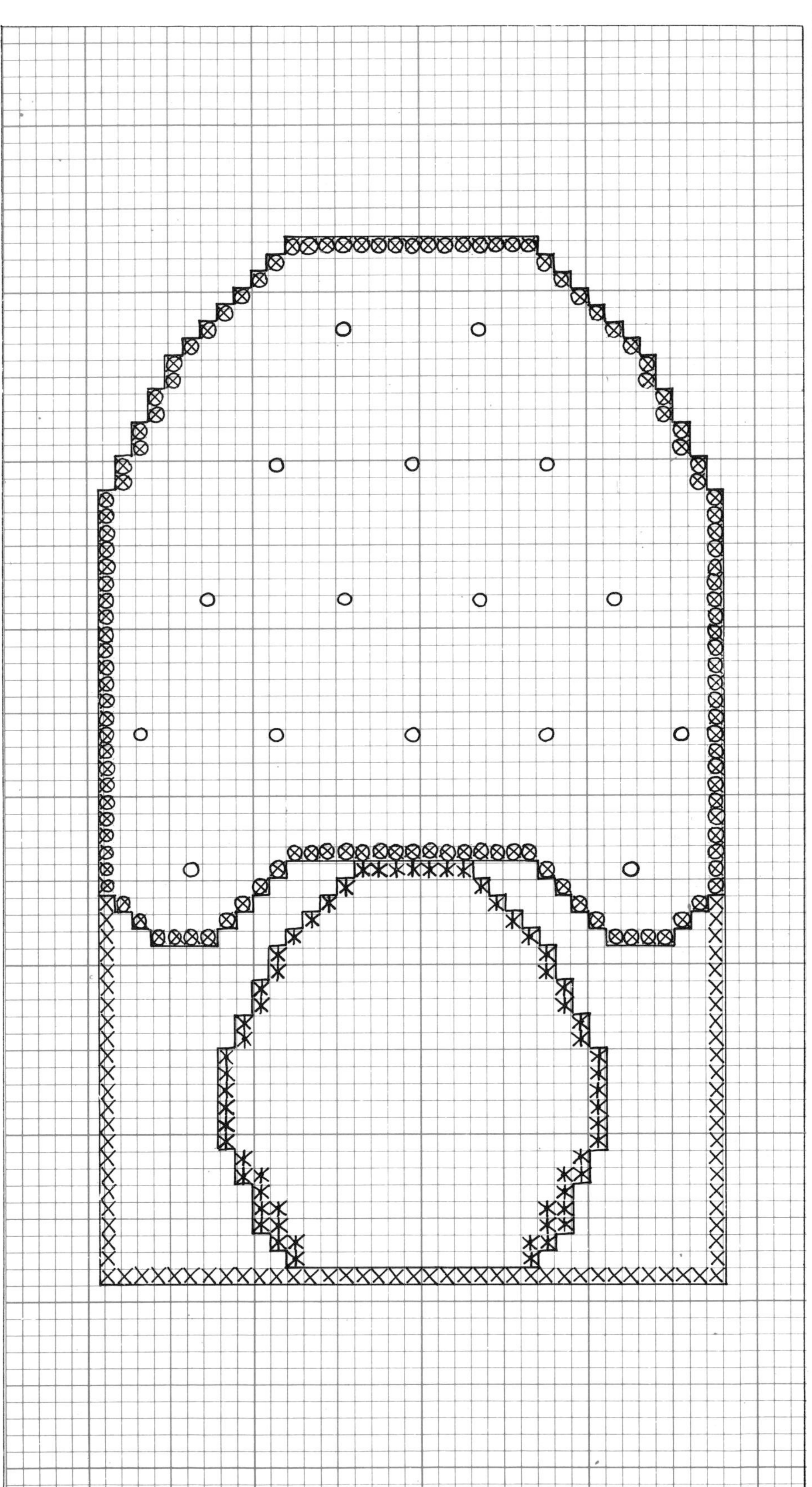

Toadstool
Crochet pot holder

Key
x pampas
✱ cafe au lait
⊗ fire
o popcorn st in pampas

DECEMBER

"In December keep yourself warm and sleep."

HOLLY AND PRIVET

Holly and Privet *Knitted Coat and Lacy Scarf*

Measurements

Coat, to fit bust	86-97	97-107cm
	34-38	38-42in
Length from shoulder	102	103cm
	40	40¾in
Sleeve seam, with cuff folded in half,	47	47cm
approximately	18½	18½in
Scarf, width		25cm (10in)
length, excluding fringe		152cm (60in)

Materials

Bulky yarn

Coat,

Light (L – cream)	13	14	100g balls
A (light green)	1	1	100g ball
B (dark green)	1	1	100g ball
C (red)	1	1	100g ball
D (navy)	1	1	100g ball

Pair of needles each Nos 9 (6mm) and 7 (5mm)

Scarf 3 100g balls

Pair of No 10(6½mm) needles

Gauge

14½ sts and 19 rows to 10cm (4in) over stockinette stitch on No 9 (6mm) needles

Abbreviations

k – knit; **p** – purl; **st(s)** – stitch(es); **sl** – slip; **psso** – pass slipped stitch over; **yfwd** – yarn forward; **inc** – increase, increasing; **dec** – decrease, decreasing; **beg** – beginning; **alt** – alternate; **gst** – garter stitch; **cont** – continue; **tog** – together; **tbl** – through back of loops; **rep** – repeat; **st st** – stockinette stitch

To Make

COAT

Right Front

With No 7 (5mm) needles and L, cast on 57 (61) sts. Work 9 rows in gst. **Next row:** k 3 (5), (m 1 [by picking up and knitting into back of horizontal strand lying before next st], k 11) 4 times, m 1, k to last 7 sts, slip these 7 sts on a safety pin and leave for border.

**Change to No 9 (6mm) needles and beg k row work 14 rows in st st on these 55 (59) sts.

Shape thus: **Dec row:** k to last 20 sts, k 2 tog, k 18. (1 st decreased.) Work 19 rows straight. Rep these 20 rows until 50 (54) sts remain. Work straight until front measures 61cm (24in) from beg, measured through center of work, ending after a p row**.

Shape front slope by dec 1 st at front edge of next row, then on every following 4th row until 43 (47) sts remain.

Shape square armhole thus: **Next row:** bind off 6 st, p to end. ***Keeping armhole edge straight, continue dec 1 st at front edge on every 4th row from previous dec until 31 (35) sts remain, then on every following 3rd row until 24 (27) sts remain.

Work straight until front measures 28 (29) cm, 11 (11¾) in from armhole shaping, ending at armhole edge. Shape shoulder by binding off 8 (9) sts at beg of next and following alt row. Work 1 row. Bind off.

Left Front

Cast on and work 9 rows in gst as right front. **Next row:** k 7, slip these 7 sts on a safety pin and leave, k 3 (5), (m 1, k 11) 4 times, m 1, k to end.

Work as right front from ** to ** but noting that dec row will be: k 18, k 2 tog tbl, k to end.

Shape front slope by dec 1 st at front edge on next row, then on every following 4th row until 44 (48) sts remain. Work 3 rows straight.

Shape square armhole thus: **Next row:** bind off 6 sts, k to last 2 sts, k 2 tog. Complete as right front working from *** to end.

Back

With No 7 (5mm) needles and L, cast on 86 (93) sts. Work 9 rows in gst. **Next row:** k 5 (3), (m 1, k 11) 7 (8) times, m 1, k to end. 94 (102) sts.

Change to No 9 (6mm) needles and beg k row work 14 rows in st st.

Shape thus: **Dec row:** k 18, k 2 tog tbl, k to last 20 sts, k 2 tog, k 18. (2 sts decreased.) Work 19 rows straight. Rep these 20 rows until 84 (92) sts remain. Work straight until back measures 61cm (24in) from beg, ending after a p row.

Work holly and privet spray thus: **1st row:** k 17 (21) L, work 1st row of chart 1, k 17 (21) L. **2nd row:** p 17 (21) L, work 2nd row of chart 1, p 17 (21) L. **3rd to 24th rows:** rep 1st and 2nd rows 11 times but working rows 3 to 24 of chart 1.

Keeping chart correct, shape square armholes by binding off 6 sts at beg of next 2 rows. 72 (80) sts.

Cont working from chart 1 until 66th row has been worked. Cont in L only for remainder until back measures same as fronts to shoulder shaping, ending after a p row.

Shape shoulders by binding off 8 (9) sts at beg of next 6 rows. Bind off final 24 (26) sts *loosely*.

Right Sleeve

(**NB:** Main part of sleeve is worked sideways.) With No 9 (6mm) needles and L, bind on 64 sts loosely. Work in st st working holly border from chart 2 thus: **1st row:** k 2 L, work 1st row from chart 2, k 51 L. **2nd row:** p 51 L, work 2nd row from chart 2, p 2 L. **3rd to 16th rows:** Rep 1st and 2nd rows 7 times but working 3rd to 16th rows from chart 2. Rep these 16 rows until sleeve measures 56 (60) cm, 22 (23½) in from beg. Bind off loosely in L.

With No 7 (5mm) needles and L, right side facing, k up 40 (46) sts *firmly* and evenly along lower edge of sleeve (ie opposite edge to holly border edge). Work in gst for 7 cm (2¾in). Bind off.

Left Sleeve

Work as right sleeve but working holly border at opposite edge, thus 1st row will be: k, 51 L, work 1st row from chart 2, k 2 L.

Right Border and Collar

With wrong side facing, slip 7 sts of lower right front onto a No 7 (5mm) needle. Rejoin L. Noting that 1st row will be wrong side, cont in gst until strip, when slightly stretched, fits up right front to start of front slope, ending after a right-side row.

Working extra sts into st st, beg k row, and remainder in gst as before, shape inner edge of collar by inc 1 st at beg of next row, then on every following alt row until there are 19 sts. Work 1 row.

Cont shaping, working holly border from chart 2 thus: **1st row:** inc in first st in L, work 1st row from chart 2, k 7 L. **2nd row:** k 7 L, work 2nd row from chart 2, p 2 L. **3rd row:** k 2 L, work 3rd row from chart 2, k 7 L. Cont in this way working from chart 2 until the 16th row of chart has been worked, at the same time inc 1 st at inner edge on every 4th row from previous increase, working extra sts into st st in L. Rep these 16 rows until there are 30 sts.

Now working inner 7 sts also in gst, cont

straight until shaped edge fits up front slope and round to center back of neck. Bind off.

Left Border and Collar
With right side facing, slip 7 sts of lower left front onto a No 7 (5mm) needle. Rejoin L. Noting that 1st row will be right side, cont in gst until strip, when slightly stretched, fits up left front to start of front slope, ending after a right-side row. Working extra sts into st st, beg k row, and remainder in gst as before, shape inner edge of collar by inc 1 st at end of next row, then on every following alt row until there are 19 sts. Work 1 row. Cont shaping, working holly border from chart 2 thus: **1st row:** k 7 L, work 1st row from chart 2, inc in last st in L. **2nd row:** p 2 L, work 2nd row from chart 2, k 7 L. **3rd row:** k 7 L, work 3rd row from chart 2, k 2 L. Complete as right border and collar.

Pockets (2)
With No 7 (5mm) needles and L, cast on 28 sts loosely. **1st to 10th rows:** k. **11th row:** k. **12th row:** k 3, p 22, k 3. **13th to 16th rows:** rep 11th and 12th rows twice. Rep these 16 rows twice more, then rows 1 to 9 again. Bind off loosely knitways.

To Finish
Press following instructions on the yarn band, including gst edges and noting that outer gst edge of collar should be slightly stretched. Join shoulders. Stitch upper edges of sleeves to side edge of armhole, joining groups of 6 bound-off sts to corresponding sections of sleeves. Join side and sleeve seams. Fold cuffs in half to wrong side and hem in position. Stitch inner edge of borders and collar to front and neck edges, joining ends at back of neck. Sew on pockets. Press seams.

SCARF
With No 10 (6½mm) needles, bind on 41 sts *loosely*. **1st row** (right side): k 2 tog, (k 2, yfwd, k 1, yfwd, k 2, sl 1, k 2 tog, psso) 4 times, k 2, yfwd, k 1, yfwd, k 2, k 2 tog. **2nd row:** k 3, p 35, k 3. Rep these 2 rows until scarf measures 152cm (60in), ending after a 1st row. Bind off *loosely*. Press following pressing instructions. Fringe the 2 short ends as desired. Trim and press fringes.

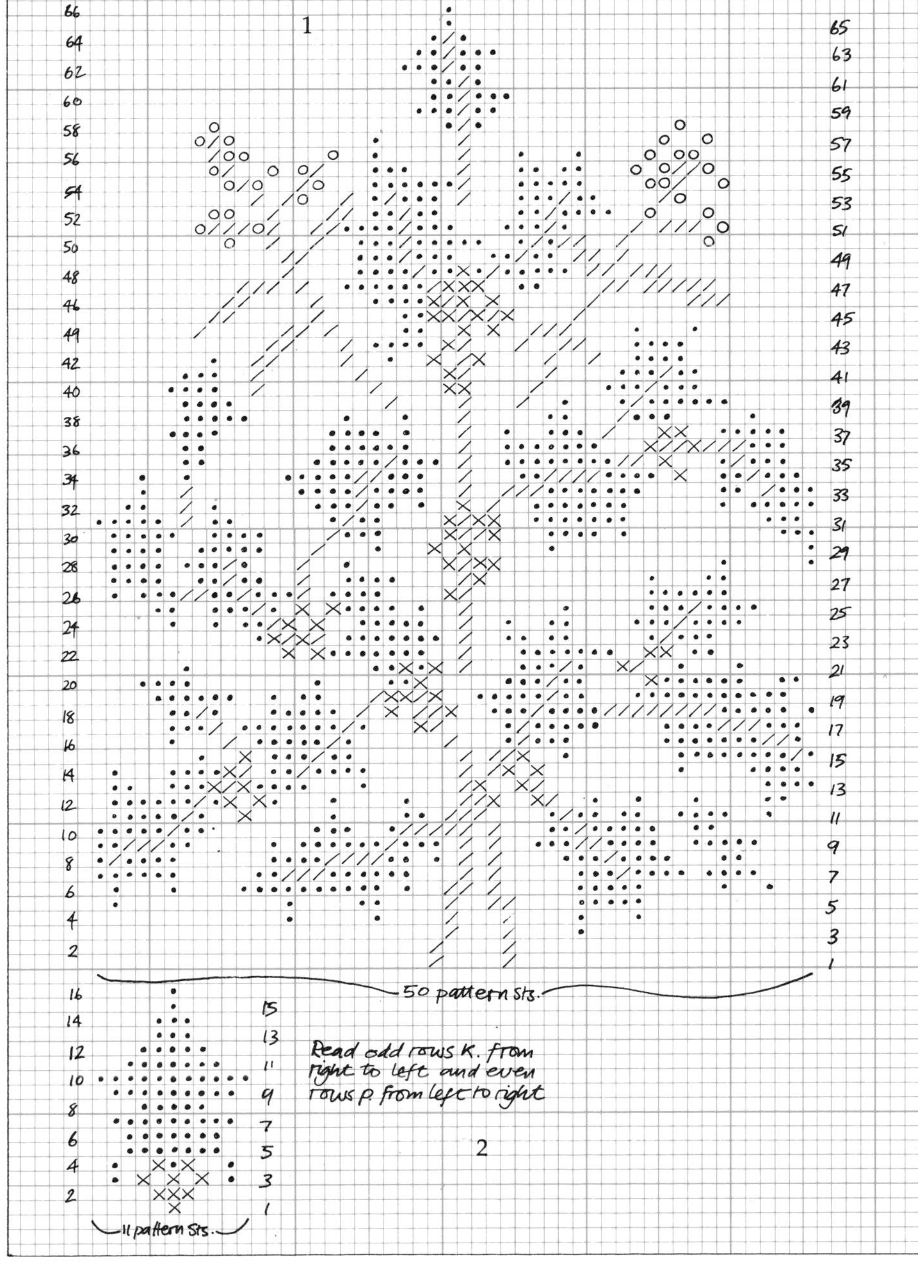

Holly and Privet
Knitted Coat

Key
□ L (cream)
⁄ A (light green)
• B (dark green)
X C (red)
○ D (navy)

Special instructions
Read odd rows *k.* from right to left and even rows *p.* from left to right

GOOD CHEER

CHRISTMAS

Christmas Morning

POMP OF EVE

Merry Jest *Christmas Crackers with Ribbons*

Measurements

Length 30.5cm (12in)

Materials for 1 cracker

Single crepe paper 17cm x 30.5cm (6¾in x 12in)
Lining paper 15cm x 28cm (6in x 11in)
One snap
One motto
9cm x 15cm (3½in x 6in) flexible, lightweight cardboard for stiffening
White glue
Two tubes: one 12.5cm (5in) long and one 25cm (10in) long, both with approximately 3.75cm (1½in) diameter (use bought mailing tubes or cardboard tubes from paper toweling, or make your own by rolling stiff cardboard and securing with cellophane tape)
Thin twine
One gift
Selection of Offray ribbons

To Make

1 Frill short ends of crepe paper by pulling between fingers to stretch paper.

2 Lay crepe paper on table. Put lining paper on top with bottom edges level.

3 Lay snap and motto across lining paper. Lay lining card centrally on lining paper with bottom edge level (A).

4 Spread glue thinly across top edge of crepe paper.

5 Lay the large tube across cardboard stiffener, 2.5cm (1in) from bottom edge of cracker papers. The right hand edge should line up with the right hand edge of the cardboard (B).

6 Lay the smaller tube on the right hand end of the larger tube, just touching (B).

7 Now start to roll the cracker up from the bottom, keeping the tubes in position. Roll firmly and then press the cracker down onto the glued edge to secure. Hold until the glue dries.

8 Carefully withdraw the small tube from the right hand end, about 5cm (2in) (C). Wrap the piece of twine carefully around the cracker, at point of edge of stiffener card. Pull the twine tight and remove small tube. This will give the cracker a 'waisted' shape (D).

9 Pull the larger tube out from the other end until it is 5cm (2in) away from the left hand end of the stiffener card inside the cracker. Insert gift. Use the twine as before to make the waist. (If preferred make the waist more defined afterwards by tying a piece of matching thread around tightly.)

10 Glue Offray ribbons around the cracker ends just above the frilled edge. Decorate cracker with lace and more ribbons, taking care to choose colors which will complement the shade of the crepe paper. Ideas for two color schemes can be seen on page 145 and these may help to inspire other variations.

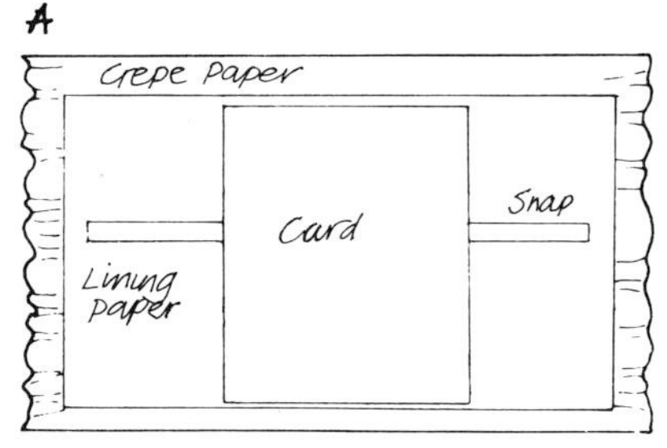

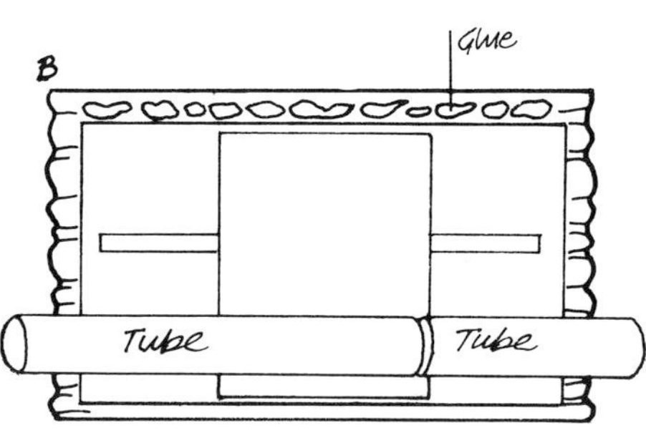

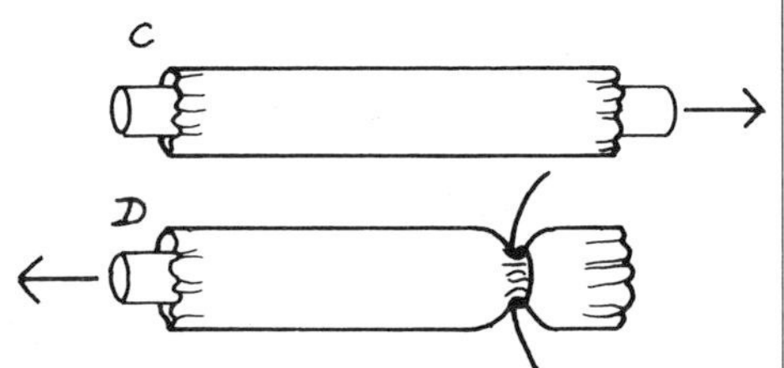

Whirling Snowflakes

Christmas Tree Ribbon Decorations

RIBBON SNOWBALLS

Materials

Selection of Offray ribbons, such as fancy Jacquards, metallic ribbons, satins, stripes and spots
Styrofoam balls available from craft shops
Pins
(Beads and sequins optional)

To Make

1 Choose a ribbon and pin one end to top of snowball.

2 Take ribbon round the ball, pinning at bottom as you go.

3 Pin again on top.

4 Choose next ribbon to go round ball. Mix colors and patterns of ribbons. Do not fill all the spaces – let some of the white snowball show between ribbons. Try pinning narrower ribbons over wide ribbons.

5 Pin zigzags of ribbon up and down round the ball (optional).

6 Pin ribbons horizontally round the ball.

7 Slip beads or sequins on to the pin before pushing it into the ribbon.

8 Pin loops of ribbons to form bows at top of snowball.

9 Pin ribbon loops to tops of balls for hanging.

10 Experiment with different ribbons to create a variety of snowballs.

RIBBON COCKADES

Materials

2.5m (2¾yd) Offray satin ribbon 25mm (1in) wide or lace edging
For smaller cockades use 3m (3¼yd) of 16mm (⅝in) wide ribbon or lace edging

To Make

1 With needle and thread, gather ribbon or lace along 1 edge (A).

2 Wind round and round to make flower shape (B).

3 Baste gathered edges together at back.

4 Add narrow ribbon loop for hanging.

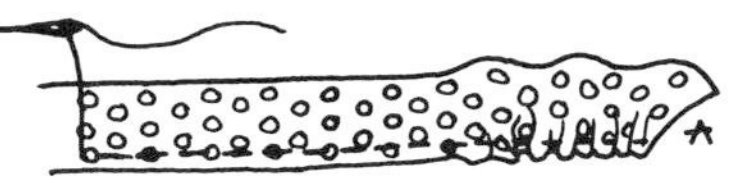

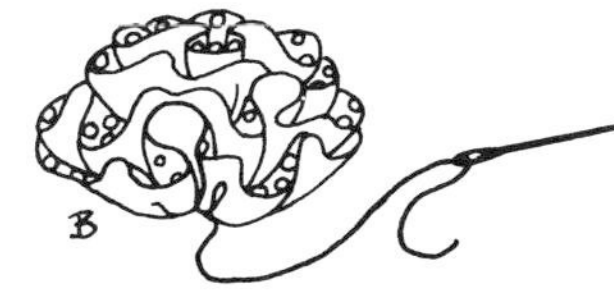

Good Cheer

Ribbon Door Wreath

Measurements

Frame 30cm (12in) in diameter

Materials

1 florist's wire wreath frame 30cm (12in) diameter *or* 1 Styrofoam ring
Offray ribbons:
1.5m (1⅝yd) 39mm (1½in) width Emerald Green
4m (4⅜yd) 12mm (½in) width Red
2.5m (2¾yd) 15mm (⅝in) width Green
Cellophane tape
Florist's stub wires, and silver rose wires (available from most florists in small quantities)
3 pine cones
3 teasels
Seed heads: poppy and nigella (love-in-a-mist)
Gold spray paint (it is essential to buy paint manufactured for this purpose for health reasons)
3 large artificial apples already on wire
Small white baubles and artificial holly berries
Styrofoam block 7cm x 5cm x 5cm (2¾in x 2in x 2in)
Artificial holly and mistletoe

To Make

1 Wind emerald green ribbon round wreath frame, starting and finishing at bottom. Fasten at back with tape.

2 Pass a stub wire round lower part of pine cone and twist ends together to form 'stem'.

3 Spray teasels, cones and seed heads with gold paint and leave to dry.

4 Make multiple loop bows with the ribbons, as shown in 'Christmas' Ribbon Centerpiece. Reserve approximately 30cm (12in) of red ribbon for the hanging loop.

5 Put hanging loop and 1 multiple bow to one side.

6 Wire Styrofoam to center bottom of ribbon frame. Insert dried materials and apples into Styrofoam to form attractive arrangement.

7 Place red bows at base of Styrofoam arrangement and insert green bows and artificial holly and mistletoe into spaces. Completely cover Styrofoam.

8 At top of wreath, directly above arrangement at bottom, sew on hanging loop and red multiple bow securely.

Crowds of Birds

Embroidered Wall Picture

Measurements

Embroidered area 27cm x 20cm (10½in x 8in)

Materials

40cm (15¾in) of 91cm (36in) wide beige fine weight embroidery fabric
Anchor Embroidery Floss: 2 skeins each of 0295; 0914; 1 skein each of 0168; 0278; 0280; 0292; 0306; 0333; 0355; 0402 White; 0403 Black; 8581
Crewel needle No 7
Picture frame with backing board to fit embroidery

To Make

1 Cut a piece from fabric 45cm x 40cm (17¾in x 15¾in).

2 Fold fabric in both directions (lengthwise and widthwise) and crease lightly to form center lines.

3 With one long side of fabric facing, transfer Chart A from page 150 onto fabric, taking care to place design centrally by matching broken lines of chart with center line folds of fabric.

4 Work embroidery following Chart B with key on page 150, working as far as possible out from center. All parts on Chart B numbered alike are worked in the same color and stitch.

5 Use 3 strands of floss throughout.

6 Embroidery is worked in 5 stitches which are listed in the key with Chart B. Refer to 'Glossary of Embroidery Stitches' on page 156 for working instructions.

7 Details of mounting and framing embroideries are on page 62.

Crowds of Birds
Embroidered Wall Picture

Key

Section		*Stitch*
1	0168	long and short stitch
2	0278	or
3	0280	satin stitch
4	0292	
5	0295	
6	0306	
7	0333	
8	0355	
9	0402	
10	0403	
11	0914	
12	8581	
13	0292	straight stitch
14	0295	
15	0306	
16	0355	
17	0403	
18	0914	
19	8581	
20	0278	back stitch
21	0306	
22	0355	
23	0403	
24	0914	
25	8581	
26	0295	stem stitch
27	0306	
28	0355	
29	0402	
30	8581	
31	0333	french knots
32	0402	
33	0403	

Shade numbers refer to Anchor Embroidery Floss.

A

Each square equals 25mm (1in)

B

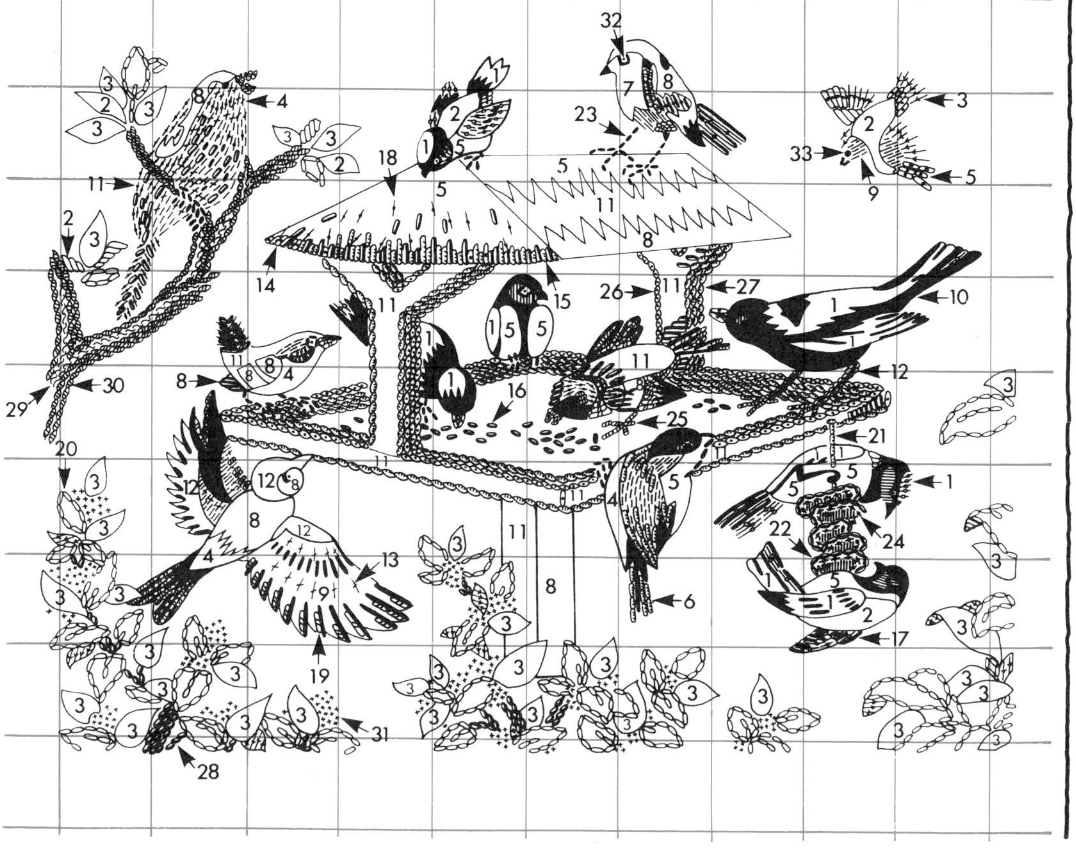

Birds *Needlepoint Wall Picture*

Measurements

Picture size (with background)
30cm x 15cm (12in x 6in)
Birds design size:
25cm x 11cm (10in x 4½in)

Materials

30cm x 58cm (12in x 23in) wide No 10 Penelope (double-threaded) canvas
Anchor Tapestry wool in 10m (11yd) skeins: 7 skeins 0386; 1 skein each of 0402 White; 0403 Black; 0441; 0497; 0401; 0398; 0399; 0564; 3197; 3195; 0392; 0568; 0985; 0649; 0351; 3166; 0427; 0426; 0702; 0837; 0849; 0432; 0848; 0984; 3013; 3230; 3229
Tapestry needle No 18
Picture frame with backing board to fit needlepoint

To Make

Important Note: read 'General Working Instructions for all Needlepoint' on page 15.

1 Fold canvas lightly in both directions to form center lines. Work basting stitches along center lines.

2 Center of chart is indicated by arrows which should coincide with basting stitches. Each square on chart represents one square of double thread canvas, or 1 needlepoint stitch.

3 Work needlepoint following chart and key for 'Birds' design below working as far as possible out from center.

4 Complete background using 0386 and work backstitch details as given on chart using half strand.

5 Remove basting stitches.

6 Model worked in traméed half cross stitch.

7 See page 62 for mounting and framing instructions.

Key	
/	0402
●	0403
ll	0441
∧	0497
⊥	0401
+	0398
S	0399
→	0564
e	3197
<	3195
T	0568
←	0985
I	0649
>	0351
↑	3166
V	0392
\	0426
ↄ	0702
O	0837
↓	0849
=	0432
ı	0848
Z	0984
H	0392
X	3013
–.	3230
•	3229
△	0649
∩	0427

Birds
Needlepoint Picture

Design 100 x 43 stitches
Design size (approx.)
10 stitches to 2.5cm (1in):
25cm x 11cm (10in x 4¼in)

Special instructions

Outline:	
bluebirds	*0398*
brown birds:	
wing	*0649*
head	*0398*
foot	*0985*
breast	*0984*
eyes	*black*
red area in eyes	*0427*
Backstitch:	
highlights in eyes	*ecru*

Broken line separates design into two for use when working greeting cards

Shade numbers refer to Anchor Tapestry wool.

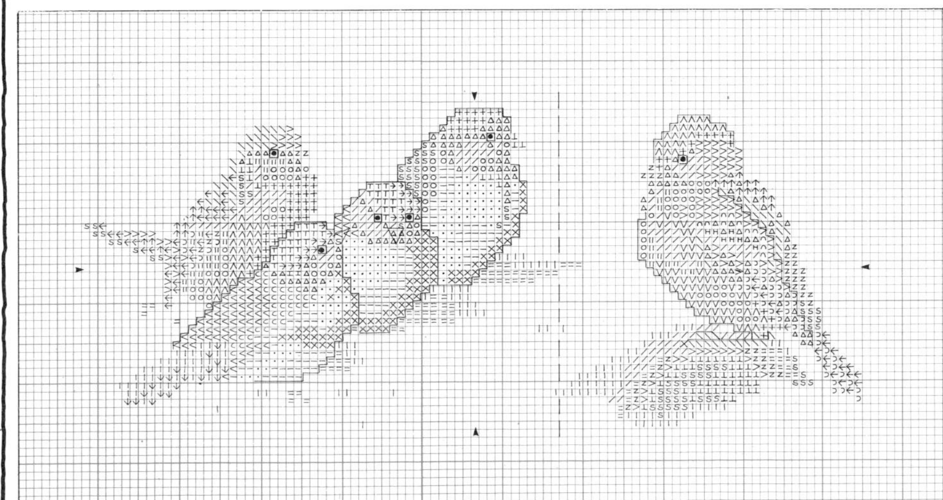

Birds

Embroidered Greeting Cards
(Picture on page 27)

Measurements

Embroidery designs (approx):
Card 1-16cm x 11cm (6¼in x 4½in)
Card 2-10cm x 11cm (4in x 4½in)

Materials

20cm (8in) square Aida fabric with 14 threads to 2.5cm (1in) for each card
Anchor Embroidery Floss:
For single bird card: 1 skein each of White; Black; 0387; 0920; 0921; 0392; 0341; 0399; 0400; 0397; 0391; 0398; 0847; 0401; 0340; 0337; 0339; 0338; 0393; 0380
For 4 birds card: 1 skein each of White; Black; 0387; 0847; 0401; 0168; 0928; 0852; 0887; 0292; 0167; 0170; 0397; 0339; 0399; 0398; 0400; 0341; 0338; 0380; 0340; 0337; 0393; 0921; 0920
Tapestry needle No 24
Greeting cards for embroidery
Double-sided adhesive tape
Fabric adhesive

Birds
Embroidered Greeting Cards

Key	
/	white
●	black
ll	0387
∧	0398
⊥	0400
+	0399
S	0397
→	0167
C	0168
<	0928
T	0158
←	0380
I	0170
>	0341
↑	0340
V	0391
\	0338
ↄ	0337
o	0847
↓	0922
=	0921
ı	0920
Z	0393
H	0392
X	0887
—	0852
•	0292
△	0401
∩	0339

Shade numbers refer to Anchor Embroidery Floss.

Designs: a) 40 x 43 stitches
b) 60 x 43 stitches
14 stitches to 2.5cm (1in):

Special instructions

Outline:	
bluebirds	*0399*
brown birds	
wing	*0401*
head	*0399*
foot	*0380*
breast	*0393*
eyes	*black*
red area in eyes	*0339*
Backstitch:	
highlights in eyes	*ecru*

To Make

Important note: read 'General Working Instructions for all Cross Stitch Embroideries' on page 16.

1 Fold fabric lightly widthwise and lengthwise to mark center lines. Work basting stitches along center lines.

2 Center of chart is indicated by arrows which should coincide with basting stitches.

3 Work embroidery following chart and key for 'Birds' design on page 151, working as far as possible out from center. Chart shows embroidery designs for both greeting cards. Broken line separates one design from the other.

4 Use 2 strands of floss throughout. Each square on chart represents one intersection of threads (1 warp and 1 weft) or one cross stitch.

5 Remove basting threads.

6 Place oval frame of card over embroidered motif. Mark where oval edges fall.

7 Trim fabric to fit inside card. Hold taut in position with double-sided adhesive tape.

8 Peel off top half of tape and press down onto front of card; smooth in place.

9 If necessary, add a smear of fabric adhesive round the inside edge of oval.

Holly

Embroidered Table Runner

Measurements

Table runner: 80cm x 40cm (32in x 15¾in)
Embroidered design (approx) 15cm x 8cm (6in x 3¼in)

Materials

80cm x 40cm (32in x 15¾in) evenweave linen with 28 threads to 2.5cm (1in) 2.5m (2¾yd) of 2.5cm (1in) wide cotton lace edging
Anchor Embroidery Floss: 1 skein each of White; Black; 0217; 0215; 013; 0216; 0214; 0358; 047; 046; 0924; 0381; 0218; 0266; 0269; 0862; 0861; 0860; 0906
Tapestry needle No 24

To Make

Important note: read 'General Working Instructions for all Cross Stitch Embroideries' on page 16.

1 With one long edge facing, fold fabric in half to make horizontal center line. Fold fabric in half in opposite direction and crease lightly. Approximately 20cm (8in) either side of center point, fold lightly to mark vertical center lines of each 'holly' design. Baste center lines.

2 Use 2 strands of floss throughout.

3 Work embroidery following chart and key for 'Holly' design below, working as far as possible out from center. Each square on chart represents 2 double threads of fabric (2 warp and 2 weft) or 1 cross stitch.

4 Work chart at right hand end of linen. Repeat design in reverse at left hand end.

5 Keeping designs centered, trim the embroidered linen to 80cm x 40cm (32in x 15¾in).

6 Remove basting threads.

7 To prevent fraying, machine stitch cut edges.

8 Press 1cm (⅜in) to wrong side around outer edge of fabric, using a damp cloth. Press folded edge under to form hem approximately 6mm (¼in) deep. Miter corners.

9 Pin, baste and machine hem in place. Press hem with damp cloth.

10 Starting with an end of lace edging protruding by approximately 5cm (2in) at first corner, pin lace on right side of runner, overlapping edge of linen by 3mm (⅛in) to cover stitching line of hem.

11 At 3 remaining corners, pin lace neatly, folding to form a miter on right side. At 1st corner, cut, fold and pin lace to match other 3 corners. Baste lace in place.

12 Stitch lace in place by hand or machine. Hand stitch mitered lace corners. Trim surplus lace and overcast raw edges.

13 Press finished runner with damp cloth.

Holly
Embroidered Table Runner

Key
△ white
black*
— 0217
ǁ 0215
Z 013
∧ 0216
• 0214
V 0358
O 047
/ 046
+ 0924
0359*
0906*
X 0381
● 0218
⁘ 0246
▲ 0269
\ 0852
ƛ 0861
= 0869

Design 46 stitches wide
81 stitches long

Design size (approx)
14 stitches to 2.5cm (1in):
8cm x 15cm (3¼in x 6in)

Special instructions
1. Outline
Berries *047*
Leaves *0906*
Small dots in berries *Black*
(Make dots by bringing needle up through hole and going back down as close as possible to it.)
2. Backstitch
Leaf veins *0906*
3. Work second Holly design in reverse if preferred.

Shade numbers refer to Anchor Embroidery Floss.

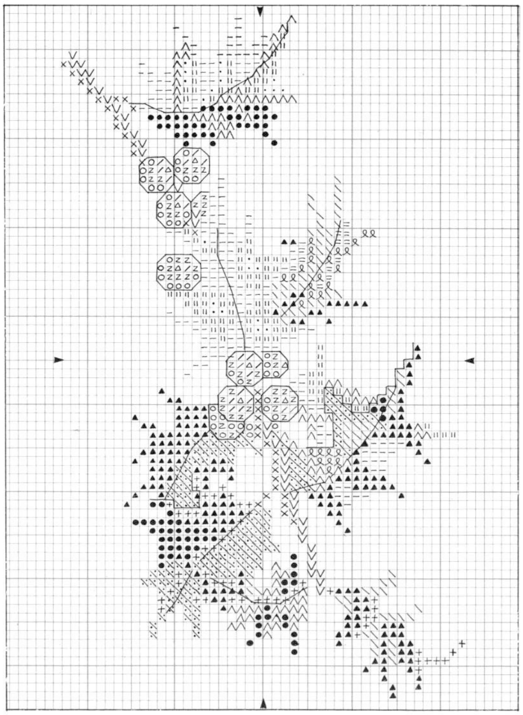

Christmas *Ribbon Centerpiece*

Measurements

Base 20cm (8in) diameter

Materials

Offray ribbons:
2m (2¼yd) of 39mm (1½in) width Red
3m (3¼yd) of 15mm (⅜in) width Green
1m (39½in) of 3mm (⅛in) width White and Silver Lurex
Florist's wires, stub wires, silver rose wires
3 pine cones
3 red glass Christmas tree balls
3 silver glass Christmas tree balls
3 teasels
Seed heads, eg poppy and nigella (love-in-a-mist)
Gold spray paint (it is important to purchase gold paint especially manufactured for these purposes for health reasons)
1.5m (1⅝yd) cream lace
Corrugated cardboard 20cm (8in) diameter (covered with green fabric, optional)
Glue
Small block of Styrofoam
1 candle
Plastic toothpicks

To Make

Following diagram A as a guide, together with picture above:

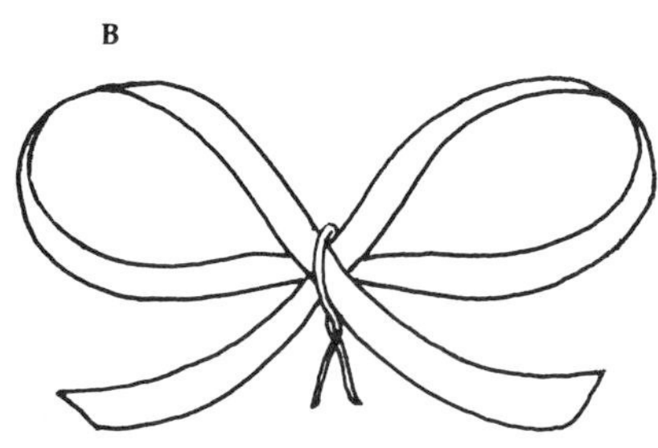

1 Make multiple loop bows with green and silver ribbons securing each with silver rose wire. Diagram B.

2 Place stub wire around lower part of each pine cone and twist ends together.

3 Place stub wire through the hanging loop of each glass ball and twist ends together ready to place in Styrofoam block.

4 Spray cones, teasels and seed heads with gold paint and leave to dry.

5 Staple ring of lace to edge of cardboard a little way in from edge.

6 Gather and secure with a florist's stub wire the remaining lace to form small cockades.

7 Glue Styrofoam to center of base.

8 Tape several toothpicks to end of candle and insert candle to center of Styrofoam.

9 Arrange other materials around candle and ribbon bows to cover Styrofoam completely.

10 Artificial holly and mistletoe can be added.

When making multiple bows, make as many loops as required, all of equal size.

Mistletoe
Knitted Pearl Sweater

Measurements

To fit bust	86	91	97	102cm
	34	36	38	40in
Length from	58	60	61	62cm
shoulder	23	23½	24	24½in
Sleeve length	47	47	47	47cm
	18½	18½	18½	18½in

Materials

Knitting worsted
18 19 19 20 20g balls
Pair of needles each Nos 4 (3¾mm) and 2 (No 1). Pearl beads for embroidery (allow 1 for every motif and approximately 100 for neck)

Gauge

24 sts and 30 rows to 10cm (4in) over stockinette stitch on No 4 (3¾mm) needles

Abbreviations

k – knit; **p** – purl; **st(s)** – stitch(es); **patt** – pattern; **sl** – slip; **yfwd** – yarn forward; **psso** – pass slipped stitch over; **inc** – increase, increasing; **dec** – decrease, decreasing; **beg** – beginning; **alt** – alternate; **rep** – repeat; **cont** – continue; **st st** – stockinette stitch; **tog** – together

To Make

Front

With No 2 (3mm) needles, cast on 107 (113, 119, 125) sts. **1st row:** k 2, (p 1, k 1) to last st, k 1. **2nd row:** k 1, (p 1, k 1) to end. Rep these 2 rows for 7cm (2¾in), ending after a 1st row. **Next row:** rib 4 (7, 10, 13), (inc in next st, rib 8) 11 times, inc in next st, rib to end. 119 (125, 131, 137) sts.

Change to No 4 (3¾mm) needles and patt thus: **1st row:** k 4 (7, 10, 13), (yfwd, sl 1, k 2 tog, psso, yfwd, k 15) to last 7 (10, 13, 16) sts, yfwd, sl 1, k 2 tog, psso, yfwd, k 4 (7, 10, 13). **2nd row:** p. **3rd row:** k 5 (8, 11, 14), (yfwd, sl 1, k 1, psso, k 16) to last 6 (9, 12, 15) sts, yfwd, sl 1, k 1, psso, k to end. **4th to 10th rows:** beg p row, work 7 rows in st st. **11th row:** k 13 (16, 19, 4), (yfwd, sl 1, k 2 tog, psso, yfwd, k 15) to last 16 (19, 22, 7) sts, yfwd, sl 1, k 2 tog, psso, yfwd, k to end. **12th row:** p. **13th row:** k 14 (17, 20, 5), (yfwd, sl 1, k 1, psso, k 16) to last 15 (18, 21, 6) sts, yfwd, sl 1, k 1, psso, k to end. **14th to 20th rows:** as 4th to 10th. These 20 rows form patt.

Cont in patt until work measures 37cm (14½in) from beg, ending after a right-side row.

Keeping patt correct, divide for 'V' neck thus: **Next row:** p 59 (62, 65, 68), p 2 tog, p 58 (61, 64, 67). **Next row:** work across 55 (58, 61, 64), k 2 tog, k 2, turn. **Next row:** k 2, p to end. **Next row:** work to last 4 sts, k 2 tog, k 2. **Next row:** k 2, p to end. Cont in this way, dec 1 st inside neck edge on next and every following alt row until 54 (57, 60, 63) sts, remain, then on every following 4th row until 42 (44, 46, 48) sts remain.

Work straight until front measures 58 (60, 61, 62) cm, 23 (23½, 24, 24½) in from beg, ending at side edge.

Shape shoulder by binding off 10 (11, 11, 12) sts at beg of next and following alt row, then 11 (11, 12, 12) sts at beg of next row. Work 1 row. Bind off.

With right side facing, rejoin yarn to remaining sts. **Next row:** k 2, sl 1, k 1, psso, work to end. **Next row:** p to last 2 sts, k 2. Complete to match first half.

Back

Omitting neck shaping, work as front to shoulder shaping, ending after a *right-side* row.

Shape shoulders thus: **1st to 4th rows:** bind off 10 (11, 11, 12) sts, work to end. **5th to 8th rows:** working center 35 (37, 39, 41) sts in garter st, bind off 11 (11, 12, 12) sts, work to end. Bind off evenly.

Sleeves

With No 2 (3mm) needles, bind on 47 (49, 51, 53) sts. Work in rib as on welt for 7cm (2¾in), ending after a 1st row. **Next row:** rib 5 (5, 3, 7), *inc in next st, rib 3 (2, 2, 1); rep from * to last 6 (5, 3, 8) sts, inc in next st, rib to end. 57 (63, 67, 73) sts.

Change to No 4 (3¾mm) needles and patt thus: **1st row:** k 27 (30, 32, 35), yfwd, sl 1, k 2 tog, psso, yfwd, k to end. **2nd row:** p. **3rd row:** k 28 (31, 33, 36), yfwd, sl 1, k 1, psso, k to end. **4th to 20th rows:** beg p row, work 17 rows in st st, inc 1 st at each end of 5th, 9th, 13th and 17th rows, working extra sts into st st. On these 20 rows 1 rep of patt has been worked.

Cont in patt, shaping sleeve by inc 1 st at each end of next and every following 4th row until there are 109 (115, 119, 125) sts.

Work straight until sleeve measures 47cm (18½in) at center. Bind off loosely.

To Finish

Do not press. Join shoulders. Allowing approximately 24 (25, 26, 27) cm, 9½ (10, 10¼, 10¾) in for armholes, sew bound-off edges of sleeves to yoke, then join side and sleeve seams. Sew 1 bead to each lace motif. Now sew remainder of beads to neck edge. If desired, front neck edge may be backed with grosgrain ribbon.

Glossary of Stitches

Embroidery Stitches

Long and Short Stitch

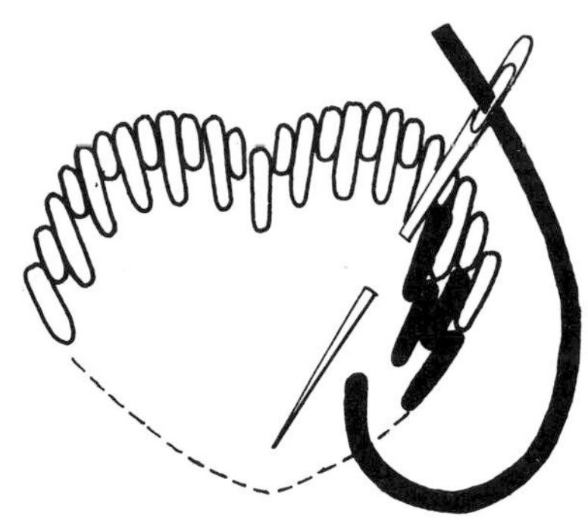

This form of satin stitch is so named as all the stitches are of varying lengths. It is used to fill a shape which is too large or too irregular to be covered by satin stitch. It is also used to achieve a shaded effect. In the first row the stitches are alternately long and short and closely follow the outline of the shape. The stitches in the following rows are worked to achieve a smooth appearance. The diagram shows how a shaded effect may be obtained.

French Knots

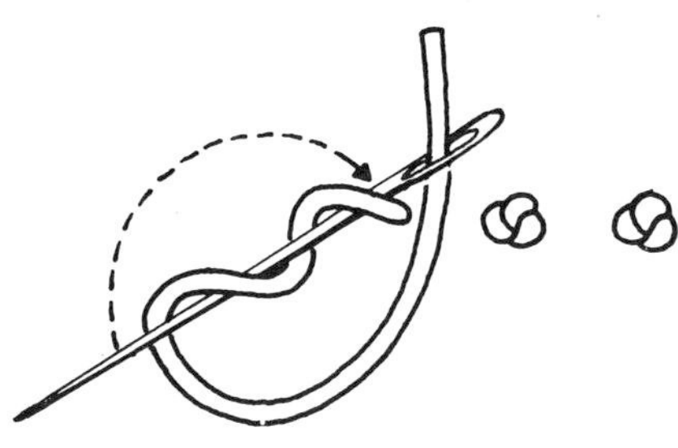

Using one strand, bring thread out at the required position, hold thread down with left thumb and encircle around needle as in fig. 1. Still holding thread firmly, twist needle back to starting point and insert where thread first emerged. See arrow. Pull thread through to back and secure for a single French knot or pass on to position of next stitch.

Buttonhole stitch or Compact Blanket stitch

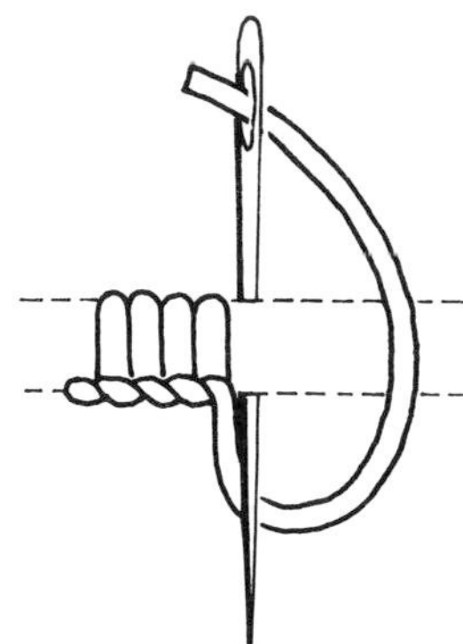

Bring needle in position on upper dotted line, taking a straight downwards stitch with thread under needle point. Pull up stitch to form loop. Repeat working stitches very close together.

Satin stitch

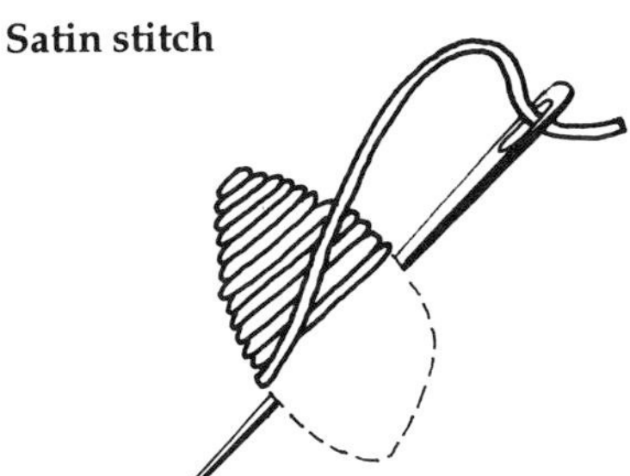

This consists of straight stitches worked side by side from one side of shape to other. Start by bringing thread up to right side at one edge of shape. Take thread back to wrong side directly opposite. Bring needle back to right side next to where it appeared for previous stitch.

Back stitch

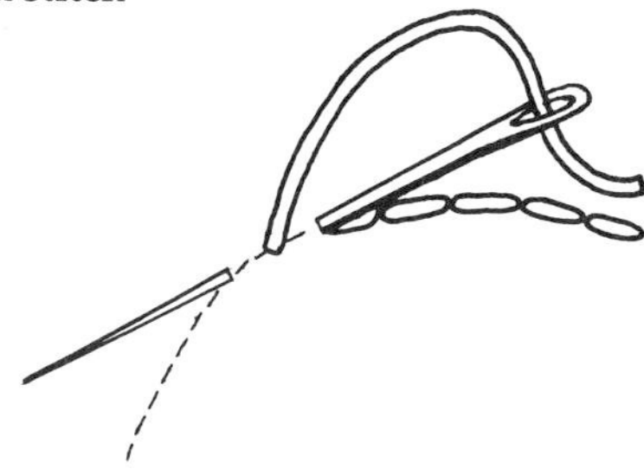

Start by bringing thread through to right side, 2–3mm (1/16–1/8in) from start of line. Take thread back through to wrong side at start of line. Bring it up to right side again 2–3mm (1/16–1/8in) further along line from where it came through previously.

Blanket stitch

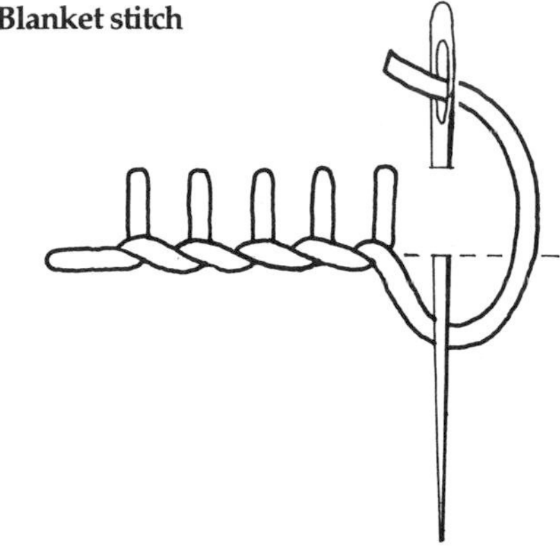

Bring needle out on lower line and insert needle in position on upper line by taking a straight downward stitch with thread under point of needle. Pull up stitch to form loop and repeat, spacing out stitches evenly.

Chain stitch

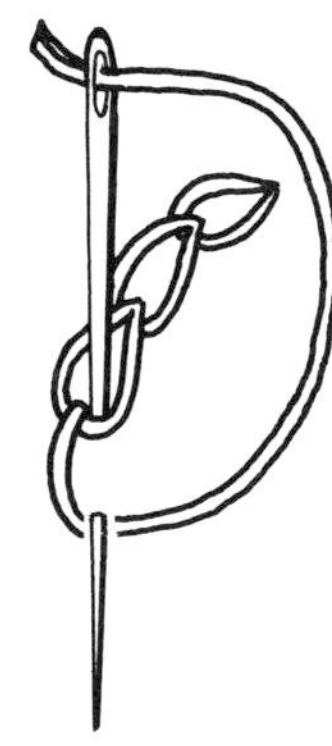

Working from right to left, bring needle up to right side of fabric at beginning of line. Insert needle back into fabric at same point and bring needle point up again further along line. Keep loop of thread under point of needle and pull gently up to form stitch. Continue along line in this way.

Straight stitch

Bring needle up at one end of line and take it back to wrong side at other end of line.

Long-tailed daisy stitch with one Straight stitch worked in center

This is made up of one chain stitch with one straight stitch worked at end. Another straight stitch is then worked in center of chain stitch loop.

Stem stitch

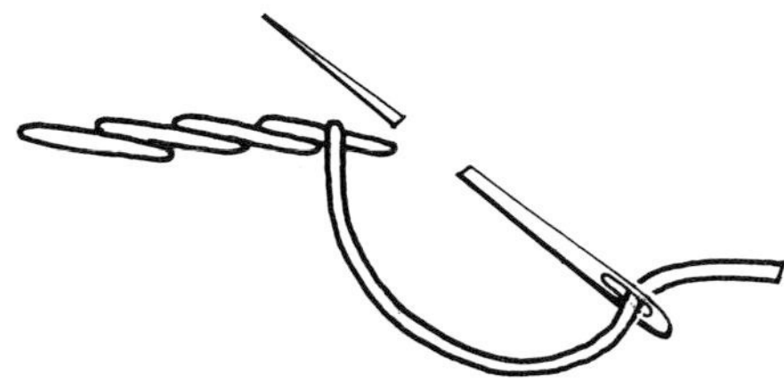

Working from right to left, bring needle up to right side of fabric at beginning of line. Insert needle back into fabric further along line and bring needle point up midway along this stitch keeping thread to one side. Continue along line in this way making sure thread is always to same side of point of needle.

Traméed Half Cross Stitch
Following diagram A and working from left to right, start by making foundation (tramée) stitches:

1 Traméed threads are taken horizontally across the canvas to lie on the surface between a pair of narrow horizontal canvas threads.

2 No stitch must be longer than 13cm (5in). Any line of one color longer than 13cm (5in) requires stitches to be split.

3 (A) Bring needle through at 1 and insert back down at 2 (no length more than 13cm (5in).

(B) Bring needle through at 3, piercing the stitch just made to form a split stitch. Insert back down at 4.

(C) Following number sequence (red for up and blue for down) continue in this way across canvas.

4 **Do not** start or finish each traméed stitch at the same pair of vertical threads on each row. This will cause a ridged effect on the right side when the work is complete.

5 When tramé stitches are complete in one color, work enough half cross stitches to cover tramé threads in the same color.

6 Following diagram B, follow the number sequence from 1 to 24 which shows 2 complete rows. Position 25 shows the starting point for the 3rd row. Back of work should show stitches all lying vertically.

(A) To Tram a canvas

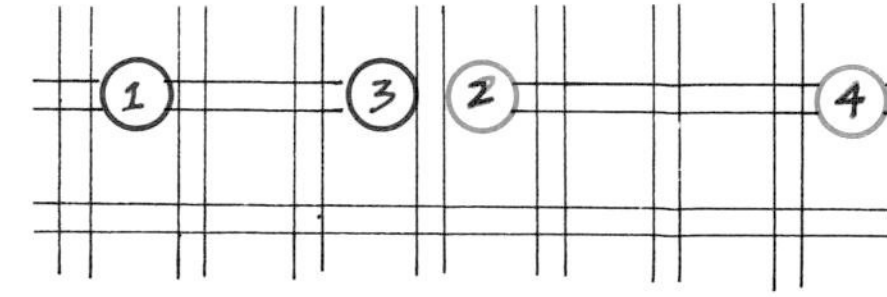

(B) Half Cross stitches

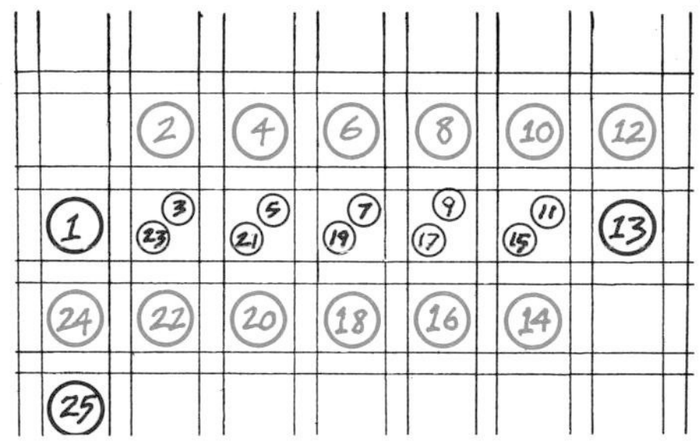

Blue circles show where needle goes down from the right side. Red circles show where needle comes up from wrong side.

(C) Traméed half cross stitch

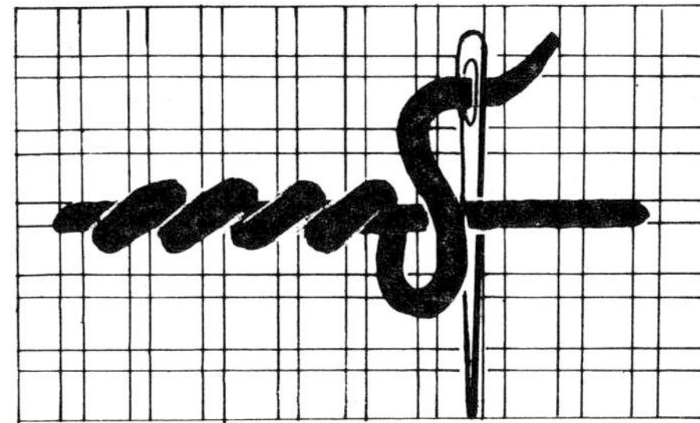

Tent Stitch
This is another popular needlepoint stitch. Follow instructions 1, 2 and 3.

1 Begin by bringing needle from wrong side of canvas; insert needle diagonally into upper line over one intersection of canvas threads (the point where a pair of narrow vertical threads cross a pair of narrow horizontal threads); bring needle through on lower line two canvas thread intersections to left. Continue in this way to end of row.

2 Follow for 2nd row.

3 Shows reverse side of correctly worked tent stitch where length of stitches is greater than those on correct side.

1

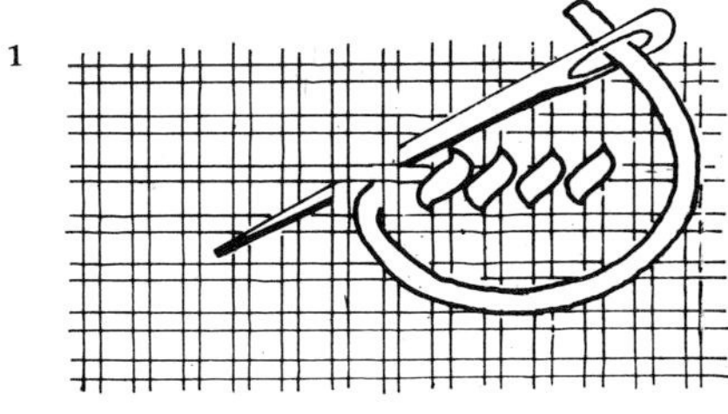

2

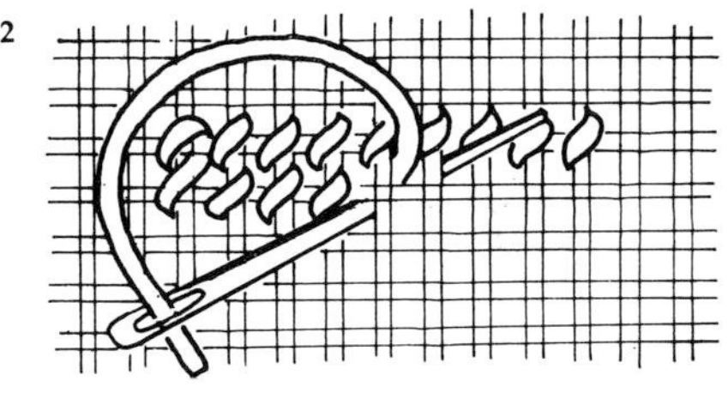

3

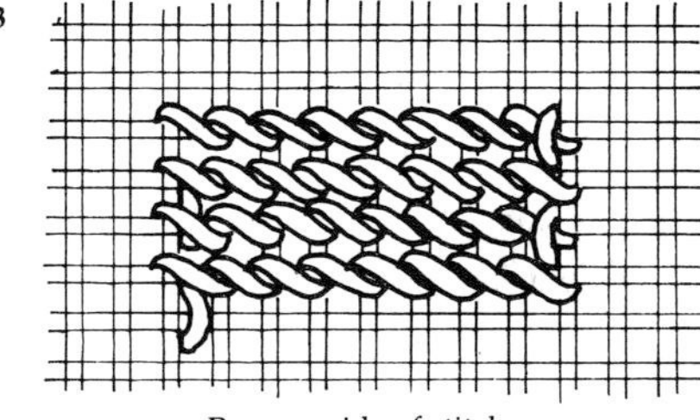

Reverse side of stitches

Note: diagram shows double thread canvas, however, the stitches can be worked in exactly the same way on single thread canvas.

Useful Addresses

For Further Information
A book like this can only offer a small sampling of craft and needlework suppliers. For more information, look first to your local crafts and needlework shops. These will carry (or can special-order) most of the items you need to complete the projects in this book. If your local shops can't help (or if there is none near you), there are many mail order sources. A few are given here. More can be found by checking the advertisements in magazines such as *McCall's Needlework & Crafts* and *Better Homes and Gardens Creative Ideas* (available at newsstands) or in the many publications devoted to individual crafts.

Knitting and Crochet

Important note: When contacting any company by mail please enclose a s.s.a.e. for reply.

Susan Bates, Inc.
PO Box E
Rtc 9A
Chester, CT 06412
Distributor of yarns by Paton and Jaeger, and the Anchor line.

Bernat Yarn & Craft Corp.
Depot and Mendon Streets
Uxbridge, MA 01569

Brunswick Worsted Mills
230 Fifth Avenue
New York, NY 10001

Pingouin
PO Box 100
Highway 45
Jamestown, SC 29453

Chat Botte
Armen Corp.
1281 Brevard Boulevard
Asheville, NC 28806

Phildar Yarns
6438 Dawson Boulevard
Norcross, GA 30093

Reynolds Yarns, Inc.
Box 696
Stony Brook, NY 11790

William Unger & Co.
PO Box 1621
Bridgeport, CT 06601

Needlepoint and Embroidery

Appleton Bros. Ltd.
P.O. Box 544
Little Compton, RI 02837

Coats & Clark Inc.
72 Cummings Point Road
Stamford, CT 06902

Columbia-Minerva Corp.
295 Fifth Avenue
New York, NY 10016
Makers of yarn and canvas

Needlecraft House
West Townsend, MA 01474
Elsa Williams silk thread

Regency Mills
259 Center Street
Phillipsburg, NJ 0885
Makers of embroidery fabrics

Patchwork and Sewing

Fairfield Processing Corporation
P.O. Box 1130
Danbury, CT 06810
Makers of Polyfil — polyester fiberfill and quilt batting

Pellon Corp
119 West 40 Street
New York, NY 10018
Makers of Quilter's Secret and iron-on interfacing

Ribbons

C. M. Offray & Son Ltd.
261 Madison Avenue
New York, NY 10016

Rug making

Paton's yarn
see Susan Bates, Inc. under Knitting and Crochet

Shillcraft
500 N. Calvert Street
Baltimore, MD 21202

Wooden Boxes
Cardinal Manufacturing
Box E
Carteret, NJ 07008

Mail Order Sources

Adventures in Crafts
PO Box 6058
Yorkville Station
New York, NY 10128

The American Needlewoman
Box 6472
Fort Worth, TX 76115

Herrschner's, Inc.
Hoover Road
Stevens Point, W1 54481

The Knitting Room
at the Heirloom
2215 Defense Highway
Crofton, MD 21114

The Needlecraft Shop
Box 6472
Fort Worth, TX 76115

The Stitchery
204 Worcester Street
Wellesley, MA 02181

To order a sew-it-yourself Teddy Bear Kit from Michael Hague's book ALPHABEARS, send $9.00 to The Toy Works, Fiddlers Elbow Road, Middle Falls, New York, 12848.

No responsibility can be taken for any materials or shades, featured in this book, that have been discontinued by manufacturers. At the time of going to print, all manufacturers gave the most up-to-date information available. Any reputable craft shop, wool shop or department store will help in choosing a substitute, should this be necessary. Please insure that all relevant details are given in order to obtain the best possible substitute and, therefore, the best possible results. Although every possible effort has been made to use currently available materials throughout this book, it is possible that certain items will be deleted from manufacturers supplies as time progresses. We apologize for any inconvenience this may cause but feel sure an acceptable substitute will be available without too much difficulty.

Acknowledgements

My sincere thanks go to all designers, company personnel and outworkers who helped to produce the many beautiful craft items which appear in this book; to Tim Bishopp for his marvellous photography; to Pam Elson for her expertise in home styling; to Amanda Cooke for her expertise in fashion styling; to Jenny Raworth for the use of her lovely home and dried flower arrangements; to Ron Pickless for designing the book; to Pam Cherry for her secretarial and administrative help; and to Sunbeam Knitting Wools for giving me the time to complete my work for this book.

Sincere thanks also go to my two dear friends Kate Harrison and Katie Fitchie, for their great kindness and help at all times.

My very special thanks go to my son Jonathan whose patience, understanding and encouragement made this book possible; to my Mother for her love and support at all times; and to my late Father to whom I owe so much.

Knitting
Pat Menchini

Crochet
Twilley's of Stamford
Louise Parsons
Ruth Swepson (*Woodland*)
Coats Domestic Marketing Division (*Butterfly*)

Embroidery
The Royal School of Needlework
Coats Domestic Marketing Division
Lady Denise Hanson (*Goldfinch*)

Needlepoint
Margaret Strang
Coats Domestic Marketing Division (*Apple*)
The Royal School of Needlework (*Blackberries*)

Quilter's
The Vilene Organisation

Dried Flowers
Jenny Raworth

Sewing
Hilary More

Rugs
Jennifer Ward and Richard Lane

Ribbon weaving and ribbon Christmas decorations
The Offray Design Studio

Tatting
Coats Domestic Marketing Division

Framing, embroidery and needlepoint pictures and covering an album
Pauline Butler

Props for photographs

Curtains
Dorma

Wooden picture frames
Framecraft

Lampbase and shade
Alma Lighting

Jug and pitcher, vase, bell
Royal Winton Potteries

Teaset and dinner set
Noritake

Cushions
Peter Colling Textiles

Country Diary products
Nigel French Enterprises